Busoni as Pianist

Eastman Studies in Music

Ralph P. Locke, Senior Editor
Eastman School of Music

Additional Titles on Music of the Twentieth Century

*The Poetic Debussy: A Collection of
His Song Texts and Selected Letters*
(Revised Second Edition)
Edited by Margaret G. Cobb

Portrait of Percy Grainger
Edited by Malcolm Gillies and
David Pear

*Music's Modern Muse:
A Life of Winnaretta Singer,
Princesse de Polignac*
Sylvia Kahan

*The Pleasure of Modernist Music:
Listening, Meaning, Intention, Ideology*
Edited by Arved Ashby

*The Substance of Things Heard:
Writings about Music*
Paul Griffiths

*Opera and Ideology in Prague:
Polemics and Practice at the
National Theater, 1900–1938*
Brian S. Locke

*Pentatonicism from the
Eighteenth Century to Debussy*
Jeremy Day-O'Connell

*Maurice Duruflé:
The Man and His Music*
James E. Frazier

*French Music, Culture, and
National Identity, 1870–1939*
Edited by Barbara L. Kelly

*Beethoven's Century:
Essays on Composers and Themes*
Hugh Macdonald

*In Search of New Scales: Prince Edmond de
Polignac, Octatonic Explorer*
Sylvia Kahan

The Ballet Collaborations of Richard Strauss
Wayne Heisler Jr.

Othmar Schoeck: Life and Works
Chris Walton

*Irony and Sound:
The Music of Maurice Ravel*
Stephen Zank

*August Halm:
A Critical and Creative Life in Music*
Lee Rothfarb

*Music Speaks:
On the Language of Opera, Dance, and Song*
Daniel Albright

*Intimate Voices: The Twentieth-Century
String Quartet, Volume 1:
Debussy to Villa-Lobos*
Edited by Evan Jones

*Intimate Voices: The Twentieth-Century
String Quartet, Volume 2:
Shostakovich to the Avant-Garde*
Edited by Evan Jones

Janáček beyond the Borders
Derek Katz

A complete list of titles in the Eastman Studies in Music series may be found
on the University of Rochester Press website: www.urpress.com

Busoni as Pianist

GRIGORY KOGAN

TRANSLATED AND ANNOTATED BY
SVETLANA BELSKY

UNIVERSITY OF ROCHESTER PRESS

First published 2010
University of Rochester Press
668 Mt. Hope Avenue, Rochester, NY 14620, USA
www.urpress.com
and Boydell & Brewer Limited
PO Box 9, Woodbridge, Suffolk IP12 3DF, UK
www.boydellandbrewer.com

ISBN-13: 978-1-58046-335-5
ISSN: 1071-9989

Library of Congress Cataloging-in-Publication Data

Kogan, G. (Grigorii), 1901–1979.
  [Ferruchcho Buzoni. English]
  Busoni as pianist / Grigory Kogan ; translated and annotated by Svetlana Belsky.
    p. cm. — (Eastman studies in music, ISSN 1071-9989 ; v. 73)
  Includes bibliographical references (p.) and index.
  ISBN 978-1-58046-335-5 (hardcover : alk. paper)
  1. Busoni, Ferruccio, 1866–1924. 2. Pianists—Italy—Biography. I. Belsky, Svetlana.
II. Title.
  ML410.B98K6413 2010
  786.2092—dc22

                                                                2009045610

A catalogue record for this title is available from the British Library.

This publication is printed on acid-free paper.
Printed in the United States of America.

Contents

Foreword

Grigory Mikhailovich Kogan (1901–1979)

I had the privilege of meeting Grigory Mikhailovich when I was a small child taking piano lessons with his wife, Sofia. Soon I became his student, as well. Since that time, and until his death, he was my teacher, my mentor, and my dear friend.

Kogan was one of the most remarkable figures of his time. As a man of extraordinary scholarship, he spoke many languages, and was also a pianist, lecturer, critic, and pedagogue, the author of many books on a variety of subjects, ranging from *The Psychological Requisites for Pianistic Success, The Texture of the Piano,* to *Ferrucio Busoni, Couperin,* and the important monograph *The Pianist's Work,* among others.

He also edited a number of piano pieces and music books, wrote articles in newspapers, magazines, and encyclopedias, wrote concert and book reviews, school curricula, and so on.

It was highly interesting and educational to hear him talk about remarkable musicians, conductors, and pianists that he had heard and met in his life.

In the late 1940s, during the well-known campaign against *cosmopolitism* in the Soviet Union, cruel and false accusations were made against many outstanding figures. Intellectuals were the prime victims of this campaign. The most prominent Soviet composers were absurdly accused of diverging from the mainstream of Russian tradition. As a result of this campaign, Grigory Kogan lost his position at the Moscow Conservatory. His constant references to foreign publications, authors, and thinkers, and his own books and articles about foreign masters such as Busoni were "sufficient grounds" for accusing and dismissing him.

Years later, upon returning to Moscow, he concentrated intensively on writing and performing. At this time, his main books were being published as well as numerous articles and concert reviews. However, he was never allowed to go abroad, which is the reason he is not yet well known in the West.

Nina Svetlanova, pianist
Professor of Piano,
Manhattan School of Music
and Mannes College

Preface

Grigory Kogan: His Life and Times

So many-sided were Ferruccio Busoni's accomplishments—as composer, author, pedagogue, and philosopher—that even his most important biographers have cast only a cursory glance at the pianistic aspect of Busoni's fascinating career.[1] This book by Grigory Kogan, offered here in English translation, is the first to concentrate exclusively on Busoni-the-Pianist, through a comprehensive summation of extant written materials (reviews, contemporary commentary, Busoni's own writings), painstaking analysis of piano rolls, and an examination of the master's editorial and pedagogical works. As such, it is of interest to every pianist, historian, and musicologist.

Grigory Kogan (1901–1979) was a leading Soviet pianist and musicologist, musical writer, and critic. A conservatory professor at the age of twenty-one, creator of the first-ever course on the history and theory of pianism, art historian, scholar, polemicist, writer—such is the short list of Kogan's accomplishments.[2] With his brilliant lectures, his concertizing, and his many books, articles and reviews, Kogan influenced an entire generation of Soviet pianists. Among his friends were luminaries such as Emil Gilels, Sviatoslav Richter, Heinrich Neuhaus, and Tatiana Nikolaeva. His greatest contribution to the study of pianism was the shifting of emphasis from the muscular and physiological aspects of the pianist's learning process to its psychological and artistic dimensions, illustrating that it is these latter facets that form a truly effective foundation of practice and performance. In the words of Heinrich Neuhaus, "Wide erudition, not only in music but in many areas of history and culture, and the ability to combine painstaking analysis with broad generalization allow Kogan to make considerable contributions to an interesting and original discipline, which, before his work, was in its infancy."[3]

Kogan graduated from the Kiev Conservatory in 1920 and remained there to teach until 1926. Later, as a professor at the Moscow Conservatory, he created his course on the history and theory of pianism, the first of its type. During this period, Kogan became very well known as a pianist, both for his highly intellectual approach to interpretation and for his huge repertoire that focused, in addition to the familiar canon, on music of the French Baroque (François Couperin, Jean-François Dandrieu, and Jacques Duphly) as well as on piano transcriptions and new works. Kogan's very intensive concert schedule also included duets with important pianists such as Grigory Ginzburg and Heinrich Neuhaus.

During Stalin's campaign against "rootless cosmopolitanism," discussed in the following pages, the Jewish Kogan, whose writing frequently referred to non-Soviet musicians, writers, and thinkers, was fired from the Moscow Conservatory and forced to seek employment in exile. Luckily, however, the distinguished composer and director of the Kazan Conservatory, Nazib Zhiganov, offered him a teaching position there, saving Kogan's professional life at some possible risk to himself.

Kogan quickly became a central figure of Kazan's intellectual life. So beloved was Kogan by Kazan's students, that even after his return to Moscow some years later, he continued to return there to give lectures.

After Stalin's death and the softening of conditions in the Soviet Union, Kogan's numerous books and articles were finally published again, and immediately became required reading for Soviet and Russian-speaking musicians. It is a privilege to bring one of these works to English-speaking readers.

No work of scholarship or literature can ever exist in a pure state, outside of its time and place, and unaffected by the circumstances of its birth. Grigory Kogan's excellent study of Busoni is a particularly telling case in point. The English-speaking reader, born and educated in the West, will, no doubt, notice certain anomalies in the book. First, there are gratuitous and unnecessary quotations from those great musicologists, Karl Marx and Vladimir Ilyich Lenin. Next, there is an incantation-like use of the word "bourgeois" to mean the embodiment of all evil. Later, in descriptions of Busoni's compositions, the words "realism" and "formalism" begin to appear, terms that could not possibly apply to Busoni's work because they appeared after his death and outside of his own geographic milieu. And finally, in the last few chapters, Kogan's tone seemingly inexplicably shifts from profound admiration of his hero to criticism of his political, philosophical, and sociological positions in matters that appear to have concerned the real, living Busoni very little indeed.

None of these things would have appeared at all strange to any Soviet reader in the 1960s and the following decades. He would have instantly recognized the attempt, on the part of the author, to offer the precise minimum number of required genuflections in the direction of the official doctrine, the smallest acceptable amount of recitation of prescribed cant, and the least possible damage to Busoni's persona in fitting him into the procrustean bed of Socialist dogma, in order to mollify the censor and allow for publication. A Soviet reader would have noted these things, but not allowed them to affect him any more than the ever-present posters exhorting him to be guided by the Glorious Communist Party in fulfilling the current Five-Year Plan ahead of schedule, or the daily newspaper warnings to watch out for the infiltration of the enemy du jour, or any other set pieces of the infinitely tedious bureaucratic catechism. The Western reader, luckily for him, does not possess this skill.

It is my belief that Kogan himself would have preferred that the passages and chapters he incorporated for the censor's benefit be removed when the times allowed it. However, since he is no longer with us, it is the translator's responsibility to present the complete and unaltered text, but also to offer at least some warning and explanation. Thus, the chapters in question are preceded by an explanatory note, and translator's notes point out the instances of purely political incrustations in the earlier chapters, which, the reader might agree, appear to have been inserted into the text post facto.

I had been shocked, along with my fellow émigrés from the Soviet Union, to discover how little knowledge and understanding of Soviet history, reality, and people there is even among the intellectuals of the West (comparable, no doubt, to the ignorance and misunderstanding of the West by the Soviet intelligentsia!). Even now, after the flood of information and the declassification of numerous documents that became available after glasnost and the dissolution of the USSR, that country is still seen as some Thule-like mysterious place, whose horrors, many assume, have been exaggerated, and its people are viewed as some strange beings, a "mystery wrapped in an enigma." The Soviet people, of course, were just people, with the same hopes and aspirations as people everywhere. They were the inheritors of a great cultural tradition, but, constrained by their reality, they learned to make whatever accommodations were necessary for success and, sometimes, survival. As for the country, at its nightmarish worst, it was George Orwell's *Oceania* (for which it was the inspiration), and, at more benign times, a threat only to its citizen's consciences, rather than their lives.

Kogan's *Busoni*, researched and nurtured over decades, was finally published in 1964, the year Nikita Khrushchev was deposed and Leonid Brezhnev assumed power, and the epoch of *Ottepel* [The Thaw], its hopes largely unrealized, gave way to the Time of Stagnation. The book could not have been published a bare dozen years earlier, and, equally, would not exist in its current form but for the events of the half-century or so that preceded it. In order to make clear to the reader the reasons and the nature of Kogan's "constraints," it is necessary to look at the events of that half-century and the social, cultural, and philosophical consequences to which it gave birth.

* * *

The question of how and why an ideology inspired by positive utopian visions of a just society and equality of all men had led to the establishment of a dictatorial regime instead has been considered by numerous historians and we need not concern ourselves with it in these pages.

What is no mystery at all is that, after the abuses and failures of the last Romanovs, the Russian Revolution and the Great New World it envisioned must have appeared to the exhausted Europe in the years around World War I to be the last hope of mankind. The loss of life in the Revolution itself and the Civil War that followed must have seemed a small price to pay. Very few observers could have predicted, as Bertrand Russell did (as early as 1919), that the whole experiment would end badly in a Napoleonic dictatorship.[4] The rest of the world, especially progressive artists and writers, offered the young Soviet Union their passionate infatuation.

The Revolution inspired a great wave of creative energy, tremendous artistic achievements in all areas, and bold experimentation. Many members of the avant-garde, those belonging to the "Left Front of Art," actively brought their creative efforts to the service of the Bolsheviks—the theater director Vsevolod Meyerhold; the composers Arthur Lourié and Nikolai Roslavets; the artists Natan Altman, David Shterenberg, and Kazimir Malevich; the cultural theoreticians Osip Brik and Nikolai Punin; the film directors Sergei Eisenstein and Vsevolod Pudovkin; and the poet Vladimir Mayakovsky.[5] During these early years, artists were "genuinely animated by the spirit of revolt against, and challenge to, the arts of the West, conceived as the last desperate struggle of capitalism, presently to be overthrown on the artistic as well as every other front by the strong, young, materialist, earthbound, proletarian culture, proud of its brutal simplicity and its crude and violent new vision of the world, which the Soviet Union, . . . was bringing to birth."[6] The composer Nikolai Roslavets, initially a dedicated Communist, explained his artistic creed of emancipating music from outdated conventions as a parallel to the new restructuring of society.[7] After all, with *épater le bourgeois*[8] as one of the guiding principles of the entire modernist movement, what better home could its practitioners have found than a society whose stated purpose was to eliminate the bourgeoisie as a class?

The period of Vladimir Lenin's New Economic Policy (1921–27) was remarkable for its considerable artistic freedom.[9] Under Anatoly Lunacharsky's leadership of the People's Commissariat of Enlightenment, the "controllers of culture did not interfere with anything that could be represented as being a 'slap in the face' to bourgeois tastes, whether it was Marxist or not."[10] The Association of Contemporary Music (ACM) sponsored performances of the music of Mahler, Strauss, Schoenberg, and Stravinsky, Berg's *Wozzeck* was produced in Leningrad, and Bartók and Hindemith visited Russia to perform their own music. There were exhibitions of modernist Western painters like Picasso and Matisse.[11]

Lenin, however, personally disliked modernism intensely. His own attitude to radical artistic experimentation was "bourgeois in the extreme." Others thought that it was the business of Socialist artists to help with the making of Communist society. The members of the Russian Association of Proletarian Writers (RAPP) produced propagandistic and educational "documentary reportage of the new life—the building of factories, collective farms, power stations, the destruction of the old installations, the production of the essentials of the socialist economy— tractors, combines, uniform food, identical clothing, mass-produced houses, books, above all good, happy, uncomplicated, standard human beings."[12] Still other experiments in the 1920s involved collective authorship of literature. Little of value remains from these movements.

In light of ensuing events, and in retrospect, the heady freedom of this period was regarded with nostalgia for years to come. But, as Nadezhda Mandelshtam, the widow of the persecuted poet, reflected in her memoirs much later: "This hankering after the idyllic twenties is the result of a legend. . . . But in reality it was the twenties in which all the foundations were laid for our future: the casuistical dialectic, the dismissal of older values, the longing for unanimity and self-abasement."[13]

Indeed, it was during the freewheeling 1920s that all the conditions that inexorably led to the horror-filled 1930s had been put into place. Vladimir Lenin died in 1924. Joseph Stalin came to power and began his rise to that very Napoleonic dictatorship foreseen by Russell. All economic areas were subjected to strict collectivization and central planning. The Russian identity was slowly and forcefully replaced with a Soviet one. And crushing ideological control began to encroach upon artistic creativity.[14]

While the arts still prospered for a time, the winds of change were already chilling literary life to the core—perhaps not change, precisely, rather a return to old familiar prerevolutionary ways. Tsarist Russia had always been a land of censorship. In fact, the only period in Russian history when censorship did not exist was from February to October 1917.[15] Freedom of the press was the first to go. Interestingly, classic Marxism considers freedom of the press integral to a Communist society; and as late as 1917 Lenin himself wrote a special article extolling it.[16] But by 1921 he was of a different mind: "The bourgeoisie (all over the world) is still very much stronger than we are. To place in its hands yet another weapon like . . . freedom of the press . . . means facilitating the enemy's task."[17] During the same year Lunacharsky made it official in his article "Freedom of the Press and the State": censorship was necessary to prevent the dissemination of counterrevolutionary ideas.[18] Personal freedom must be sacrificed for the same reason. According to published data for August 1922, during that month alone, state security agents opened and read around 150,000 letters sent to citizens from abroad (about half of the total) and every one of the 285,000 letters mailed out.[19]

The writers and poets never stood a chance at all. In Stalin's famous phrase, writers are the "engineers of human souls." This was an echo of Lenin's earlier (1905) statement[20] that the literature of a Communist state must be the "'gear and screw' of the revolutionary propaganda mechanism"[21] and thoroughly subordinated to the state's political goals. These goals in literature, formulated in 1924 and later part of the charter of the Union of Soviet Writers,[22] are clear and leave little room for individualism (which the collectivist Socialist state must regard as a perversion in any case): "Socialist Realism, being the basic method of Soviet literature and literary criticism, demands from the artist a truthful, historically concrete depiction of reality in its revolutionary development. At the same time, the truthfulness and historical concreteness of the artistic depiction of reality must coexist with the goal of ideological change and education of the workers in the spirit of socialism."[23] And so the word *realism*, which Kogan must use as the highest compliment to his hero, and which will color, guide, and contort the development of Soviet literature and the other arts, is first enshrined at the heart of official (and the only permissible) doctrine.[24]

This is not to say that great works could not be written within the confines of Social Realism. The remarkable poetry of Russia's greatest revolutionary poet, Vladimir Mayakovsky—direct, individual, original, profoundly sincere, unforgettable—was a perfect fit, at first. Interestingly, Lenin did not care for it, not even the verses that were passionately pro-Soviet. He called Mayakovsky's political credo a "special form of Communism . . . Hooligan Communism."[25] But Stalin took a broader view. Mayakovsky's appeal to the masses was undeniable. He could be very useful—with a bit of supervision. He proved adaptable—and was suitably rewarded with publication in premier newspapers, lucrative contracts, a Moscow apartment and a car, and the rare opportunity to travel abroad. The public perception of one's revolutionary fervor must inevitably suffer, of course, if one is seen as pursuing, to cite Kogan's often reiterated quote from Busoni's own writings, "the aims of gain." As another, and less adaptable Russian writer, Evgeny Zamyatin, wrote much later: "Writer X wrote revolutionary verses—not because he truly loves the proletariat and wants revolution, but because he loves and wants a car and public stature. Writer X in my opinion is a prostitute."[26] As for what his accommodation with the mighty did to his own soul, we can only guess. Mayakovsky's old friend, the émigré artist Yuri Annenkov recalls seeing him in Paris in 1929. The conversation turned to a return to Moscow. Annenkov said, "'I no longer think about that: I want to remain an artist, and in Bolshevik Russia that is impossible.' Mayakovsky, looking grim, replied, 'Me, I'm going back . . . since I've already stopped being a poet.' And sobbing like a child, he added softly, 'Now I'm . . . an official.'"[27] Mayakovsky shot himself on April 14, 1930. Sergei Esenin, the still-well-loved lyrical Russian poet, killed himself on December 27, 1925.

For the living, and those wishing to remain so, open ideological resistance to the strengthening regime had become impossible. By the end of the 1920s, the country had a "system of total, all-embracing control over the actions and thoughts of scientific and cultural figures, with a special role played by the 'punitive sword of the revolution'—the organs of the VChK-OGPU [forerunners of the KGB]."[28] If an artist, a writer, or a composer wished to lead a reasonably normal life, he had to learn not only to coexist but also to collaborate—and if his collaboration was not of the voluntary kind, the regime was perfectly willing to accept the forced variety. Arts and letters had become "political currency; and the gap between what was proclaimed in public and spoken in private grew greater than ever before."[29]

And then came 1929, "the year of the great watershed," in Stalin's words. This was the beginning of forced collectivization of agriculture, the brutal elimination of "kulaks" (successful peasants) as a class, and the mass starvation that followed.[30] Trotsky was exiled abroad; Nikolai Bukharin and the opposition he headed were completely destroyed. Stalin's power became absolute. All spheres of cultural life now came under direct central control. All existing artistic pro-letarian organizations were dissolved, to be replaced by unions, with a cadre of Communist bureaucrats to impose orthodoxy.

Grigory Kogan had joined the Academy of Arts (Akademiia khudozhestven-nykh nauk) in 1927. Formed in 1921 with the support of Lunacharsky as the premier body of scholars to lead the artistic life of the country, it was subjected to a campaign of personnel purges starting in 1929. Anyone accused of research not "based on Marxist methodology and dialectic materialism" was removed. *Vechernyaya Moskva*, which kept score, counted twenty-four members "cleaned out" out of a total membership of between thirty and thirty-five.[31] A Marxist cell was formed within the academy, whose job it was to supervise the work of the non-Marxists.[32] Kogan, the author of "Marxism and Art," survived.[33]

The Union of Soviet Composers was founded in 1933. Its official mouthpiece was the periodical *Sovetskaia muzyka*, whose mission was to oppose "the ideology of mod-ernists" and to promote "the development of a Marxist-Leninist musicology."[34]

The Union of Soviet Writers was formed in 1932, with the great Russian writer Maxim Gorky (1868–1936) as its first chairman. Gorky's international fame and prestige were invaluable to Stalin, who seemed to have a sincere respect for the illustrious author. So Gorky was convinced to return from his self-imposed Euro-pean exile to take charge of Soviet literature.[35] His first charge was the organiza-tion of the First All-Union Congress of Soviet Writers.

This "Congress of deceived hopes," as it soon became known, the very one that called for "Social Realism" as the only allowable aesthetic, opened on August 17, 1934. One of its various goals was to show the participants themselves (and the world outside Soviet borders) just how deeply the government respected its writ-ers.[36] If these writers hoped that there would be some beneficial reforms or some relaxation of censorship, they were cruelly disappointed. Recently declassified documents reveal disheartening information about what went on. It appears that Stalin received almost daily bulletins from the NKVD (the secret police) on what the writers were saying in the corridors of the congress. The common sentiment was expressed by Isaac Babel, a writer soon to be murdered as an enemy of the people: "We must demonstrate to the world the unanimity of the Union's literary forces. And since all of this is being done artificially, under the stick, the congress is as dead as a tsarist parade, and no one abroad, naturally, believes the parade."[37]

But Babel was very wrong about international reaction. There were a number of foreign celebrities present as special guests of the Congress—including Louis Aragon, André Malraux, and Martin Andersen-Nexø. According to the declassi-fied reports, a leaflet was handed to them, an "appeal from a group of writers," which read, in part: "For the last seventeen years the country has been in a state that absolutely precludes any possibility of free expression. . . . We Russian writ-ers are like prostitutes in a brothel, with the only difference that they sell their bodies and we sell our souls; and as they have no way out of the brothel except a hungry death, neither do we."[38] The famous foreigners did not respond. After all, at this time Germany and Italy were rearming, threatening to swallow large chunks of Europe whole, and burning books. To the European progressives, their own mostly free and mostly prosperous states did not seem adequate to resist Hitler and Mussolini. Stalin did not hold public bonfires—he merely prevented the writing of new books and the publication of old books that the regime found offensive. The wholesale destruction of books and manuscripts and the imprisonment and murder of their authors were still in the future, and never public. So, Stalin and Communism appeared to their admirers to be the only bulwark against the growing threat of Fascism. Other major Western writers shared this opinion—Romain Rolland, George Bernard Shaw, and Theodore Dreiser.[39] The pleas of a handful of discontents were not likely to change their worldview and their deeply held beliefs. In any case, it is unclear whether any foreign pressure could have prevented the catastrophe that unfolded in 1936.

Isaiah Berlin called it "a kind of St. Bartholomew's Eve."[40] By the time it was over, millions were destroyed, simple workmen, high-ranking Communist officials, most of the army officer core, eminent scientists and poets, distinguished writers, composers, directors—this slaughter halted only by the greater slaughter of World War II.

In the world of culture, it all began with an opera. Shostakovich's *Ledi Makbet Mtsenskogo uezda* (Lady Macbeth of Mtsensk) was composed earlier, between 1930 and 1932, and premiered in Leningrad in 1934 to critical and popular acclaim, hailed immediately as "a great achievement of Soviet Culture."[41] In two years it received over 200 Russian performances, and was produced internationally in New York, London, Stockholm, Prague, Zurich, and other cities.[42] The story, by Nikolai Leskov, which takes place, safely, in prerevolutionary Russia, is one of lust, greed, rape, and murder, a sort of Russian *Lulu*. It inspired one of Shostakovich's most expressive and expressionist scores. Stalin went to see it in January 1936. It is possible that, petrified by the august presence, the musicians did not perform well. Equally possibly, Stalin's very Victorian sensibilities were scandalized. However, it is more likely that the unfortunate opera was merely a convenient vehicle for the start of a carefully planned and prepared campaign.

The first salvo was fired on January 29, 1936, by the newspaper *Pravda*. This was the infamous article "Muddle Instead of Music," which criticized the "dissonance and confusion" of the music and its "pornographic" qualities. The composer "missed the demands of Soviet culture to banish crudity and wildness from every corner of Soviet life." And, most important for our discussion, the article introduced that dreaded word *formalism,* which, as an epithet embodying all things anti-Soviet, became the rallying cry for the artistic repression to follow. *Pravda* followed with a number of seminal assessments of other arts in quick succession. On February 13, it published an attack on film, "A Crude Scheme Instead of Historical Truth," on February 20, it featured "Cacophony in Architecture," followed on March 1 by "On Mess-Making Artists," and, finally, on March 9, "Outward Brilliance and False Content" dealt with theater.[43]

Formalism was present everywhere, and had to be rooted out. The definitions of Formalism are many and varied. The most basic is, essentially, that formalist art is too complicated and incomprehensible to the masses, and thus useless in the construction of Soviet culture.[44] According to Sergei Prokofiev "formalism is . . . the name given to that which is not understood at first hearing."[45] Or, best of all, in Glenn Gould's inimitable words, formalism is "whatever one's colleagues are writing."[46]

In the 1936–37 season, ten out of nineteen new plays in major theaters were taken off the stage, including the ballet *The Limpid Stream* with music by the ill-fated Shostakovich. (This work is about the happy life in a kolkhoz, full of bright tunes and as Social Realist as anything Shostakovich ever wrote, so its banishment can only be seen as a punishment.[47] In light of punishments handed out to others, Shostakovich could consider himself supremely lucky.) In that same season more than ten theaters were closed down in Moscow alone and ten others in Leningrad. In the 1937–38 season, fifty-six plays were removed from the repertoire and banned.[48]

And what was it exactly that Soviet writers were supposed to write? All those calls by *Pravda* for "directness and clarity" were finally explained by the lead article on March 3: "Directness and clarity are the characteristic traits of all statements and speeches of Comrade Stalin." And for those still confused, *Literaturnaya gazeta* spelled it out: Stalin's style was a "marvelous and artist-inspiring classic example of simplicity, clarity, and chiseled expression, and of splendid and courageous power of truth. This is our good fortune: for us Soviet artists, these are the examples from which we can learn courage, strength and truth."[49]

And so the midnight arrests and the executions of the intellectual elites began. The number of writers alone destroyed in 1936–39 is estimated to be above 600, nearly one-third of the Writers Union's total membership.[50] Most of them, along with musicians, scholars, and scientists, were rehabilitated posthumously, and their works republished. However, it is impossible to estimate the loss of those manuscripts confiscated and destroyed at the time of the arrests, and the works still in their minds or those that could have been written later. Kogan, who was not one of the victims, nevertheless published nothing between 1937 and 1948. The damage to the cultural life of the country, indeed to the world, was profound; the damage to its social values was worse.

The prominent theater director Vsevolod Meyerhold, who is mentioned in Kogan's book, was arrested in 1939. He was brutally beaten, and shot on two absurd charges—spying for Japan and formerly working for the tsarist Okhrana (security agency). Under torture, Meyerhold "confessed"[51] to everything his interrogators wanted, and gave statements against other cultural figures. None of those he named as "Trotskyite agents" were ever arrested. Why Meyerhold and Babel died, while Akhmatova, Shostakovich, and Pasternak survived was never explained. For Soviet intelligentsia, life became a lottery. In the atmosphere of uncertainty and fear, "a pall of death in life hung over the cities of the Soviet Union, while the torture and slaughter of millions of innocents were going on."[52]

The norms of civilized behavior shifted. If you denounced your colleague, or signed a letter of condemnation, maybe, just maybe, you might be safe. Anna Akhmatova told Isaiah Berlin ". . . you come from a society of human beings, whereas here we are divided into human beings and. . . ."[53] And it mattered little if one chose to be a "human being" rather than Akhmatova's unspoken "and. . . ." Boris Pasternak, the future author of *Doctor Zhivago* and Nobel Prize winner, was ordered to sign a collective letter from writers approving of the death sentence for Marshall Mikhail Tukhachevsky. When Pasternak refused, pressure was applied. As he recalled later, his pregnant wife fell to his feet begging him to save the life of his unborn child and sign the letter. He could not bring himself to do so. He even wrote in a letter to Stalin himself that he "did not consider himself capable of judging the life and death of other people."[54] He had made his choice to ". . . to die with the masses, with the people." After this, Pasternak, obviously, could do no more but wait for the dreaded middle-of-the-night knock on his door—which did not come. Instead, the newspaper published the letter from writers in support of the execution—with Pasternak's signature! Reportedly, Pasternak wept in despair, repeating, "They've killed me."[55]

*   *   *

As the news of the cataclysmic events in the Soviet Union began to leak out to the West, idealist Progressive intellectuals chose to support Stalin. The evidence was either simply too overwhelming to believe or still insufficient to tip the balance between the promise of Utopia and the reality.[56] To his dying day George Bernard Shaw continued to praise Stalin as the personification of Socialism.[57] Romain Rolland, another intellectual mentioned by Kogan, found Stalin to be "simple, attentive, cheerful, even gentle."[58] Hardly a simpleton, however, Rolland did have his doubts. He wrote in his diary: "I feel pain and indignation arising within me, but I suppress the need to write and speak about it. All I would have to do would be to make public the slightest criticism of this system, and its mercenary enemies . . . would seize upon my words as a weapon, poisoning them with the most criminal ill will."[59] In other words, the Soviet Union must be defended from all critics as a "bulwark against the danger of fascism in Western Europe," no matter what the cost, because "the cause is bigger than they [Stalin and his henchmen] are."[60]

Keeping one's doubts and suspicions suppressed for the benefit of "the cause" is one thing. Allowing oneself to be used blatantly for propaganda purposes is another. The writer Lion Feuchtwanger traveled to the Soviet Union in 1937 and was immediately welcomed and feted by Stalin himself, whom Feuchtwanger found to be a "simple, good-natured man," who "appreciated humor and was not offended by criticism of himself,"[61] and who "was always profound, wise, and thoughtful."[62] He came to Moscow to witness one of the show trials Stalin was putting on. Apparently, Feuchtwanger had been skeptical about all those confessions the accused were making in earlier trials (under what torture, what threat to family, what weight of despair?). As he described in his book *Moscow, 1937,* the trial he witnessed in the courtroom "converted" him to faith in Stalin's justice.[63] Stalin immediately had the book translated into Russian and published. The author received a large fee, both for this book and his novels,[64] a situation not at all usual at the time.[65] And as for Feuchtwanger's doubts, his original line of reasoning was to quote Socrates on the difficult passages in Heraclitus, the Greek philosopher of the sixth century BCE: "What I understand is superb. Hence I conclude that the rest, which I do not understand, is also superb."[66]

To those Western observers who were not "imprisoned in Stalinist ideology," to quote music historian Peter Gay, the Stalinist Soviet Union, far from being a bulwark against the rising Nazi regime, seemed to possess "astonishing and disheartening affinities" to it.[67] To them, the Nazi–Soviet Non-Aggression Pact of August 1939 came as no surprise. One wonders if the pro-Soviet writers had any sort of a crisis of faith. In any case, Hitler broke the pact and invaded the Soviet Union on June 22, 1941.

* * *

The war years were a time of comparative artistic freedom, either because the Soviet Union needed the support of the Allies or because Stalin was busy with other things. If writers and musicians expected that this creative freedom would continue after the war, they were quickly and thoroughly disabused of their hopes. This time, the first attack was directed at literature, under the leadership of Andrei Zhdanov (1896–1948), the Politburo member in charge of ideology.[68] On August 14, 1946, the Organizational Bureau of the Central Committee of the All-Union Communist Party issued a special resolution, which denounced Mikhail Zoshchenko as a "scoundrel of literature" and Akhmatova's poetry was declared "alien to our people."[69] To the writer Lydia Chukovskaya, the authorship of the resolution was unmistakable: "his [Stalin's] most august mustache protruded from every paragraph."[70] Zhdanov elaborated in a number of speeches, which were issued as a brochure that became "a mantra of Soviet ideology."[71] Although written eighteen years earlier than Kogan's *Busoni,* Zhdanov's formulations on literature were considered holy writ, and only formally disavowed in 1988.[72] At the same time, the campaign of "struggling against cosmopolitanism" unfolded, during which anything even suspiciously not Russian was persecuted; anti-Semitism was encouraged from above; and even progressive Western authors became anathema while Soviet writers found themselves completely fenced off from the mainstream of Western civilization. Nonfiction became limited to Russian and Soviet matters, and as for fiction, writers were to compose, to quote the incomparable Berlin yet again:

novels dealing with exploits in kolkhozes, factories or at the front; . . . patriotic doggerel or . . . plays which [condemn] the capitalist world or the old and discredited liberal culture of Russia itself, in contrast with the simple, now wholly standardized, type of tough, hearty, capable, resolute, single-minded young engineers or political commissars ("engineers of human souls") or army commanders, shy and manly lovers, sparing of words, doers of mighty deeds, "Stalin's eagles," flanked by passionately patriotic, utterly fearless, morally pure, heroic young women, upon whom the success of all five-year plans ultimately depends.[73]

An attack on music followed soon after. The pretext was another ill-fated opera, Vano Muradeli's *The Great Friendship*. The great irony was that this opera, neither formalistic in any way at all nor a magnum opus, was composed with the specific and obvious intent to flatter Stalin, an ethnic Georgian. Its subject matter was a fawning portrayal of Georgian Communists. It seems that something about the libretto displeased the Great Leader—or perhaps, this time, he decided to use a work that was not already proclaimed a masterpiece, by a composer little known in the West. Poor Muradeli offered his *mea culpas* and remained in official favor. Instead, the wrath fell on more prominent and greater composers.

A meeting of the Central Committee of the Party was convened in January 1948, with over seventy leading Soviet musicians in attendance, including Nikolai Miaskovsky, Sergei Prokofiev, Dmitri Shostakovich, Aram Khachaturian, Dmitri Kabalevsky, Yuri Shaporin, Vissarion Shebalin, and Tikhon Khrennikov. Zhdanov read excerpts of the earlier "Muddle Instead of Music" to them and added, ominously, that "now it is clear that the direction in music condemned back then still lives, and not only lives, but sets the tone for Soviet music." He elaborated further: "we have a very acute even though seemingly covert battle between two directions in Soviet music." One direction was realistic, developing in a profound organic connection with the people; the other was formalist, based on a refusal to serve the people "so as to serve the profoundly individualistic feelings of a small group of select aesthetes." The representatives of the formalist direction wrote music that was "crude, graceless, and vulgar," resembling, in Zhdanov's elegant definition "either a dentist's drill or a musical gas chamber."[74]

The ultimate blow fell on February 11. *Pravda* published a final list of composers of the "formalist, anti-people direction." Shostakovich, Prokofiev, Khachaturian, Shebalin, Gavriil Popov, and Miaskovksy, in that order, were condemned for: "disseminating among figures of Soviet musical culture tendencies alien to it, leading to a dead end in the development of music, to the liquidation of musical art."[75] Khrennikov, the general secretary of the Composers Union, lectured the miscreants in more detail: "Enough symphony diaries, pseudo-philosophizing symphonies, hiding boring intellectual navel-gazing beneath a veneer of profound thought! . . . Our audiences are tired of modernist cacophony! It's time to turn our music back on the path of clarity and realistic simplicity! . . . We will not permit further destruction of the marvelous temple of music created by the composer geniuses of the Past!"[76] Shostakovich was fired from the Moscow and Leningrad conservatories, his works removed from the repertoire. He and his "formalist" cohorts became "enemies of the people," in need of immediate and radical reeducation.[77]

Musicologists came under fire soon after, in 1949. Russia's best musical scholars were scolded for their interest in foreign music, and for daring to analyze Russian music using foreign ideas. They too had to learn to see historical developments in light of the official Party line.[78] Grigory Kogan, with his obviously Jewish name and well-known interest in foreign pianists was among the victims. He was fired from the Moscow Conservatory and exiled from Moscow.

One cannot help but wonder how much further the regime would have gone, and how much more damage Soviet culture could have sustained if Stalin had lived much longer. But on March 5, 1953, he died, and a new era began.

* * *

This was the era of Nikita Khrushchev's Thaw, which lasted approximately from the time of Khrushchev's historic speech exposing Stalin's actions in 1956 to Brezhnev's trial of two authors, Andrey Sinyavsky and Yuly Daniel, for the crime of publishing their works in the West, in 1965. Grigory Kogan's *Busoni*, published in 1964, is a true child of its time—its very existence made possible by the new freedoms, and, simultaneously, its content shaped by the old restrictions.

Khrushchev made his historic speech, "On the Personality Cult and Its Consequences," on February 25, 1956, at a secret session of the Twentieth Party Congress. In it he denounced Stalin's mistakes and crimes, revealed the extent of the Great Purges and the repressions, and blamed the Cult of Personality[79] Stalin had created around himself for the damage to the country and its people.[80] Hundreds of thousands returned from labor camps, jails, and exile, including members of the intelligentsia. Censorship was weakened, and contacts with the West were allowed. The people began to believe that a new and better life, of which they could only dream before, was beginning.

These hopes blossomed in May 1958, when Khrushchev cautiously disavowed the Zhdanov resolution against Shostakovich, Prokofiev, and other composers.[81] The resolution against Pasternak, Akhmatova, and other writers, however, remained in place. Their hopes were soon to be dashed even more. Boris Pasternak's famous novel *Doctor Zhivago* could not have been published in the USSR, but had been smuggled to the West (a story worthy of a suspense novel of its own!) and won the Nobel Prize in Literature in 1958. The official fury reached epic proportions. A vicious article appeared in *Pravda* under the title "Noise of Reactionary Propaganda Around a Literary Weed," Pasternak was forced to turn down the prize and expelled from the Writers Union.[82] It was as if Stalin's days had returned. In 1962, Khrushchev attended an exhibition featuring the works of young artists and sculptors in Moscow, and was not amused. In the storm that followed, the accusations of "formalism" rang out with abandon equal to that of 1938. There were no executions, but Culture and the Government were at war again.

The Thaw was not only short-lived, it was also superficial, and offered no guarantees against a return to the old ways and no security against government interference. In 1964, Leonid Brezhnev came to power in a bloodless coup, and the epoch of hope was over.

But in that short interval, Kogan was able finally to publish his work of a lifetime—the great study of Busoni, and if he had to fill it with accusations of "formalism" and praise of "realism," and to fluctuate between approving Busoni's antibourgeois stance and berating him for not adopting the Marxist-Leninist creed, the reader will surely understand.

Svetlana Belsky

Acknowledgments

This book is the brainchild of my dear teacher, Nina Svetlanova, internationally acclaimed pianist, student of Grigory Kogan and Heinrich Neuhaus, and the teacher who inspired a generation of young pianists. It was she who introduced me to Kogan's writings, to *Busoni,* and to the pianistic concepts contained within it. I have since worked hard to pass their wisdom on to another generation of piano students.

So many others have supported this project during its long journey from idea to book, and I would like to thank you all. I am especially grateful to my father, James Belsky, for technical and computer expertise and endless enthusiasm. To George Livadas, for his knowledge of all things Busoni and his very helpful discography. To Peter Spragins and Kevin Kenner for their editorial suggestions, and to Alex Stephenson for all his help with music notation software. And finally, to my husband, Alex Korsky, who has had to put up with very long hours and extra domestic chores, and yet has supported me through every stage of the project.

Busoni as Pianist

Grigory Kogan

Translated and Annotated by Svetlana Belsky

Introduction

"... In order to receive a work of art, half the work must be done by the receiver himself."

F. Busoni, "On the Future of Opera"*

Among the most prominent performing musicians whose fame history has preserved, it is difficult to name one whose art aroused as stormy and contradictory a reaction among contemporaries as that of Ferruccio Busoni, the German-Italian pianist of the turn of the century. His activities—not only performance but also composition, pedagogy, and musicology—constantly attracted the attention of the musical world, sparked passions, and created an extensive literature. His book *Entwurf einer neuen Ästhetic der Tonkunst* [Sketch of a New Aesthetic of Music] excites a lively polemic in the press;[1] his idea for the reform of keyboard notation (*Versuch einer organischen Klavier-Noten-Schrift*) stirs up a protracted debate;[2] a short article "Wie lange soll das gehen?" [How Long Will It Go On?], criticizing the atmosphere of concerts, incites passionate arguments.[3] "I begin this letter with yesterday's concert of Ferruccio Busoni, which, in its interest, eclipsed all preceding ones and aroused such hot arguments and such a difference of opinion, that it is necessary to deal with it first," writes the Berlin correspondent of the *Russian Musical Gazette*. "Although the 'Concerto'[4] ... is more than an hour long, and the listeners could not have understood everything upon first hearing, they became ever-more drawn in, electrified, reaching by the end a state of physical excitement—chaos reigned in the coatrooms, strangers spoke to each other, remarks were heard such as 'but this is the tenth Symphony!' [5] one saw bewildered faces, people bumped into one another, without even noticing—in general, the deep reaction was felt everywhere."[6] "The appearance of Busoni here became a major event. Our musical anthill came to life. Passionate debates and judgments were ignited among the music lovers. The public became divided into two fiercely hostile camps. Some exalted Busoni to no end. . . . Others were, if not skeptical, then, at least, cool. . . ."[7] Busoni's participation in the Liszt celebrations in Heidelberg, his cycle of six Clavierabende in Berlin (during October–December 1911) became events that for a long time captivated the attention of the German musical press.[8] Otto Lessmann's[9] musings about one of Busoni's recitals grows into a large essay on "whether further development of piano-playing is possible."[10] A critical analysis by B. L. Yavorsky[11] of Busoni's

Moscow concerts (October–November 1912) becomes a thorough discussion of the problems and types of the performer's art.[12] Two Liszt Clavierabends held by Busoni in Berlin in 1909 culminated in a sharp exchange on the subject of "Busoni and the interpretation of Liszt's music."[13]

Critical response to Busoni is amazing for its wildly divergent opinions. Otto Lessmann in the previously mentioned article remarks that no other currently concertizing pianist encounters either such ecstatic admiration or such energetic renunciation. Indeed, for some, Busoni is a "demigod," "the greatest virtuoso of our day," infinitely above all others, the only worthy successor of Liszt, one of the three (Paganini, Liszt, Busoni) "most illustrious names in instrumental mastery of the past hundred years," a genius who stands "on the other side of all other pianists, who ushers in a new era of piano-playing";[14] "Never, undoubtedly, never will anything like this be heard again," writes the famous French musicologist Jean Chantavoine after the artist's death.[15] But for others, the Italian pianist is a "passing idol," a dry technician, an over-intellectual and extravagant interpreter, lacking a "spontaneous musical gift" and even elementary musicality. "There is much that is artificial in him, vogue . . ." affirms one critic. "He could blossom only in the contemporary German soil—the soil of perceptible decay of the spirit of music, and a decay of sincere love for musical beauty. . . . Mutilating and deforming Chopin's Etudes, robbing them of poetry and specifically Chopinesque flavor, Busoni turned them into simple exercises for finger dexterity, his pedaling, meantime, far from irreproachable. It sometimes seemed that the pianist, from the pinnacle of his worldwide renown, mocks both Chopin and the public—but, above all, musicians." "The musical experiences of Busoni," seconds another reviewer "or, rather: his feeling of musical beauty, does not reach in him that brightness, that abundance, due to which they demand to be expressed, and freely and easily find the necessary means and devices for expression. . . . Music appears to be difficult for Busoni, and therefore he must over-exert himself in all regards, both physically and spiritually (that was particularly evident in the performance of Chopin). . . . And in Busoni's book,[16] there is much about feelings, spirit, temperament and thoughts, which music expresses, but not one word mentions musical <u>beauty</u>, and that immediately throws a certain shadow over both his esthetics and his musical nature." From Busoni's concerts joins in the third, "where you might be shown Chopin's Etudes in a deformed fashion, why, almost as if in a broken mirror," . . ."in the end the listener goes home cold and disappointed . . . only hypnotized, not moved. . . . Mannerism remains mannerism. . . . Each work is approached with some sort of perversity, which leaves in his playing no divine simplicity."[17]

Even more than his playing, Busoni's literary and compositional efforts encountered bitterly divergent opinions. Some see in the author of *Fantasia contrappuntistica* and the *Sketch of a New Aesthetic of Music* a great and original composer of the caliber of Mahler, Scriabin, Debussy, a visionary thinker, a spiritual guide of the new musical generation; they term him the "strongest, most all-encompassing mind among contemporary musicians," an extraordinary personality that calls to mind the images of Liszt, Leonardo, Raphael, and Goethe.[18] Others see nothing in these works but "senseless confusion," "nonsense," "amateurish attempts in the 'category of the pitiable.'"[19]

What can explain this diversity of judgment, such contrast in the public perception of Busoni's art? What about him so irritated and so offended his contemporaries?

Certainly no one today would blame it on his lack of genius. His great gift—especially pianistic—has long been accepted and outside debate; and, anyhow, without such a gift it would not have been possible for him to rouse the attention of his society, to heat it to such a degree. "Without possessing a positive content," reasonably notes Heine in his tenth letter about the French stage, "it is not possible in this world to evoke either favorable or hostile passions. It is necessary to possess a fire to ignite hatred, as well as love."[20]

Obviously the answer lay not in the limitations of Busoni's talent, but in its orientation toward the very new, which differed dramatically from the fashionable, the habitual, and the accepted in contemporary tastes, views, and ideas. Originality permeated all aspects of Busoni's multifaceted creativity. His articles, books, and letters contradicted established thought; his music broke accepted formal schemes and the usual conventions of the harmonic language; familiar warhorses sounded different in his hands. Upon his first acquaintance with Busoni, the reviewer of one of St. Petersburg's papers states with surprise "he is like no other pianist St. Petersburg has ever heard."[21] Other critics also note the "extremely individual" character of his playing, "incredible originality," "unusual originality and independence" of interpretation, the ability to "see and understand differently than anyone else," to interpret "disregarding traditions," bringing in "the unexpected, the new," "breaking the mold," audaciously "parting with tradition, the commonly accepted, consecrated by the ages and the tradition of the great interpreters."[22] "Yes, Busoni is original and new in his interpretation—in his whole attitude toward the music he performs. It is precisely this originality that some judges and critics will not forgive him."[23]

Originality and novelty distinguished not only Busoni's interpretation but also the technical side of his pianism. Acting, even here, "against all tradition," according to Adolf Weissmann[24] he "created for himself a new technique, contradicting all the rules. . . ."[25] "Busoni the Pianist, . . ." confirms another critic, "much like Busoni the Composer, or Busoni the Interpreter, does not fit into any mold: his method of playing the piano is wholly original. He contradicts all theoretical arguments about the physiologically correct methods of developing technique or the most pleasant, in the acoustical sense, ways of sound production on the piano."[26] This applies to all aspects of the piano technique—the so-called position of the hands, their movement, fingering, pedaling: "the pedaling of this giant-pianist breaks with the most essential elements of usual pedaling. . . ."[27]

Thus, Busoni was an innovator in his art. But to say that is to say very little. As we know, all innovation is not alike. The novelty of some event by itself says nothing of its character or of its value. To decide the latter, to establish Busoni's place in music history and our own attitude toward Busoni's art it is not enough to show its novelty for its time; it is necessary to investigate whence Busoni came and where he finished; what his springboard was, what aspects of the old he rejected, what precisely his innovations were, and what the content of his contributions was.

This book is dedicated to the investigation of these questions, a description of the creative path of the master, and the characterization of his aesthetic and his art.

Chapter One

Busoni did not become an innovator all at once. The beginnings of his activity took place under very different artistic ideals. Let us look first at this time—the childhood, adolescence, and youth of our hero.

In the north of Italy, in Tuscany, near Florence lies a little town called Empoli. There, on April 1, 1866, the future great pianist was born. He was the only son of the Italian clarinetist Ferdinando Busoni and the pianist Anna Weiss, who was Italian on her mother's side and German on her father's. The boy's parents concertized and led a wandering life, which the child, too, was obliged to share. Eleven months after birth he was taken away from his native town, and, traveling from place to place, in 1869, found himself in Paris where the family planned to settle. However, the Franco-Prussian War that began in 1870 forced Busoni's parents to abandon this intention. The boy's father set off on an extended concert tour of Italy, while Ferruccio and his mother settled in Trieste in the home of his grandfather, Giuseppe Weiss.

In Trieste—an Italian city, then part of the Austro-Hungarian Empire— Busoni's musical education began. His abilities, as is usual among great musicians, manifested themselves early. By four years of age he already played the piano by ear. The first lessons of piano and musicianship were given by his mother, and soon the pupil could perform small four-hand pieces of Diabelli with his teacher.

Busoni's mother was a good pianist, quite successful on the stage (eight days before her son's birth she performed in Rome in the presence of Liszt);[1] her son remembered in her playing a faultless technique, great facility, and a certain "salon" approach "in the spirit of Thalberg's art."[2]

In 1872, after an absence of two years, suddenly his father came back, and the boy's life underwent great changes.

Busoni's father was a colorful, original personality. Far from lacking in talent, but deficient in general education and professionalism, he continually nurtured grand plans, which usually greatly exceeded his rather modest real gifts. He did not wish to play in an orchestra, considering that beneath him, and, quite possibly, could not, for, according to his son, he could not manage rhythm or sight-reading any too well.[3] But solo concerts, which had brought him "small fame,"[4] could not entirely satisfy his ambition, either. In search of the road to fame he tried many and various ventures: now attempting to write and publish poetry, then "making" his son's career, and so on. Ardent and outspoken, unceremonious and despotic, always "temporarily" without a penny to his name, but nevertheless full of unwavering faith in the future, he often evoked ironic smiles in those around him and materially complicated the lives of his family members.

His father's fantasies left their mark on Busoni's life from the very start. By his wish, the newborn was given four names: Ferruccio-Dante-Michelangelo-Benvenuto—in the naive belief that the "patronage" of the three great Tuscan artists (Dante Alighieri, Michelangelo Buonarroti, and Benvenuto Cellini) would guarantee the child's glorious future. Naturally, having reached the age of awareness, Busoni hurriedly discarded the "heavy responsibility" tactlessly laid upon him by his father, rejected the two middle names, and, eventually, also the fourth, leaving himself only the name Ferruccio.

Back with the family, his father immediately commenced furious activity. Having insisted on moving the family away from the home of his father-in-law to a separate apartment, he dismissed his wife from further instruction of the child, and, thoroughly unembarrassed by his incompetence in questions of pianism, undertook the boy's education himself. These lessons are colorfully described in Busoni's "autobiographical fragments":

> My father knew little about piano playing, and, in addition, did not have very good rhythm, but he compensated for these faults with absolutely indescribable energy, severity, and pedantry. He could sit by my side for four hours a day, controlling every note and every finger. There could be no indulgence, rest, or slightest inattention on his part. The only pauses were precipitated by explosions of his unusually irascible temperament, which were followed by reproaches, dark prophecies, threats, an occasional box on the ear, and ample tears. Finally, there was repentance, father's consolation, and assurance that he wishes only the best—and the next day it all began again.[5]

Having put it into his head at all costs to make another Mozart out of his son, Busoni's father decided that the boy was most likely to reach this goal by following, step by step, the artistic path of the author of *Don Giovanni*. The latter, of course, studied music from the age of four and performed at six. Busoni's lessons began at the "correct" time. It only remained to prepare him successfully for a public debut, which took place—alas, with a certain delay in "the plan"—in Trieste, on November 24, 1873: the seven-year-old Busoni took part in his parents' concert, playing the first movement of Mozart's C-Major Sonata, the F-Major Sonatina of Clementi, and two pieces from Schumann's *Album for the Young*: "Armes Waisenkind" and "Soldatenmarsch." The little pianist appeared under the dual name Weiss-Busoni—the father's new idea, in the belief that the combination of two "big names" would create good publicity for the young prodigy.

Around the same time, Busoni began to test himself in composition. In the summer of 1873 he wrote a few little piano pieces, which were soon followed by several other compositions for the piano, or for voice and piano.

The successful Trieste debut opened the door to future performances by the young Ferruccio. On May 18, 1874, he performed "quite distinctly and with subtle details"[6] the C-Minor Concerto of Mozart under his father's baton, and on February 8, 1876, gave his first full recital in Vienna, which included Haydn's Trio in D Major (Busoni played the piano part from memory), a Rondo of Mozart, Hummel's Theme and Variations, and five small pieces of his own. A few other artists participated in the concert, including young Arthur Nikisch (the future famous conductor) who played the violin part in the Haydn and accompanied two singers on the piano.

The Viennese concert of young Busoni did not pass unnoticed. On February 13, a detailed review by Edward Hanslick appeared in the *Neue Freie Presse*. The Austrian critic noted the boy's "brilliant success" and "unusual abilities," which set him apart from the crowd of "wonder-children . . . whose wonder ends with their childhood." "For a long time now," writes the critic, "no other child prodigy had elicited as much sympathy from me as little Ferruccio Busoni. That is because he is so little a prodigy and so much a good musician. . . . His playing is fresh, natural, with that difficult to define but immediately obvious musical instinct, which always finds the correct tempo, the correct accents, catches the spirit of the rhythm, and clearly brings out the voices in the polyphonic episodes. . . ." The critic also praised the "incredibly serious and masculine character" of the performer's compositional experiments, which, together with his predilection for "lively figurations and combinatorial contrivances" testifies to a "loving study of Bach"; the same features distinguished the free fantasy, which Busoni improvised after the program—"mainly in imitation and counterpoint"— on the themes given by the author of the review.

This description of the early art of the Italian musician is confirmed by the later admission of Busoni himself that "from earliest childhood [he] played Bach and studied counterpoint," which had then become his "mania," so that each of his childhood compositions contains "at least one *fugato*."[7] Because of these "Bachisms," Busoni's early works appeared to the contemporary critics as if "written two hundred years ago."[8]

The judgment of an authoritative critic made an impression on the musical world, particularly on the music publishers: they began to bring out Busoni's works from 1876–77.

The stay in Vienna was commemorated for Busoni by one more important event—meeting Anton Rubinstein. Upon hearing the young artist, Rubinstein wrote his opinion that the boy "possesses a most remarkable talent, both as a performer and as a composer" and "some day will bring glory to his country"; at the same time, the great Russian pianist persistently recommended that his young colleague be relieved of public performances "to earn a living" and given an opportunity to "work seriously," obtain "a thorough education," but without "shoving" him into any conservatory.[9] Rubinstein's sensible advice was not followed: Busoni was compelled to continue concertizing to feed not only himself but also his parents. Almost four years passed before circumstances allowed him to devote somewhat more serious attention to his musical education. At the end of 1879, the thirteen-year-old Busoni left Trieste for another Austrian town— Graz, the capital of the province of Styria, where, on November 23 he conducted the performance of his *Stabat Mater* for chorus and string orchestra. A few days later he became a student of the noted local musician Dr. W. Meyer.

Wilhelm Meyer (1831–1898),[10] better known as W. A. Rémy, in those years enjoyed great popularity not so much as a composer, but as a superb teacher of music theory and composition; among his students were such outstanding musicians as Reznicek, Weingartner, and Kienzl.[11]

Busoni studied with Meyer-Rémy from December 1879 to March 1881, writing during that time many fugues, quartets, cantatas, a six-voice choral Mass a cappella, and thoroughly familiarizing himself with the theory and history of music; in the future, the student remembered with gratitude his demanding and able teacher.[12] This year and a quarter was the extent of Busoni's "school" education in composition and general musicianship; as for the piano, after his mother and father, he took no more lessons from anyone, thus remaining practically self-taught.

At the end of his studies with Rémy, Busoni undertook a concert tour of Italy, which was a great success. Here, his father reappeared on the scene, with his maniacal aspiration to copy the biography of Mozart. As the latter was elected to the famous Philharmonic Academy in Bologna in the fifteenth year of his life, so the fifteen-year-old Busoni was required to seek the same honor. After passing an extremely difficult examination, in 1881 he, too, became a member of the Bolognese Academy—the first one since Mozart to be awarded this honorable title at such an early age. The junior academician lingered in Bologna for some time and wrote the most extended of his works of those years—a gigantic, 300-page-long score of his cantata for chorus, soloists, and orchestra *Il sabato del villaggio* on the text of a Leopardi poem. Unpublished, as were many of Busoni's early works, the cantata was performed in Bologna in 1883 under a well-known conductor, L. Mancinelli. The same year saw the publication of Busoni's transcription of the funeral march for the death of Siegfried from Wagner's musical drama *Götterdämmerung*—his first experiment in the transcription genre that was destined to bring him so much fame in the future.

As he grew older, with each passing year Busoni, feeling more and more burdened by his father's eccentricities, tried persistently to leave his guardianship and to begin an independent life. In the search for his own road in life, from 1884 he more noticeably separated himself from Italy and became "Germanized." Living in Vienna and in other Austrian cities, he was drawn into the circle of noted local musicians, artists, and literati, and fell under the strong influence of Brahms, to whom he dedicates his piano etudes Opus 16 and Opus 17.

At this time, Busoni commenced another endeavor: from 1884 various newspapers and magazines (*L'Indipendente* of Trieste, *Grazer Tagespost*, *Zeitschrift für Musik*, *Neue Zeitschrift für Musik*, and others) published—under the name of the author, and under his anagrammatic pseudonym Bruno Fioresucci—his correspondence, reviews, and articles on music ("The State of Music in Italy," "Giovanni Sgambati," "Verdi's *Otello*," "On the Anniversary of *Don Juan*," etc.). Among these articles, the detailed reviews of Anton Rubinstein's Vienna concerts of February 1884 are of particular interest. The interpretations of the eminent Russian pianist made a great impression on Busoni, especially those of Chopin—the B-Minor Sonata and the C-Minor Nocturne; these performances were "more valuable than an entire course of study."[13] According to Schnapp, for the next few years, Rubinstein's playing became young Busoni's "ideal," which he occasionally copied; as late as the winter of 1890–91, listening to Rubinstein's performance of "Erlkönig," among other works, Busoni, as his wife related, "wept, like a child; tears of fascination and joy ran down his cheeks."[14]

At his meeting with Rubinstein in February 1884, Busoni played his barely completed large Piano Sonata in F Minor, dedicated to Rubinstein, who liked the work, but it remained unpublished.

Busoni's first performance in Berlin took place on April 14, 1885; the program included the *Chromatic Fantasy and Fugue* of Bach, Beethoven's *Appassionata,* and the performer's own Variations and Fugue on Chopin's C-Minor Prelude. The public reception was cold. The young artist had to face the fact that by the age of nineteen the fame achieved by a "wonder-child" loses its value, and his position in the musical world must be won anew, on a different, more solid basis than the one that was useful in childhood.

In 1886 (1887, according to other sources), Busoni finally realized his long cherished plan to "get away from troubled and unsettled home conditions":[15] he finally left the parental home and settled in Leipzig. Life there was far from easy. In need of money, he accepted every sort of employment: he played, composed, wrote articles, produced piano scores of operas, piano transcriptions of Mozart and Mendelssohn symphonies, Schubert's overtures and dances, and the orchestral part of Schumann's Concert Allegro. Busoni's letters give a lively description of conditions in Leipzig:

> Food, not only in quality, but in quantity leaves much to be desired. . . . A few days ago my Bechstein arrived, and I had to give the movers my last taler by the next morning. The night before, I am walking down the street and run into Schwalm (the owner of C. F. Kahnt publishing house—G. K.). I immediately stop him: "Please take my compositions—I need the money." "I can't do that right now, but if you would like to write a little Fantasy on the *Barber of Baghdad*[16] for me, come to me in the morning, and I'll give you fifty marks in advance and a hundred after it's ready." "Agreed!" We said our goodbyes.
>
> The next morning I come for the fifty marks: "Does our agreement still stand, Mr. Schwalm? One hundred after the job is done?" "Of course! Here are the fifty!" "And here is the finished work," and I take the manuscript out of my pocket. I worked from nine at night to three thirty, without a piano, and not knowing the opera beforehand.[17]

Life in Leipzig also had its bright side. There, Busoni found good friends—the Dutch violinist Henri Petri (1856–1914) and his family. Their closeness left its mark on the biography of the Italian artist. The head of the family—a concertmaster and leader of a then-popular quartet—became an ardent admirer and the first promoter of Busoni; the grateful composer dedicated two of his works to him—the second String Quartet Op. 26 and the Violin Concerto Op. 35a. Henri's wife—the pianist Kathy Petri—suggested to Busoni the happy idea of undertaking piano transcriptions of Bach's organ works; the inspirer is the object of the dedication of the first transcription—of the D-Major Prelude and Fugue finished in 1888, and premiered by the transcriber for the Leipzig Bach Society. Another composition of those years is connected to the Petri family—the four violin Bagatelles Op. 28, written, as the dedication informs us, "for the seven-year-old Egon Petri, for easy violin"; Egon, the son of Henri and Cathy, is the very Egon Petri (1881–1962),[18] who eventually gave up the violin and became the famous pianist, the best-known student and follower of Busoni.

In Leipzig, Busoni also met with other gifted musicians of his generation, then still as young as he, at the start of their careers, and destined to achieve renown later; among them were Sinding, Delius, Nováček, and Mahler. Among older musicians visiting Leipzig in those years, Grieg and Tchaikovsky took a particular interest in Busoni. Tchaikovsky heard Busoni's first String Quartet Op. 19 performed by Petri's quartet and related his impressions of the work and its author in the ninth chapter of *Autobiographical Description of Travels Abroad in 1888*. The great Russian composer calls the twenty-two-year-old Busoni "a remarkably interesting personality," possessing, besides talent, "strong character [and a] brilliant mind," who "I have no doubt . . . will soon be talked about"; he considers it "highly desirable" that this "superb pianist appear among us in the near future." As to the purely creative potential of Busoni, Tchaikovsky notices in him "a very strong talent in composition" and "an unusual seriousness of direction," but faults him for "forcing his nature," striving to "seem German . . . be profound in a German manner," instead of "inventing new musical forms in the spirit of his own people, . . . rich in peculiarly Italian melodicity."[19]

Despite all this, Busoni's position in Leipzig remained so uncertain and materially insecure that in 1888 he accepted with pleasure the post offered to him due to a recommendation of the well-known theoretician Hugo Riemann, a professor of piano at the recently opened music institute in Helsingfors (now Helsinki).

Chapter Two

His two-year long sojourn in Finland's capital played a large role in Busoni's biography. An acquaintance with the country's folk music,[1] closeness with a number of Finnish musicians—Wegelius, Kajanus, Järnefelt,[2] and others, a closeness, which, with one of them—Sibelius—grew into lifelong friendship, opened new horizons for Busoni, and began the process of eroding the foundations of his then rather conservative musical worldview.

Among other events of Busoni's life in Helsingfors,[3] in 1889 he met the daughter of the Swedish sculptor,[4] Gerda Sjöstrand,[5] who, in one year's time became his wife.[6]

During the stay in Finland, which was then a part of the Russian Empire,[7] Busoni's first ties with Russia took shape. In 1890 he performed in St. Petersburg on a few occasions (one of these being a symphonic assembly of the Russian Musical Society, playing the Schumann Concerto under Rubinstein's baton), and in August of the same year and in the same city he took part in Rubinstein's first international competition for pianists and composers.

This competition took place under circumstances quite different from those of the competitions of today. Only men between the ages of twenty and twenty-six were allowed to enter; there were only two prizes: one for composition and one for piano, each in the sum of 5,000 francs.[8] Six contestants took part: five pianists and one composer, including one entrant in both categories. That one was Busoni. For the composition prize he submitted a *Konzertstück* for Piano and Orchestra Op. 31a (dedicated to Rubinstein), a Sonata for Violin and Piano Op. 29, two solo works for piano Op. 30 (*Kontrapunktisches Tanzstück* and *Kleine Ballettszene III*), and two cadenzas for the Fourth Piano Concerto of Beethoven (in G Major, Op. 58); at the piano competition he performed the D-Major Prelude and Fugue of Bach, Mozart's A-Minor Rondo, Sonata Op. 111 of Beethoven, the C-Minor Nocturne, F-sharp Minor Mazurka and the F-Minor Ballade of Chopin, the first two numbers of Schumann's *Kreisleriana*, *Waldesrauschen* of Liszt, and the Fourth (D-Minor) Concerto of Rubinstein.

Busoni did not receive the piano prize; the jury awarded it to a certain N. A. Dubasov, the scion and future professor of the St. Petersburg Conservatory, whose later activity left no trace in the history of pianism.[9]

Now, with many decades' hindsight, the jury's decision seems strange, ridiculous, and shameful: Busoni and Dubasov—these two names can hardly be mentioned in the same breath in the twentieth century! Honesty, however, compels us to admit that both as a composer and a pianist, Busoni at the time of the competition was not the same Busoni who was later to attain renown. Busoni emerged from his youth a serious, solidly erudite, and well-trained professional, a somewhat dry technician, and skillful contrapuntist, nothing more; his academically faultless playing and compositions lacked that most important aspect for which his art was celebrated years hence—individuality, originality, and creativity. In this respect, the contemporary press did not single him out from among the other competitors, who "were trained in more or less the same German school. . . . We noticed no individuality in the contestants. Before us were faceless pianists, that is to say—with an imprint of the German spirit, with their tastes developed in Germany or under her influence. . . . All imparted the same expression to what they played. . . ."[10]

And yet, despite his important shortcomings, as a pianist, Busoni, even in those years, already towered above, or, in any case, markedly surpassed his competitors. At least the newspapers and magazines of the time quite unanimously acknowledged him "the strongest of the contestants," indicating that his mastery, his "polished playing," and "deep understanding of the spirit and character of each work" placed Busoni "ahead of his comrades."[11] For this reason, the announcement of the results of the competition aroused the simultaneous objections of the critics.

Most likely, the decision of the jury was influenced by Rubinstein's candid and insistent wish that at least one prize go to a Russian musician; since the only Russian competitors were in the piano category, bestowing the piano award on Busoni was impossible. In addition Rubinstein did not much like Busoni's interpretation of the classics.[12] The weighty authority of Rubinstein, his domineering nature, the patriotic coloring of his arguments, and, finally, his position as the competition organizer and chairman of the jury, which gave him two votes, plus one more vote of a foreign jury member who did not come—all this, of course, determined the outcome of the vote. These circumstances were no secret to the contemporaries: some newspapers unambiguously suggested that Rubinstein "exerted a certain pressure," and argued that "in an international competition the question of nationality must take second place."[13]

The lack of objectivity of the jury's decision was so obvious even to the jury itself that it attempted to correct it by awarding to Busoni—by recommendation of the same Rubinstein—the prize for composition! This awkward maneuver was easily apparent to the musical world, which expressed the "not terribly courageous hypothesis" that the composition prize was given Busoni, "to relieve a guilty conscience . . . for his exceptional qualities as a pianist."[14] For, according to the general opinion, Busoni's compositions, performed at the contest, did not deserve an award, since they were "nothing exceptional in their musical content," even though they were professionally far above the "rather insignificant" creations of his only competitor, a certain Cesi.[15] So, the second injustice on the part of the jury helped not to conceal, but to further highlight the first. In general, the official results of the competition were characterized in the contemporary press as "quite unexpected," "unjust": "Busoni played best, he should have been given the laurel crown among the other pianists. . . . As to the composition award, it should have been given to no one at all"; "One could have sooner supposed that Mr. Bussoni (*sic*) will be awarded the prize for his piano playing, while the composers will be left with their hopes."[16]

After the competition, Busoni did not return to Helsingfors, but, in September 1880, obtained a position as professor of piano at the Moscow Conservatory, a position for which Rubinstein had recommended him earlier. This is the picture of the young professor as drawn by one of his students:

> . . . This was a remarkable person, of un-Italianate patience, unwavering striving toward a goal . . . and energy, energy without end. If in the early morning hours you chanced to walk by the house where [Busoni][17] lived, you would hear that he has already begun his two-hour work (in the mornings he played scales), and upon hearing the start of this work, you could check your watch, for it reliably indicated the time—ten minutes to eight. At ten minutes to ten, [Busoni] went to the Conservatory and worked there from ten to two o'clock. After lunch and a light rest, he played again, gave lessons again, and, as became known later, wrote, working on editing a huge classic opus, which occupied, by his own admission, ten years of labor.[18] During his lessons, he amazed his students with his astonishing knowledge: anything his students played, he knew by memory, and how!—with precision, to the last note, last detail. Without thinking long, he sat down at the piano and performed any work in question with that immaculate precision which was his trademark. He knew by memory all the concerto accompaniments, trio and quartet parts—all without hesitation, without risk of ever forgetting or making a mistake, with that same serenity that described both his performances for the students in class, and before 3,000 people in the concert hall of the Noble Assembly Hall (presently—the Hall of Columns of the House of Unions.—G. K.).[19]

Busoni stayed in Moscow only for one school year (1890/91). During this time he appeared repeatedly on the local concert stage, exciting, however, more the respect than the warm sympathy of the audience: ". . . Busoni, 'remembered a music critic afterward' was perceived in Moscow as an authoritative pedagogue rather than an outstanding creative personality, an artist, a talent. One often heard the 'old' Busoni judged as a cerebral pianist, in whom pianistic culture and mastery are more evident than a spontaneous pianistic gift."[20] The imperious director of the Moscow Conservatory, V. I. Safonov,[21] too, conceived a dislike for the Italian pianist; he busied himself composing "witty" puns on Busoni's name: "Bezruccio Beztoni" [loosely translated as "No Hands, No Tone."—Trans.]. All this forced Busoni to quickly leave Moscow and to move in 1891 to the United States—first to Boston, as a professor of piano at the New England Conservatory, and later (in 1892) to New York. It was there that Busoni underwent the transformation that made possible the birth of a new Busoni—a great artist who astounded the world and brought forth a new epoch in the history of pianism.

The transformation, of course, did not happen instantaneously, it had been brewing for a number of years. The metamorphosis began in Finland. There, the first doubts were born about the validity of those academic traditions in whose spirit he was brought up and began his career. At this time, his friend Martin Wegelius, the director of the institute where Busoni worked, brought to his attention the creative figure of Liszt. Until then, Busoni, as a pious man of Leipzig, and a "Brahmsian," held a rather naive, almost Philistine view of the great Hungarian and displayed a more or less skeptical indifference to the fruits and principles of his art. Now both appeared to the young artist in a new light. Busoni's newborn interest in the composer of the *Mephisto Waltz* received a new impetus in America; a local collector introduced Busoni to the rare first editions of Liszt's works, laying the foundation for his intensive studies of the older man's musical legacy. The effect was so powerful that Busoni, like Liszt before him upon his encounter with Paganini, left the stage for a while to think in solitude, to digest the discoveries, and to fertilize his own art with them. "This was a time in my life," he wrote later, "when I discerned such gaps and errors in my own playing, that, with an energetic decisiveness, I began to work on the piano on a thoroughly new basis. Liszt's works were my teachers, and opened for me the door to an intimate understanding of his special art; from his 'texture' I created my 'technique.' Gratitude and admiration made Liszt my master and my friend."[22]

Liszt's influence not only renewed the pianistic technique of Busoni; it manifested itself in his entire musical outlook and led to a radical rethinking of the school rules and ideals absorbed by the Italian artist with the mother's milk of German musical culture. "Mi sento molto meno Tedesco . . ." (I feel much less German), he writes in Italian to his friend Wegelius.[23]

The first fruits of Busoni's "transfiguration" were a transcription of the *Spanish Rhapsody* for piano and orchestra, aspiring to imitate Liszt's own transcriptions of Schubert's Fantasy and Weber's Polonaise, born of "my impulse of enthusiasm for Liszt,"[24] and the famous, now classic, edition of Book I of the *Well-Tempered Clavier*. In the copious notes and supplements of this edition, Busoni developed his "widely understood school of the highest mastery of piano playing," where, for the first time, he explained his new views of the problems of music history and piano pedagogy, transcription and interpretation, tone production and "contemporary technique of piano playing."[25]

Both of the above works were completed in 1894. During the same year, Busoni left America, returned to Europe, and settled in Berlin.

Thus ends the first period in Busoni's life and career. From now on, a student's observance of the canons of "academic Romanticism" is behind him. The master leaves the paths of others to follow his own direction.

Chapter Three

Now settled in Berlin, Busoni renewed his concertizing, appearing before the public as a much-transformed pianist. During the years described in the previous chapter, his playing offended or irritated no one, nor did it make a particularly strong, extraordinary impression. Now it had become an important artistic phenomenon, which, while it provoked heated arguments, also attracted ever-greater world attention.

The first considerable success came to Busoni in 1898, after his Berlin cycle dedicated to the "historical development of the piano concerto"; the cycle consisted of four evenings, during which the artist performed with orchestra fourteen concertos of Bach, Mozart, Beethoven, Hummel, Chopin, Mendelssohn, Schumann, Liszt, Brahms, Rubinstein, and Saint-Saëns. Musical circles began to talk about a new star in the pianistic heavens. The pianist's fame was confirmed and augmented in numerous concert tours of Germany, Italy, France, England, Canada,[1] the United States, and other countries, especially in 1912 and 1913, when, after a long absence, Busoni again appeared on the stages of Moscow and St. Petersburg, where his concerts started the famous "war" between Busonists and Hofmannists.[2] These were the last encounters of the Russian audiences with the great artist; soon World War I began, and Busoni never visited Russia again.

By this time, Busoni's piano career had reached its apogee; its culmination was the Berlin cycle of six *Klavierabends,* with which the artist celebrated, in 1911, the centennial of his still much-respected teacher and inspirer.[3] The musical press promoted the Italian virtuoso from a "star" to the "sun" of contemporary pianism, now pronounced, by the pen of an ever larger number of authoritative critics, a "king," a "tsar" of the piano world, "the first," "the greatest pianist of our days," "the most outstanding artist of the piano in our day," "outside all competition," "apart" from "all living pianists." "In our day, the laurel crown belongs, without a doubt, to Busoni. Hofmann, d'Albert, Sauer, Paderewski, Godowsky, Rosenthal—all these are outstanding artists, yet none of them has acquired the importance . . . of Busoni." ". . . In the world of piano we have but one. . . ." "The word 'pianist' sounds much too ordinary when applied to this artist. Busoni is a great poet of the piano. His phenomenal technique is only a vehicle for impressing the soul of the listener by the colossal power of internal pathos of the genius soul of the artist. The fascination of his playing, the creative rapture, which permeates Busoni's interpretation of different composers, places him far above all other pianists. I have never heard Liszt or Rubinstein. Perhaps their playing reached still higher poetic revelations than Busoni's. But that is hard to imagine."[4] There were many such reactions.

However, this opinion was by no means shared by all. The arguments about the master's playing never stopped. A number of listeners felt no sympathy toward Busoni's pianism, were bewildered and left cold; some sharply criticized and rejected it. But even the enemies felt compelled to give their due to the power of the artist's creative personality, to admit that he was "a giant" with whom "one may not agree," "one might argue," even "be indignant about the whims of the genius," but "it is not possible to deny that Busoni is a wonderful pianist," not possible to "avoid succumbing to his charm," "not to be captivated by the hypnotic power of his performances." "Busoni, even when one does not agree with him, bestows more than the agreeable ones." "It is a great deal more interesting and educational to disagree with Busoni than to agree with a pack of mediocre pianists." "The vividness of the concept, the creativity reaches a rare puissance in the remarkable personality of Busoni. For that, you forgive him those fancies of execution that would be unforgivable in anyone else."[5]

The concessions of the opposition speak even louder than the plaudits of supporters. Of course, there is no unanimity; but then, when has that ever existed in the history of pianism? During the lifetime of Liszt, many preferred Thalberg. Among the contemporaries of Busoni, various names were lauded, each favored by a group of adherents over the transcriber of the Chaconne.[6] A story of ancient Greece comes to mind. In an attempt to discover the foremost painter in the land, each city was asked to name its favorite. Each city came up with a different candidate—its own citizen, naturally. However, the second favorite was the same man in each city; and he was proclaimed the finest painter in Greece.

Something of this nature also happened in the first decades of the present century. Each country had its darling, whom the largest part of the public placed above all pianists of its time; but the names varied from country to country, whereas the name of their greatest rival remained the same. So, in the German opinion, superiority was contested between d'Albert and Busoni, in that of the French—between Paderewski and Busoni, in that of the Russian—Hofmann and Busoni.[7] The reader is left to draw his own conclusion.

Of course, the question of Busoni's place in the pianistic hierarchy of his epoch has little meaning today. It is more important to uncover the character of his playing, to detect what about it so captured his contemporaries, and what so greatly offended many of them.

Chapter Four

The most indisputable quality of Busoni's pianism was his technique. There were no disagreements in its estimation. Both the rapturous admirers and the fierce detractors of the artist were united in the opinion that the technical achievements of his playing "defy description and comparison with any of the contemporary pianists," that such technique was "never before possessed by any pianist." "His technical perfection is fantastic, especially the octaves. There can be no doubt that Busoni has no competition—Rosenthal's technique seems childish after Busoni." "One needs to play the piano for thirty years to properly appreciate Busoni's playing," as a famous professor of piano assured the critic Y. Engel.[1]

But even thirty years of piano playing were not always enough to solve the riddles of Busoni's mastery: "Busoni elevated pianism to such head-spinning heights, that even seasoned professionals can hardly make out with the naked eye what precisely he is doing up there." Accomplished experts, stupefied, threw up their hands: "What this artist has achieved in piano technique borders on the supernatural," "it seemed thoroughly inconceivable that this was done by one man with two hands," "it seemed incredible that a mortal sat at the piano!"

Specifically, critics noted "his uncommon playing of scales," "filigree-like clarity and elegance," "lightning finger passages," "magic speed" of octaves, the rapidity and evenness of which were beyond the limits of achievability "even for Teresa Carreño" and other notorious octave players.[2] Furthermore, Busoni's *prestissimo* was "significantly faster than the *prestissimo* of other people"; "you had to hear with your own ears the coda of the Fourth Ballade (of Chopin—G. K.), to believe that ten human fingers are capable of producing such a tempo."

Nevertheless, as great as were the dexterity, lightness, and velocity, "the supernatural perfection of his finger and wrist mechanism,"[3] which distinguished Busoni's playing, they paled and took second place to his art of "piano orchestration." Precisely here, in this area, the artist's mastery amazed the listener the most. Newspapers and journals of those years vie with one another in singing praises to his "thoroughly astonishing," "almost magical" variety of "nuances of sound color," admit that "one cannot get enough" of the "incredible richness," "remarkable luxuriance and originality of the piano palette," "the sumptuous rainbow of brilliant, ringing, sharp, or clouded, veiled sonorities," with which the pianist positively "hypnotizes, bewitches" the audience. "He enriched the piano resources with unheard-of devices and transformed piano sonority to entrancing beauty. It is doubtful whether any among modern piano masters—including Godowsky and Hofmann—can boast such enchantment of sound as Busoni.

He can coax out of his monochrome instrument such an opulent spectrum of brilliant and radiant colors, such delicate nuances of charming tones, and such a blinding interplay of caressing shades that rapture and awe even a listener spoiled by the gigantic achievements of contemporary pianism."

The nature of Busoni's coloring should not be understood simplistically. It was not merely that the piano under Busoni's fingers "became an orchestra," that "the sounds of a harp, of woodwinds, of strings, the harmonies of bells can be envisaged in his piano," that "you hear now horns, now bassoons, or a quartet, doubled by winds, or, finally, two or three different timbres simultaneously." First of all, Busoni did not *imitate* "bassoons or horns" or other orchestral instruments, but, rather, *transmuted* their actual sound, gave its artistic realization, its poetic *idea*—much like the famous *Lilacs* of Monet, next to which real lilacs "appear to be a weak," coarse imitation.[4] Second, and most important, Busoni went beyond imitation, even the ennobling kind, of existing sonorities; his wondrous sonorous imagination gave birth to (and materialized at the keyboard) sounds having no prototype, never-before heard, only dreamed-of sounds, which would transform the concert Bechstein into some unknown instrument. "The piano is not at all that instrument we know so well, when Busoni is playing it. . . ." "The artist seems to be able to vary the very sound of this instrument. . . ." "As if conjured by a charm, unusual, novel sounds emerged from the piano—as if an inventor had enhanced the instrument with entirely new timbres."

The illusion was so powerful that among the artist's colleagues' suspicions arose that the pianos he used had nonstandard hammers or some sort of altered mechanism; on one occasion, after a concert of Busoni[5] in Paris, a group of pianists rushed to the stage to examine and scrutinize the instrument, refusing to believe that it was no different from all other concert grands of the same brand.

Busoni's control in the world of pianistic colors was unlimited; but some colors were noticeably preferred. Among these favored tones of Busoni's palette were the aforementioned "caressing shades" and "clouded, veiled sonorities," "half-shadows," "lightest, airy pianissimo" of the passagework, "sounding like an aeolian harp," "entirely special matte velvet of the chords," "whole scales of distinctively Busonian matte nuances." Y. Engel compares the artist to the legendary knight who "conquers nations, overcomes cities, unlocks castle doors, which, as in an Anderson tale, confine within them not only tumultuous storms but also the most tender, sweetest of zephyrs (the latter, by the way, being Busoni's best)." "What amazes most in Busoni's playing is the *piano,*" confirms another critic, "He compels his already extremely flexible, pliant touch, capable of the most exquisite shades, to the maximum of subtlety. He succeeds in obtaining, in *piano,* a whole scope of the slightest, wondrous nuances, magic, enticing sonorities. You listen, and it seems that whole cascades of pearls, shimmering with some singular matte radiance are flowing from his fingers. Truly, Busoni is a poet of the pianistic whisper." Almost verbatim, we read in a third review: "His *piano* astounds the most. No one else has this 'pianistic whisper.'"

In the same sphere, the special attention of reviewers is attracted by the "marvelous *portamento,* which the artist plays as if dripping drops of sonorous rain on the piano" and the "remarkable *perlé,*[6] which I have heard from no other contemporary pianist"; "His flitting passages, his glittering playing—it is emeralds and pearls in sounds."

Busoni's technique, his mastery of coloring the piano sound astonished the listener so much that it obscured other, more important qualities of the pianist. "There is no doubt that Busoni's success as a performer was due, initially, to a misunderstanding. . . . The public and the critics for a long time thought that, in fact, Busoni is merely a great virtuoso—he lacks a soul, a creative artistic spark."[7] Even in later years, some nearsighted critics "saw him as no more than a brilliant technician," a master of "superficial virtuosity," who "flaunts" the beauty and variety of sonority without reference to the musical content of the works performed.

Time had shown how far from the truth were the judgments of those who failed to see the forest while admiring the trees. "They did not understand the spiritual essence of this performer-creator, this free poet of the keyboard," "they heard the external, without recognizing the driving force; wondered at the perfection of the technical means, without realizing that they were only the expression of a singular concentration of the spiritual expressive impulse." The more penetrating critics already saw clearly then that "Busoni's strength is not in technique alone. He is not a virtuoso," but, "before all, an artist," whose "grandiose, limitless technique serves not as a goal, but as the means" of realizing certain artistic conceptions, who does not "parade" sonorities, but "discovers new perspectives not just in the world of pianistic colors, but *also in the interpretation of that which is painted with them*" (italics mine—G. K.).[8]

Those who refused to see Busoni as a creative artist did not see these "new perspectives," the new interpretations; did not see, because they looked through the glass of the familiar, the clichés in common use on the pianistic stage. Busoni's interpretations, like all his musical thinking, differed sharply from these clichés, demanded a different approach from the listener and an ability to assume another creative viewpoint. An artist, such as a writer, composer, or painter, "must be judged according to the laws he himself recognizes" (Pushkin,[9] in a letter to Bestuzhev[10]). The wing of an aircraft cannot be evaluated for its appropriateness in an automobile; to appreciate the shape of the latter, it is necessary to understand the construction of the airplane. It is not surprising, then, that the critics who ignored Pushkin's rule, unable to do their "half of the work,"[11] who judged Busoni-the-interpreter according to the canons of a style entirely foreign to him, were baffled by the pianist's "incomprehensively gigantic" artistic designs, which remained a "complete enigma" to such critics; unable to solve it, to understand what the performer wanted to say, they self-confidently decided that there was nothing to understand, that behind that blinding technique, behind that "kaleidoscope" of sonorities lies no artistic interpretation, no musical content. Not the first case in the history of art, and surely not the last. . . .

Who, then, was Busoni-the-interpreter, what were the "laws" that he recognized, and how did they differ from those followed by other performers at the turn of the century?

To answer these questions, to understand and correctly evaluate the *new* that the Italian pianist brought to the pianistic art, it is imperative first to understand the *old* that served as his launching pad—in other words, to understand the style of piano playing then prevalent on the concert stage.

Chapter Five

Despite individual (sometimes significant) differences between the virtuosos of that epoch, the vast majority of them were trained in the traditions of Romanticism. However, the times of the flowering of this style in piano playing, the times of Liszt and Rubinstein were already past, and the style leaned toward decadence. The concert repertoire consisted of a limited number of composers and compositions. The classicism of the eighteenth century seemed a cold and obsolete art, Bach—an esteemed museum relic. "How many of his works can no longer appeal to us!" wrote the famous pianist Eugen d'Albert in the foreword to his edition of the *Well-Tempered Clavier.* "I know that there are those who can listen to the cantatas without showing boredom. But they are either hypocrites or pedants."[1] Not surprisingly, Bach and Mozart were almost never performed in concert, or were played for formality's sake at the very beginning of the program, as a prelude to the "real" concert. The piano repertoire began "seriously" with Beethoven, and reached its apogee in Mendelssohn, Schumann, and Chopin, in whose compositions Hofmann, Paderewski, and many other renowned performers of the day gained their laurels. Liszt was popular chiefly as the author of transcriptions and effective virtuoso pieces; his more important original works appeared in the programs much more rarely. The above-mentioned names, represented usually by the same, much overplayed compositions (the "Moonlight" and "Appassionata" of Beethoven, Schumann's *Carnaval,* the seventh Waltz, fifteenth Prelude, and A-flat Major Polonaise of Chopin, Liszt's sixth Rhapsody and "La Campanella," and so on), were supplemented by a certain number of the "most modern" composers, mainly of the salon variety (Moszkowski, Paderewski, Sauer, Schutt,[2] etc.). All these were tossed together, like a salad, to arrange recital programs, which would come out guilty of a certain tastelessness, as a result. Here, by way of example, are a few randomly selected piano recital programs of the decades in question from St. Petersburg, Moscow, and Kiev: Bach-Tausig, Chopin, Schumann, Rubinstein, Tchaikovsky, Gabrilowitsch, Leschetizky, Mendelssohn-Liszt (Gabrilowitsch, 1898); d'Albert, Beethoven, Weber, Chopin, Tchaikovsky, Rubinstein, Liszt (d'Albert, 1898); Schumann, Beethoven, Brahms, Chopin, Paderewski, Liszt (Paderewski, 1904); Gluck-Saint-Saëns, Beethoven, Mendelssohn, Chopin, Tchaikovsky, Hofmann, Schitte, Liszt (Hofmann, 1910); Beethoven, Chopin, Rachmaninov, Tchaikovsky-Pabst; Bach-Tausig, Gluck-Brahms, Weber, Schumann, Tchaikovsky, Pabst; Beethoven, Chopin, Mendelssohn, Schubert, Rubinstein, Hofmann, Liszt; Bach, Schubert, Schumann, Chopin, Rubinstein, Hofmann, Debussy, Moszkowski (Hofmann, 1912).

The character of performance underwent a similar evolution. The larger questions of interpretation narrowed, became smaller, and were most concerned with detail. Next to this concentration on the interpretation of detail, be it "academically" thorough, or, instead, capriciously "improvisatory," the central idea of the composition, in whose profound and lucid revelation Liszt and Rubinstein saw the principal task of the performer, grew dim and lifeless. Diverging in *particulars*, the interpretation of the *whole* became standardized, lost the imprint of the artist's personality; creative exploration and individuality of interpretation all gave way to canonical reproduction of what was once discovered by the great progenitors of Romantic pianism. Even in a master as remarkable as Hofmann, the critics, including his most rapturous admirers, found an absence of "creative conception," "the creative 'self'": ". . . Revelation . . . is not to be expected of Hofmann," "far from often does he speak a new word, far from often is he profound," "Hofmann represents the typical in piano playing," even if "in flawlessly ideal perfection."[3]

Generally, interpretation, where the work of the artist's mind was in evidence, met with suspicion and was qualified as "artificial" or "cerebral." Thinking was the job of a scientist, not an artist. In art, the great sovereign was emotion, seen as an antipode of thought. In piano performance, "emotion" was of two varieties. One was expressed in playing of elegiac, exquisite, more-or-less "salon-like" character; the pianistic embodiment of these qualities was achieved by a soft wrist attack, a singing tone, preferential use of *legato*, rounded phrasing, detailed nuance, "wavy" dynamics and rhythm, frequent *crescendos, diminuendos, ritardandos, rubatos, arpeggiandos,* and similar effects, systematized by the celebrated school of Leschetizky. The pianists of this type—de Pachmann, Leschetizky students headed by Paderewski and Essipova, and others—earned the greatest fame as "Chopinists."

The specialty of the second group of pianists was the virtuoso works of Liszt. The best pianists of the group attempted to follow in the footsteps of young Liszt and Rubinstein, conquering the listener with technique and temperament, "tempest and chaos," "heaven-storming bravura" of performance.[4] But, little by little, Rubinstein's pathos was replaced by rhetorical declamation, Rubinstein's grandeur—by an artificial pose, Rubinstein's thunder and lightning—by theatrical effects. "Baroque, nothing but Baroque—all decorative embellishment and tinsel of sound . . ."—thus the critic and theorist of pianism R. Breithaupt[5] characterizes the "pompous" playing of the famous pianist Reisenauer. "Something like a theatrical king from a historical drama: with clanging armor and shining shield, a lofty step and proud gait, and pathetic howling."[6]

Busoni approached interpretation quite differently. "He is unlike any pianist St. Petersburg has heard," notes a surprised critic after his first Busoni concert. The questions the pianist posed to himself and the demands placed by him on the listeners were entirely new to them: "the public has not gotten accustomed to him yet; it came to hear the customary 'salon' performance and found itself hearing a serious concert."

The principal difference between Busoni's pianism and the "customary 'salon' performance" began with the content and organization of his concert programs. Admittance was denied to Moszkowski, Schutt, and other such composers of lightweight salon pieces. Exclusivity did not stop there: the bigger names, too, underwent a "cleansing," especially the German Romantics—Mendelssohn, Schumann, and (with one exception) Brahms, to whom the "new" Busoni cooled to such an extent that he began to consider them second rate.[7] In his maturity the master played almost exclusively Bach, Mozart, Beethoven, Chopin, and Liszt, adding a few selected works of Franck (Prelude, Chorale, and Fugue), Brahms (Paganini Variations), and Busoni himself. However, the works of the above-named five favorite composers were presented in Busoni's programs in depth, including the less familiar, rarely performed compositions; the latter were subject to special partiality, causing him to search archives, private collections, and second-hand stores for forgotten or unpublished works, printed or manuscript variants of known works, and so on. Thus, Bach's Chorale preludes, the first, not yet published edition of Liszt's "Gondoliera and Tarantella,"[8] his Fantasy on the *Marriage of Figaro*, of which the unpublished manuscript was found and first performed (after the author) by Busoni, appeared on Busoni's programs; in the same spirit of broadening the audience's horizon, in Beethoven, the artist changes the emphasis from the popular sonatas of the middle period to the more difficult last opuses (Sonatas Op. 106 and Op. 111, and Bagatelles Op. 126).

In addition, Busoni grouped the works performed according to one consideration or another. This, too, was novel at the time and attracted the attention of reviewers: ". . . Mr. Busoni takes his programs seriously, trying to give them unity and structure," "Busoni's programs were constructed interestingly, in large integral chunks."

The truth of these assertions is evident in the typical Busoni programs:

1. Sonata Op. 106 of Beethoven, 24 Preludes of Chopin, and the Liszt B-Minor Sonata;[9]

2. Beethoven Sonata Op. 109, Brahms-Paganini Variations, and Liszt's "Don Juan" Fantasy;

3. Two Beethoven Sonatas (Op. 53 and Op. 111) and one of the *Années de Pélerinage* of Liszt (complete);

4. Six Paganini-Liszt Etudes, six Bagatelles Op. 126 of Beethoven, four Bach-Busoni organ Chorale Preludes, and 12 Chopin Etudes Op. 25;

5. All-Beethoven evening: Sonata Op. 111, Bagatelles Op. 126, and Sonata Op. 106;

6. Two Liszt evenings: the first two *Années,* "Switzerland," and "Italy," both complete) on one; the third *Année* (complete) and the B-minor Sonata on the other;

7. Liszt transcription evening: first half—transcription of works by German composers (Bach, Mozart, Schubert, and Meyerbeer), second half—by Italian composers (Rossini, Bellini, Donizetti, and Verdi);

8. "Italian" Liszt evening: "Italy" from the *Années,* Gondoliera and Tarantella (first edition) on the first half, transcriptions of Italian composers on the second;

9. An evening of Liszt Etudes: the twelve "Transcendental" and six "Paganini."

Busoni was the first pianist to perform together as a whole the eighteen Etudes of Liszt, his *Années,* the 24 Preludes of Chopin, his four Ballades, and so on.

Busoni would not limit himself to planning such groupings within one program, but often went further, uniting the programs of several recitals into a unified, even more monumental cycle; to the previously mentioned examples of such cycles (the cycle on the history of the piano concerto, Liszt cycles) may be added: the Basel cycle of four "monographic" concerts (1910), tours of Italy with a group of eight *Klavierabends* dedicated to the development of piano literature from Bach to the present (1913), and so on.

Chapter Six

The peculiarities of Busoni-the-interpreter, clearly evident in the matter of *what* he played, stand in even sharper relief in *how* he played it. Here, the performer's "great personality," his "giant, brilliant, and original individuality" left an inimitable stamp on his "unusually personal," "uniquely special and independent" renditions. "Going to hear other pianists, even the great ones, we usually know quite well exactly how this or that piece will be played and get ourselves on a particular track in advance. Busoni, however, pushes us off that track: everything with him is more or less unexpected . . . acquiring a new character and thoroughly different lighting. This is the principal charm of Busoni's magical art." "The most valuable in him is that which is unexpected and yet happily discovered, deeply convincing." "Busoni's performance creates the impression of a brilliant improvisation—and this is his foremost strength!"[1]

Indeed in this, in the "free flight of poetic fantasy," in the creative nature of performance was the "foremost strength" of Busoni-the-interpreter, "perhaps, his most substantial distinction from other pianists." "The work of composition is continued by the performer. But it does not reach such brilliance as in Busoni in any other"; "no contemporary pianist is capable of this creative transformation." "The creative 'self'" of the pianist was the very leitmotif of the preference many great musicians, such as F. M. Blumenfeld, M. F. Gnessin, B. L. Yavorsky,[2] felt for Busoni over the great favorite of the prerevolution public,[3] Hofmann: "that creative 'self' is absent from Hofmann's playing," "Hofmann, without a doubt possesses much less creative power," Busoni's renditions "stand no comparison even with those of Hofmann: compared with Busoni's, Hofmann's appear routine, common, and dry." In Beethoven's Sonata Op. 106 "the inspired 'improvisation' of the great Busoni" sounded like "a revelation," after which Hofmann's interpretation "seemed rather shallow, superficial, and insignificant." This is why musicians acknowledged Busoni as an "artist of a higher rank than Hofmann" and why "for many it became impossible after Busoni's performances to be carried away by the impersonality of the formally perfect playing of Hofmann."

Not surprisingly, what, by popular consent, was the strongest feature of Busoni-the-interpreter, as often happens, was also the most vulnerable aspect of his playing. A sizable proportion of critics reproach the artist for interpretations that are often so original and individual, have a character so personal and subjective, differ so sharply from "accepted norms and sanctified traditions," that the "free flight of fantasy" of the pianist becomes capriciousness and contradicts the conventional notions of a given composer and his composition. "It has been a

long time since I have heard an artist . . . change a composition to such a degree
with his playing. Change, that is, not in the sense of altering notes, harmony,
and form, but rather its tempo, its spirit, its mood. . . . In many Chopin Preludes
he improvised in this sense so freely, that of the individuality of Chopin, the
Chopin we know and love, there was nothing left. Instead, we were shown something unusual and foreign."

Matters stood thus not only in Chopin. "He recreates them (the authors—
G. K.) in his own image. They all 'become Busoni' . . . He uses their works as
canvas for his own performing creativity"; "having gone through his creative lab-
oratory, they metamorphose so much, as to become to a much greater extent the
creations of his own genius than that of the authors whose names figure in the
program." Many other reviews speak of this: "whoever's works this amazing artist plays—he expresses mostly himself"; "Busoni never plays Chopin, Beethoven,
and Liszt; he always performs Busoni-Chopin, Busoni-Beethoven, and Busoni-
Liszt"; and again: "All that Busoni plays is not Chopin, not Mozart, not Liszt, not
Bach. All is Busoni-Chopin, Busoni-Mozart, Busoni-Liszt, Busoni-Bach."

The "Busonization" of all composers engendered numerous reproofs.
". . . Busoni instead of Liszt, Busoni instead of Mozart, Busoni instead of Chopin—is that not too much Busoni?" protested one critic. "No matter how rich,
how varied in its manifestations his genius may be, there is no doubt that Bach,
plus Mozart, plus Beethoven, plus Chopin, plus Liszt, each performed in its own
style, would present much more variety." "I, personally," echoes another, "would
prefer simply Chopin. Without any improvisations. Even if they were the improvisations of Ferruccio Busoni himself."

Busoni's willful renditions sometimes seemed so "strange," even "incomprehensible" to some reviewers, that the latter suspected artificiality in their
conception, deliberate novelty, which "crosses the line of naturalness in the
attempt to see and understand differently than others." "He purposely strives
to produce interpretations that contradict tradition, the accepted view, the
inheritance of the great interpreters. . . . In search of originality he often borders on such deviations that it seems that the artist simply grimaces, poses,
desiring at all cost not to resemble anyone." "Occasionally, it appeared as if the
pianist, from the heights of his international fame, mocks Chopin, the public,
and, above all, musicians."

The special indignation of these critics was aroused by the fact that Busoni
not only departed from the accepted understanding and from the traditions
but also indulged in altering the original text. The above-cited reviewer was mistaken, when he asserted that Busoni's changes did not involve "notes, harmony,
and forms" of the piece. In reality "he interprets all music, all compositions in his
own way, often 'correcting' compositions that do not belong to him." "The number of 'corrections' and 'improvements' introduced by this remarkable pianist
is enormous," confirms a review of Busoni's performance of Beethoven's Fifth
Concerto. Busoni "sharply changes the tempo during a single movement" of

Beethoven's Sonata Op. 111, metrically lengthens the melody in the *Erlkönig* of Schubert-Liszt, begins the recapitulation of the Funeral March from Chopin's B-flat-Minor Sonata *fortissimo* instead of the author's *piano*, permits himself "inclusions and changes" in Chopin's A-flat-Major Polonaise, repeats various phrases in the C-Major, G-Major, A-Major, and E-flat-Minor Preludes, makes small additions in the B-Minor Prelude and some of the etudes, and, instead, deletions in other etudes of the same composer and in the B-Minor Sonata of Liszt, and, in a number of the latter's works "uses a combination of various editions," and, in many cases doubles the bass or the melody, fills in and doubles chords, changes hand distribution, and does other similar "retouching."[4]

Although these sins against the letter of the text were, for the most part, insignificant, academically trained musicians reacted highly emotionally. "An involuntary feeling of indignation seizes the listener," we read in one review; another critic finds Busoni's changes in the A-flat-Major Polonaise of Chopin "repugnant"; "one would consider any changes in the original text of Chopin as artistic blasphemy," writes a third on the subject of the same changes.

Nevertheless, Busoni's "heresies" turned out occasionally to be artistic achievements that knocked the ground from under the "literalists." It was necessary to admit that, not always, but "sometimes" and even "often" Busoni re-creates the works of others "inimitably, with genius," "uses his whims to highlight a given work in a new way, and with captivating brilliance." In Beethoven's Fifth Concerto, the B-Minor Sonata and other works of Liszt he "conquers," "persuades," and "forces one to believe in the rightness of his interpretation," which is "unusually brilliant, profound, and convincing," though quite far from the "orthodox" and abundant with "improvements," "different from the prototype created by the author, but of equal genius." More than that: ". . . there are moments, when it seems that his genius suggested to him something better than what was in the original." And if so, what if all composers performed by him "turn into Busoni?" "It is not so bad at all." Of course, "there is a risk": "in the hands of those less able and less talented" performers who lack Busoni's "persuasion and puissance," this manner "may become, and, undoubtedly, will become only pretentious contortion. . . ." But the "artist of Busoni's caliber," "equal in genius" to the composer being re-created, has the right to his "genius distortion," "the victors are above judgment," "talent makes its own laws," "one can not argue with a talent this magnificent." And should someone dispute the "legality" of this or that of Busoni's "corrections," "while fully aware of the righteousness of this criticism, one wishes to grumble at the musical hypocrisy, the excessive piousness. . . ." "Let it be said hundreds and thousands of times that much is questionable in this performance, that the image of Chopin was entirely contorted. . . . Let it be so. But the mighty gift of Busoni lifted us up to the heights of art, which took our breath away, and which we were loath to leave. . . ."

The differences in attitudes toward Busoni's liberties were determined by differences in the aesthetic positions of critics. But what can explain the vacillations in the evaluation of these liberties by the same critics? Why was the "re-creation" of compositions by Busoni "sometimes the work of genius, sometimes only fortunate and interesting, and other times unfortunate but interesting"?

Partially, of course, it depended on the performer's state at a given concert—whether or not he was "on." "At his first concert, Busoni played without enthusiasm, and the extreme subjectivity of his playing left a perturbing sensation . . . ; during the second concert, where the artist played equally freely, played 'himself,' . . . you could no longer say that. That was because Busoni played with a high level of creative energy, with genius."

The most important reason, however, was something else—namely, what Busoni played and how spiritually close to him the particular composer was. "If the spiritual makeup of the composer being performed contains features that are powerful in the individuality of Busoni himself, we, as a result, have captivating revelations and attainments, if this contact is not present—Busoni can enthrall but not convince!"

The critics unanimously acknowledged Bach and Liszt to be the most closely related to Busoni. They were not mistaken: the artist had long admired the Leipzig cantor and the Weimar magician (one—from his very childhood, the other—from the time of his turning point), referred to them as the "alpha and omega," the "foundation and the summit" of performing art,[5] paid them the most attention in his research, editions, and transcriptions. No wonder, then, that they became also the twin foundations of his performing "throne." "These two composers are lucky. Their closeness to Busoni ensured that, in him, they acquired a genius interpreter." Here Busoni is "in his element," "especially great . . . simply unmatched," "incomparable," "has no equals in the depth of understanding and in artistic beauty of interpretation," indisputably owns "the world crown," "leaving far behind Hofmann and all other virtuosos I have ever heard." Reviewers of various schools never tire of admiring "the uncommon poetry," "the spiritual lucidity, the transparency in a complex contrapuntal texture," "the amazing differentiation of the timbre of each voice"[6] in the chorale preludes of Bach, the "unforgettable" interpretation of Liszt's A-Major Concerto, the "captivating," "magically grandiose," "titanically unified" rendition of the *Totentanz,* the *Dante Sonata,* the B-Minor Sonata, the "singular," "demonic" performance of *Norma* and *Don Juan,* the *Petrarch Sonnets,* "sung with inexpressible tenderness," the "dazzling technique . . . incomparable elegance, exquisite taste, and lavish detail" in the Liszt Etudes, "which were something wondrous to hear." With all that, in these and other works of the two composers, no one objected to the performer's "highly individual, bold" treatment of the author's "prototype," now quite compatible with the remarkable "penetration to the very depth of the composer's creation." And while Busoni imparts the "impression of his mighty individuality" even on Liszt, he "does not distort the creative image of the composer"; on the contrary, "in this reincarnated state, Liszt's inspiration assumes its true character. . . ."

Busoni's approach to Beethoven was more debatable. A number of critics considered him, like Bach and Liszt, among composers who were "the most compatible with the mighty personality of Busoni," called the latter "a superb Beethovenist," "the greatest Beethoven interpreter of our time." However, this opinion was shared by the majority only in regard to the grandiose *Hammerklavier* Sonata (Op. 106), the performance of which by Busoni was unanimously believed to be "a revelation," created "on heights unattainable to others."[7] In other Beethoven works, on the other hand, particularly those belonging to the early or middle periods, Busoni's innovations were not so easily accepted; the merits were noted ("remarkable for the subtle and originally conceived details," "seductive perfection in the beauty of piano timbres and musical 'diction' of Sonata Op.111," "brilliant and impressive rendition of the Fifth Concerto"), but so were the "suspicious" experiments of "modernization," which "could interest . . . but could not convince, or carry away."

The most disapproval was conferred upon Busoni for his Chopin. If in Bach, Beethoven, and Liszt he was indisputably Hofmann's superior, here Hofmann, equally indisputably, could claim his revenge. Only a handful of devoted "Busonists," fanatically loyal to their idol, unconditionally revered his "revolution in Chopin interpretation," arguing that this composer, too, was played "superbly," "splendidly," and "masterfully," passionately debated the "silly" assertion that "Busoni does not succeed in Chopin." Nevertheless, the vast majority of critics were of the opposite opinion. Acknowledging the technical perfection and aural charms of Busoni's Chopin, admiring the many discoveries and certain successes of the artist, the majority still found his interpretation of Chopin on the whole unsuccessful, unconvincing, so far removed from the spirit of Chopin's music as to occasionally resemble a caricature. "The most objections could be aroused by the performance of the two series of Chopin Etudes. Here Busoni's fanciful interpretation disharmonized with Chopin's creative plans, there the insanely quick tempos shocked, not to mention the breaking of the long line of the etude, the additions and deletions." "Marring and breaking Chopin's Etudes (with his own additions), depriving them of poetry and the specific Chopinesque aroma, Busoni turned them simply into exercises for finger velocity." Other reviews are also full of complaints about the same Etudes, displayed by the pianist "in a broken form," at the "overly capricious, arbitrary" performance of the Chopin Preludes, at the "repulsive mannerisms" in the A-flat-Major Polonaise. "But there was a composer who proved to be a stumbling block to this magnificent talent. I speak of Chopin, understood very strangely, or, rather, understood not at all." "It was not Chopin, but some impersonation of Chopin."

Thus, Chopin was the composer in whose works Busoni was least successful, whose works, if the numerous reactions of reviewers are to be trusted, he "distorted" the most. The careful reader has, probably, already noted the fact that the previously quoted indignant philippics of various critics regarding the textual "liberties" of the artist concentrated mainly around the works of Chopin; in the composers—Bach and Liszt above all—whose creative being was close to the performer, the deviations from the text were regarded, as we have seem, as artistically justified, arousing no thoughts of "blasphemy." Does this not imply that, contrary to the point of view of purists, deviations by the performer from the letter of the text are not bad and unacceptable in all cases, in and of themselves, but, rather, only where and when they are dictated by a lack of understanding of the spirit of the music, a lack of inner "contact" with it?

This question is so serious in itself and plays such an important role in Busoni's performing aesthetic, it requires more in-depth consideration.

Chapter Seven

As related in the previous chapter, Busoni was criticized for "liberties" of two varieties: departing from the commonly accepted, traditional interpretations, the "inheritance of the great interpreters," on the one hand, and altering the original text, on the other.

The first reproach should not be taken too seriously. Any true artist, an artist-performer included, without exception, differs in some way from his predecessors and necessarily departs from their accomplishments; otherwise, his "creations" would have no greater value than exact repetitions of the Ninth Symphony or *War and Peace.* "The 'new' is included in the idea of 'Creation.' . . . One follows a great example most faithfully if one does not follow it, for it was through turning away from its predecessor that the example became great,"[1] contributing something new. Beethoven would not have become Beethoven if he merely repeated Haydn and Mozart.

This, of course, does not devalue the creations of the great artists of the past; but these creations can be only admired, not duplicated. Through repetition, the discoveries of great artists pale, lose their life's breath, their potency: "tradition is a wax mask taken of life, which, passing through many years and the hands of countless craftsmen, finally loses the look of the original."[2] Busoni compares "keepers of traditions" with those poor "poets," for whom Goethe's Forkiada (Mephistopheles), in Part II of *Faust,* gathers up the clothes of the fallen Euphorion:[3]

A Lucky Find! 'Twas Now or never;
The flame is gone, it's true—however,
No need to pity mankind now.
Enough is left for many a poet's tiring,
Or to breed envy high and low;
And though I have no talents here for hiring,
I'll hire the robe out, anyhow.[4]

The efforts of "musical officialdom" crown, in place of art, sameness and routine that "destroys all creativeness," "transforms the Temple into a factory"; this routine "flourishes in the theater, in the orchestra, with virtuosi and in the 'Schools of Art,' that is to say those institutions which are arranged excellently for the maintenance of the teachers."[5] There can be either such routine, the copying of academic "examples," or a creative, thus somehow different, reading of a work—there is no third alternative.

The second reproach is more difficult to dismiss. Busoni defends himself by pointing out a fact well known to all musicians—that musical notation cannot be seen as the *original* of the musical composition (in the sense in which this term is used to describe, for instance, a painting), because it constitutes a very inexact, only approximate (in tempo, rhythm, dynamics, accentuation, tone color, length of sound, even intonation) guide, a rough outline of the actual composition. "Music cannot be notated precisely" (Scriabin).[6] Furthermore, the version fixed on paper is not necessarily always best in all ways, and is not the only possible form of expressing a given musical thought. Naturally, form is closely related to content, but it would be ludicrous to expand this correct principle dogmatically *ad absurdum* to claim infallibility and irreplaceability of every detail in every work. Technique may advance and suggest a more convenient approach (for example, a division of a passage between two hands—when it does not contradict the character of the music), the composer may be insufficiently familiar or proficient at a particular instrument (remember Chopin's or Schumann's orchestration), or, finally, he might simply not have "come up with" the best alternative. Composers themselves are often much less strict than their too-diligent defenders: otherwise, how could they (Liszt,[7] for instance) have permitted performers to make numerous alterations (from textual adjustments to transcriptions of entire compositions), how could there exist published variants by composers themselves (*ossia,* different editions), or improvised modifications in performance of their own works by Rachmaninov, Scriabin, and other composers? Apparently, "literalists" are more Catholic than the Pope . . .

Notation, the writing down of musical compositions is, above all, an inventive way to catch an improvisation so that is can again be reproduced. But the former is to the latter as a portrait is to the living model. The performer must free himself of the rigidity of the signs and to animate them. But lawgivers require the performer to reproduce the rigidity of the signs, and consider the reproduction the more perfect, the closer it adheres to them.

That fraction of the composer's inspiration, which has of necessity been lost in notation, must be restored through the inspiration of the performer. To the lawgivers, the signs themselves are of the utmost importance, and are becoming more and more important still; the new art of music is derived from the old signs—so they are now seen as art itself.

If the lawgivers had their way, a composition would always be played in exactly the same tempo, no matter who, when or under what circumstances were playing it. But, that is impossible. . . . Each day begins differently than the previous one, yet always with the dawn.[8] Great artists play their own works differently each time, transform them on the spur of the moment, accelerate and retard,—in ways that they could not notate,—and always according to the conditions of "eternal harmony." Then the lawgivers rage and reproachfully refer the creator to his own handwriting. As of today, the lawgiver has the upper hand.[9]

Thus, from Busoni's point of view, performance is not merely the sounding of notes, but a creative act, a *translation* of the notation into the *spiritual language of the individual performer:* the "performance of a work is also a transcription."[10] The artistic translation is incompatible with literalism; a *portrait* of a Beethoven sonata by Hofmann or Busoni must be judged by a different standard than a photo ID. For this reason, it is difficult to name a truly great performer who has not "sinned" in making larger or smaller departures from the letter of the text. The alterations of Wagner and other conductors in the instrumentation of Beethoven symphonies are well known, as are the freedoms taken by the young Liszt. Later, at a more mature age, Liszt, now more dignified, condemned those freedoms that contradict the "spirit" of the work; but he never forbade them in principle, either to himself or to his students (as the above-cited evidence of Siloti indicates).

Purists try to claim Anton Rubinstein for their camp, based on his comment to Hofmann: "First play what is written (when working on a piece—G. K.); if you have completely assimilated it, and you still wish to add or change something, than go ahead and do so."[11] This quote, however, the first half of which is usually emphasized at the expense of the second, constitutes, not a prohibition, but, instead, a permission to take liberties, *on the condition* that the text has previously been thoroughly absorbed. As for Rubinstein's own playing, it was famous for its freedom, and a cause of embarrassment to the musicians of an academic inclination, an embarrassment copiously registered in oral and printed statements;[12] Busoni followed in the footsteps of the great Anton, a fact often pointed out in the contemporary press.[13]

Other eminent pianists of the post-Rubinstein epoch defined their creative rights equally broadly. Cortot shocked the dogmatists all his life with his liberties with the text, always true to the maxim taught to him in his youth by Rubinstein: "Little one, remember what I tell you: Beethoven can not be performed, he must be re-created, found anew. . . ."[14] Casals,[15] in full, almost verbatim agreement with Busoni, remonstrates with the "fetish of objectivity," the "imaginary objectivity of a musical work," which "bears much responsibility for unsuccessful performances": "How many excellent artists are sill confined by the text, whereas this text is merely a very imperfect method of expressing a musical thought." He notes, as did Busoni, that he has heard many composers who "themselves did not always play their works the same way and did not obey their own directions." The great cellist demands "renunciation of routine and tradition," enjoins the performer "instead of following the letter of the text," to "decidedly reject all models and traditions . . . consciously and patiently searching for his own understanding."[16] Carl Flesch[17] recorded in musical notes examples of liberties committed in Bach and Beethoven by Eugene Ysaÿe.[18] L. Lebedinsky,[19] transcribing Chaliapin's[20] recording of the bell scene from *Boris Godunov*, illustrated how far the legendary singer departed from Mussorgsky's text.[21] Even the principled opponents of "liberties" often committed them; Rachmaninov's recordings of

Paderewski's Minuet or the B-flat-Minor Sonata of Chopin bear out this contention. In the Chopin Sonata, Rachmaninov follows Rubinstein in the recapitulation of the Funeral March in replacing the composer's *piano* with *fortissimo,* a sin attributed to Busoni, as well.

Many of these alterations have become traditional—to such an extent, that occasionally, a return to the original is perceived as "heresy" by the "orthodox." Such was the case with a number of places in the *Well-Tempered Clavier,* where Busoni's restoration of the original text was vigorously opposed by some conservative pedagogues, who continued to guard from Busoni's "distortions" . . . Czerny's distortions of Bach's text.[22]

Does all of the above constitute a license to unlimited freedom for a performer? Hardly. Busoni rejects those inventions born of the desire to innovate at all cost, rather than of artistic considerations or understanding of the spirit of the composition; ". . . conscious avoidance of the laws," he warns, "can not imitate, much less give birth to creative power."[23] It must be noted that Busoni himself was innocent of this transgression: Busoni's "liberties," whatever one's attitude to them may be, were engendered by the considered interpretation of the composition, not an "intentional avoidance of laws." The suspicions of some critics in that direction have by now been relegated to their own biographies. Nevertheless, the source of these suspicions is understandable: the novel, the unusual appears contrived and unnatural (and, of course, sometimes it is) because it does not correspond to the nature of the listener, who is incapable of fathoming it.

Busoni also rejected the tendency ascribed to him to "modernize" classical works. "You make a wrong assumption, thinking that my intention is to 'modernize' compositions," he wrote to the Belgian critic Marcel Remi, on the contrary, by cleansing them of the dust of tradition, I attempt to make them young, the way they were at the moment when they emerged from the head and pen of the composer. The *Pathetique,* a sonata revolutionary in its day, must sound revolutionary; it is impossible to put too much passion into a composition like the *Appassionata,* in which passionate expression reached its apogee in its time. In my performance of Beethoven, I attempted to approach the nervous humanity and freedom that characterized him in contrast to his predecessors. I imagined the character of Beethoven-the-man, mentally reconstructed what that communicated of his playing; in this way I created for myself an ideal, which is incorrectly labeled "modern," but is simply "alive." I do the same with Liszt. . . .[24]

In other words, the "innovations" of Busoni's interpretations were the result of "communion" with the composer, the work of creative imagination based upon Knowledge. He considered knowledge a necessary prerequisite, a sine qua non of any "free" or "literal" performance. His war was on two fronts—against wingless academism on the one hand and vulgar dilettantism, on the other; "by the 'right of individuality' I never meant the noisy expression of any blunderer,"

he warned in one of his open letters.[25] Tasteless virtuosity, the vulgar mannerisms of a de Pachmann were as odious to Busoni as the dogmas of the purists.
This was understood not only by the artist's devotees, those occupying different
stylistic positions also saw that Busoni's departures from the text are "not the
whimsies of a mediocrity failing to rise to understanding of the original," but
"carefully thought-out," always justified modifications founded upon the high
culture of the pianist, his huge erudition, that "painstaking, constantly renewed
study of the composition,"[26] which, according to Rubinstein and Casals, was
the necessary prerequisite to the performer's prerogative to freely interpret the
musical notation.

Even Busoni's opponents could not be entirely unsympathetic to the above-
mentioned qualities. "Everything we saw and heard here," notes an unfriendly
critic of the Moscow weekly *Muzyka*, "represents the result of such long and
hard labor, is so extraordinary and serious, that it demands respect. . . . Possibly, no other contemporary pianist treats his performances with such seriousness and feeling." B. L. Yavorsky sees "an example of conscious and
conscientious focusing of the performer's powers on interpretation of a composition," a "notable example of meticulous study of a composition and thinking through of its external performance." Indeed, Busoni studies the text and
"biography" of musical compositions with meticulousness, unprecedented in
contemporary pianistic practice; he rummages through manuscripts and early
printings, compares editions, correlates variants, and hunts for discrepancies
with the "scrupulous conscience"[27] of a musicologist. How fundamentally this
work was done can be judged from the solid critical apparatus of his editions
and the bibliocritical research that grew out of it. Obviously, any carelessness,
imprecision in the recreation of the written text was organically impossible in
this playing that was "deliberate to the smallest detail." In his editions, Busoni
castigates the player for any evidence of such faults and pedantically demands
"unambiguously exact" observance of the meter, sustaining of the full value of
notes, rests, and so forth.[28]

Closely related to seriousness, culture, and good taste, which distinguished
the programs and playing of the Italian artist was another quality, undisputed
by anyone—"the uncommon profundity of his mind." The reviewers term him
a "great pianist-thinker," a "genius poet-thinker of the piano." This intellectual
side of his playing made him "always very interesting": "as it is very pleasurable
to spend an evening with an intelligent person, one rushes to Busoni's concert,"
"listening to him, you always feel a keen interest in the artist's interpretation. . . ."
Always—even at unsuccessful moments, when the pianist is "unconvincing and
only interesting, which he remains at any moment of his playing."

However, this virtue of Busoni, much like his "creativity in performance," was
seen as a major defect, his second serious weakness, that weakness being the
hypertrophy of the intellectual impulse, the predominance of mind over sensibility, the lack of "heartfelt warmth" in his playing.

Chapter Eight

"Of course, technically he is practically flawless. Undoubtedly, his interpretation is original, personal and individual. Still, this sun does not give warmth, it blinds. Busoni's performance lacks spontaneity, enthusiasm, pathos, as well as expressivity, gentleness, or grace. Listening to him, one always feels acutely interested in his interpretation, but almost never—impassioned or captivated."[1]

The same opinions are heard in a number of other reviews: "The most power in his performance belongs to thought, not to the heart. . . . But what we want from music is what is felt, not what is thought. . . . And here, Busoni satisfies less"; "The root of Busoni's charm is willpower and intelligence, intelligence which is always at work, weaving complexities, whereas what you demand from art is above all spontaneity, reflective poetry"; "He has neither lyricism, nor drama. He does not move or inspire passion. . . . Busoni delights with the estheticism of his delivery, but does not captivate with its expressivity."

These quotes explain some of the reasons why the greater number among the public and critics expressed so much unhappiness with Busoni's interpretation of Chopin, and generally preferred that of Hofmann. "The cerebral, or 'brain' category plays a much greater role in the art of Busoni than of Hofmann, whose 'feeling' category, the heart, is primary. . . ." "As opposed to Busoni, Hofmann is, above all else, a poet. . . . 'Prayer' is the word that best describes the playing of Hofmann. . . . This flame does not rage with eruptions of furious elements. . . . It glimmers quietly, like an inextinguishable light."

The distinctions between the two pianists were noticed also in the sphere of pure piano sonority. In the opinion of the majority, Busoni's sound was superior to Hofmann's in variety and richness of colors, but inferior in warmth and intimacy, on the one hand, and in "thunderousness," on the other. The Italian artist's tone was "not as broad, cushioned, and rounded," it lacked the power of Hofmann's; "Hofmann's attack is more gentle, deeper . . . his *legato* is more singing. . . . Hofmann has more power in *forte*, more effective fullness." "After the concert one remembers that Busoni's sound did not have power, did not have a real *forte*. . . . Equally, fullness, roundness, richness were alien to this sound." "His attack is noble, but not rich. This is noticeable especially in *legato*, which is not remarkable for its singing quality. But *staccato* possesses much sparkle. . . . While he has an enchanting *pianissimo* . . . the pianist does not reach the necessary fullness in *forte*. . . . Thus, there is much brilliance, but little depth and singing."[2]

The frequent assaults of the press regarding the "inadequacy of emotion" in Busoni's playing provided him with the occasion to enter into a debate with his critics, much as he did in the matter of his "liberties." In his "open letter" to *Signale*, trading offense for defense, he criticizes the hackneyed notions of emotion and art:

> What is usually termed *feeling* is: tenderness, pathos, and extravagance of expression. But how much more than this is contained in this wonder-flower—feeling! Restraint, moderation, sacrifice, strength, activity, patience, generosity, joy, and that all-controlling intelligence from which, in reality, all feeling springs.
>
> And before all else it (feeling—G. K.) must be made obvious! It must be underlined so that no one can fail to notice, see, and hear it. It must be projected, greatly magnified, on a screen in front of the public, so that it dances obtrusively and indistinctly before its eyes. For in life, too, obvious expressions of feeling in gestures and words are practiced more often; rarer and more genuine is that feeling which has no need for words, most precious is the feeling that conceals itself.[3]

The author continues to ridicule the over-sensitive philistines, who recognize only the tasteless tearfulness and pomposity, and the habit of wasting emotion on the unimportant and the trivial, which arose under their influence.[4] "What the amateur or mediocre artist is concerned about is only feeling on a small scale, in detail, for short stretches. Feeling on a large scale is mistaken by the amateur, the semi-artist, and the public (and unfortunately the critic also) for want of feeling; because they have not the power to hear large stretches as parts of a still larger whole."[5]

Thus, while many contemporaries of Busoni saw a "deficiency" of feeling, they were being confronted, instead, with a different conception thereof. This new conception guards scrupulously against the excesses of the performing arts (among others) of the epoch—effeminacy, bombast, tear jerking, and pomposity. Busoni replaces the thoughtlessly "elegant sentimentality,"[6] the petty emotions of some; the false pathos, artificial "fire," and "drrrramas"[7] of the others, with a masculine and powerful art, permeated with Bach's and Beethoven's joyful, alive, enormous, but controlled, energy, which reins in "the full measure of its power,"[8] and with grand passions welded to the artist's thought;[9] as if the artist summons the listener from the stuffy "comfort" of fin-de-siècle interiors,[10] from the Sturm und Drang of theatrical storms into a clear day, bright, wide-open spaces, clean and refreshing breeze.

Busoni's wariness toward "overflowing feelings" in art, his "aversion to any sugary sentimentality" was well documented. "As soon as he suspects the smallest danger of falling into sentimentality, he immediately crosses himself thrice and becomes ironic." In his editions he constantly emphasizes, "contrary to the accepted views," that "elegant" nuances and "overindulgent phrasing" "are, and will remain, manifestations of poor taste, wherever they are found"; in performance of Bach they are "appalling mistakes." "Correctly understood, the style of

Bach . . . is characterized above all by masculinity, energy, immensity and grandeur"; performance of Bach must be "vast in plan, broad and robust, preferably too severe than too gentle," entirely free of "contemporary elegance" and "coziness" that contradict Bach's character and "cannot be reconciled with Bach's style." "Without excessive expressivity," writes Busoni above Prelude XVI of Book I of the *Well-Tempered Clavier*, knowing full well that this direction will appear at first glance "striking, even offensive, to some"; but "often enough, there is extravagant emotion where there is no true expressivity. Therefore, it is not superfluous to take measures to suppress the emotional zeal."[11]

The performing suggestions to other works of Bach are of a similar nature: "'Expression' must not be exaggerated. . . . Here, as in all other slow Bach works it is necessary to take care that it does not become sentimentality: expression must always and everywhere manifest a healthy masculine character"; "The manner of performance . . . must not be falsely (that is effeminately) softened. Only the two lyrical moments allow and demand strong, abundant expression, which, however, must constantly maintain masculine character"; "The entire piece breathes of sadness, but not sentimentality and slackening. There must be nothing feeble, floating or hesitant. The powerful nature exhibits even sadness in thoroughly different tones than a sickly, languishing soul."[12] "But certainly without emotion!" the performer is warned by a note to one of the episodes of Fugue XVII. In Fugue XII, Riemann's *Adagio pensieroso* (Slowly, pensively) is replaced by *Molto sostenuto, ma fermo in tempo e carattere* (Very sustained, but strong in tempo and character). *Bedächtig, doch nicht schleppend; dolce ma serioso, con un certo sentimento severo, ernst, severo, deciso, risoluto, energico, ardito, con fermezza, robusto, kräftig, lebhaft, frisch,*[13] instruct other editorial comments in Busoni's Bach editions.

The same point of view obtains in the problems of sound production, touch, and the like. The particularities of his playing—the preference for *staccato* over *legato,* lack of fullness, roundness in the sound—are not inadvertent defects, but deliberate choices. Like Liszt, who persuaded his student Valerie Boissier about the advantages of *piqué* over *lié,* detached playing over connected,[14] and who did not wish to resort to the "velvet" touch a la Henselt or Thalberg,[15] Busoni "avoids the singing *legato* on principle, resorting to it only rarely." In his note to Prelude VI of Book I of the *Well-Tempered Clavier* he argues that

> *legato* playing favored by the old school is not practically achievable on the piano, though it is possible—in some cases—to create an illusion of a *legato*-like effect. The "connected ideal" was born at the time when the violin school of Spohr[16] and Italian vocal art mercilessly dominated performance. There was (and still is) an erroneous view among musicians that instrumental technique must seek its prototype in singing, that it is the closer to perfection, the more it resembles this arbitrarily selected model. But the conditions on which vocal art is based—breath, connection and disconnection of syllables, words and sentences, the differences of registers—are, to a large extent,

meaningless even for the violin, and have no significance at all in the case of the piano. Different principles lead to different effects (*Wirkungen*). These effects must be cultivated and developed, in order to fully expose the inherent character of the instrument.[17]

Based upon these principles, and upon the "*staccato* nature of the piano," toward which "the importance of wrist and octave playing has increased immensely in the past decades," Busoni condemns "overly refined *legato*" and emphasizes "non *legato* playing"—"the sort of touch, where the finger makes a flexible attack with no help from the wrist, so that the active finger bounces off the key before the next finger descends. At the same time, this touch differs from the actual *staccato* in that, while the sounds must sound detached from one another, they must be gentler and longer." Here, according to Busoni, "lies the secret to the so-called *jeu perlé*, which is based on the same aspects of detachedness, softness, and uniformity."[18] This technique, as we have seen, found its brilliant confirmation in the playing of Busoni himself (see Chapter 4).

Thus, it was not a singing connectedness, but, rather, an instrumental detachedness of playing seemed to Busoni as the most appropriate to the nature of the pianoforte.[19] If Leschetizky saw *glissando*[20] as the sound-ideal for passagework, in Busoni's opinion, even a *glissando* must sound (and did sound) like a "pearly" passage. "All four eighth notes of each measure must be heard distinctly," Busoni demands in a note to Liszt's *Don Juan; perlato, granulato* appear often in other notes.

Polemics (theoretical and practical) against "elegant nuances" and "singing *legato*" were only one form of Busoni's struggle against the prevalent contemporary style of playing; as the reader will recall, this struggle also had a second front. Busoni's persistent attempts to suppress romantic sensibility were supplemented by an equally determined effort to curb romantic pathos. He interprets Fugue X of Book I, *Well-Tempered Clavier,* not as "rather contemplatively" as does Riemann, not *allegro capriccioso* (quickly and capriciously) as in Bischoff, not *allegro con fuoco* (quickly and with fire) as in Tausig, but *allegro deciso* (quickly and decisively); "the editor leans toward the opinion of Tausig, but sees fit to replace 'fire' with 'decisiveness.'"[21] The introduction to his edition of Liszt's *Don Juan* "compellingly urges" the player not to make a "bombastic piece" out of the fantasy, to strive to reproduce the "lucidity and subtlety of Mozart's *Don Juan.*"[22] "Avoidance of the pathetic and the sentimental" becomes a virtual leitmotif of Busoni's interpretation of the piece: "The figuration of the right hand is not to be thrown in a 'bravura, improvisatory' manner. . . ."; "This octave passage must not sound bravura or noisy"; "Stormily, but still under control," read some of the notes.[23] Playing the B-Minor Sonata, the second *Legend* and other works of Liszt, Busoni often startles the listeners with his "very modest, very simple" performances of places where tradition led them to expect pathos and thunder. But if his playing had less thunder than other pianists, it had more lightning.

His sound did not cover, but pierced through the orchestral *tutti,* in which, in Cortot's opinion, it again resembled Liszt.[24]

Polemics have their laws. Possibly, even probably, in his performing "polemic" against the salon-virtuoso direction in pianism Busoni went too far. For fear of expressive "warmth" or artificial "fire" he tended toward the opposite extreme— became prudish, overly cold. Nevertheless, it is clear that Busoni's playing was an expression of a specific style, with its "virtues" and "defects" arising from a single aesthetic ideal, inseparable. He can be accepted or rejected, but it is pointless to view him as a conglomeration of accidental elements, to miss the essential unity. For that reason, it is difficult to suppress a smile at the naive wishes of some musicians of the past to "supplement" Busoni's merits with the "expressivity," "impulsiveness," "spontaneity," and "impetuosity" of one or another performer of an entirely different orientation: "If he (Busoni—G. K.) and Eugen d'Albert could be . . . combined into one whole, the result would be one of the greatest musicians of all time. . . .";[25] "Kreisler . . . is the opposite . . . of the king of pianists, Busoni. Ah, if Nature gave us an artist that would unite fully the advantages of both!"[26] This method of discussing performers is still alive and well today. Let us pay homage to its founder, the unforgettable Agafya Tikhonovna Kupedryagina: ". . . If one could combine Mr. Anutchkin's lips with Mr. Podkolyossin's nose or Mr. Zevakin's assurance with Mr. Omelet's solidity, a girl might know how to choose!"[27]

Chapter Nine

The questions of rhythm and dynamics play an important role in any system of musical interpretation.

Most pianists in the epoch in question built their playing on rhythmic and dynamic "waves," made into a principle by Leschetitzky. Busoni rejects this principle.[1] He classifies constant *rubatos*, "coquettish" "long established" quickenings and retards, "well-rounded" *ritardandos* and *accelerandos*, "surging" beginnings and "melting" ends as bad taste. Himself playing, according to the critics, "extremely metrically," he demands of others—especially in Bach—"consistent motion," "strictly rhythmical playing," distinct articulation of every eighth note, conjunct, nonarpeggiated chords: "it is especially important to make sure that all the notes of the chord sound strictly simultaneously."[2] His favorite comments include *molto misurato, senza espressione, ni licenza alcuna; recht schnell, doch geschwind; mässig bewegt und klar phrasirt; mässig geschwind, mit rhytmischem Accent; ruhig, ruhig bewegt, in gleichmässiger Bewegung, egualmente, misuratamente, ritmicamente, articolato, marcato, ben in tempo, mit festem Rhytmus, mit praecisem Anschlag, zusammen, non arpeggiato, non accelerando (nicht eilen!), non rallentando (nicht schleppen!)*.[3] Busoni's propensity for even, clear, well-defined rhythmic character compels him to translate Bach's cadenzas, trills and fermatas strictly metrically, and, in places, to change the layout, to bring it into a sharper metrical "relief," to emphasize a metallic sharpness, or an even stream of *pizzicati* (as in the ninth Variation of the A-Minor Etude of Paganini-Liszt).[4]

Busoni's special hostility was reserved for the habit many pianists had of retarding endings and concealing sudden changes of tempo with gradual alterations; "retarding the tempo at the end of the penultimate measure . . . is out of the question," "the editor prefers to strive energetically for the end without slowing the tempo," the final cadence "must sound strictly in rhythm, highly energetically, like a sudden decision." In Prelude X of Book I of the *Well-Tempered Clavier*, Busoni protests against using the two transitional measures (from *Sostenuto quasi Andante* to *Presto*—G. K.) to soften the contrast by means of a "well-rounded" *accelerando;* on the contrary, it is better to maintain the original quiet tempo up to the *Presto;* the ending of the Prelude, he suggests, should be played either strictly in rhythm (*deciso*), or exactly twice slower: "a compromise (in the form of an ambiguous *allargando*) is out of place: in both cases the tempo must be meticulously observed."[5] Busoni's own playing, as we have seen, was also remarkable for sudden changes of tempo; not surprisingly, some critics characterize his rhythm as "more than sharp," "at times barbed and angular."

Thus, the rhythmic waves and curves of Leschetizky become, in Busoni's hands, a series of straight lines and angles. The transformation of dynamics is of the same nature. He comments ironically about the phrasing devices of his colleagues—"affected swelling of the phrase," "the beloved short increase and decrease of sound (< >)," "endlessly divisible scale of shades and nuances, optimally in possession of the contemporary pianist"; instead, he recommends—in playing Bach—in most cases, that the whole construction (*Satz*) be colored without change, with the same shade, which should be maintained with a "faultless uniformity," a "still singleness of sounds" similar to the registers of the organ, where the pipes are "balanced with painstaking care" to the point that a sound even slightly louder than its neighbors would seem a scream. It is necessary to possess a great variety of gradations of sound, to obtain the richest possible "scale of dynamic steps"—but, the alternation of sonorities, augmentation and diminution of sonority must occur in "clear units, impulses (terraced), without minor dynamic transitions," "as if resulting from a change of organ stops."[6] Busoni's editions instruct the performer: *non crescendo, non diminuendo, plötzlich leiser, subito f, più piano senza transizione.*[7]

These markings and indications are borrowed from Busoni's editions of Bach. They have since acquitted themselves so well in practice that they have become commonly accepted.[8] It would be incorrect to think that Busoni followed this philosophy only in Bach: he also used "terraced" phrasing and nuances—to a greater or lesser extent, with greater or lesser success—in performing the works of other composers, especially Liszt. The significance of this approach in Busoni's playing is momentous; in particular, it opened the door to the torrent of sound colors, which, to the amazement of contemporaries, erupted from under his fingers. The small-range, "overly musical"[9] nuancing of his colleagues erased the boundaries between these colors, blended them into a unified tone, buried in the wavelike homogeneity the contrasts of the many "instruments" in the piano "orchestrations" of Liszt and of the individual "voices" in the compositions of Bach;[10] by eliminating smoothed-out transitions (here, again, walking in the footsteps of Liszt),[11] Busoni liberates the "captive" colors, and they sparkle in all their blinding purity.[12]

Terraced construction of the whole from "layers," separated from one another by clear boundaries is the basic creative principle of Busoni's playing; it gave rise to clarity that astonished reviewers: "Busoni's playing is remarkable for the exceptional precision of lines, of the picture. He does not play, he sculpts"; ". . . everything sounds . . . in relief"; "his playing captivates the ear with the strikingly precise relief of his musical pictures"; "his nuances can be painted; he can be called the great sculptor among the living pianists."[13]

The great Romantic pianists aroused associations of the literary variety in their listeners, associations with a poem, a ballad, a story; Busoni's "picturesque," architectural performing style, on the other hand, is compared with the art of various painters, with the grandeur of cathedrals; it evokes "colorful canvases," "frescoes," "sound sculptures"; it is "as though carved in marble." ". . . I felt a kinship to the graphic arts in Busoni's playing," writes professor M. N. Barinova,[14] "Liszt's 'Sposalizio,' 'Il pensieroso,' and 'Canzonetta del Salvator Rosa' from the second *Année* were performed sculpturally. . . . The clear contours of the form (in the interpretation of Liszt's B-Minor Sonata—G. K.) could be likened to an architectural plan."[15] These combined impulses of architecture and visual arts are considered to be the central feature of Busoni's artistic thinking by such musicologists as Weissmann, Martienssen, and Leichtentritt: "to understand music graphically was natural to him . . . in architecture, in sculpture, in painting, he found the source of fruitful pianistic effects . . . his musical conceptions were based on a visual image." The last remark is confirmed by the words of Busoni himself: "the listener is also a spectator," he writes in a note to Liszt's *Don Juan.*[16]

The explanation for the bewilderment that Busoni's playing stirred in his audiences can also be found here. Busoni belonged to that type of artists, described by M. F. Gnessin[17] in his most fascinating essay "On the Nature of Musical Art and Russian Music,"[18] who are "boundary seekers," that is, those who incline in their work—as opposed to the "primary" artists—not to the "heart," but, rather, to the margins of their art, to that point where it touches other, adjacent arts (among such artists Gnessin lists, for example, Rimsky-Korsakov, contrasting him to the "primary" Tchaikovsky). Like the composer of *Sadko,* Busoni thought in images, akin to the visual arts, where the "total" is a result of perception of the form as a whole, and of correlation of its parts. This type of creative thinking is no less valid than any other; but, as any other, its effect is directly proportionate to the receptivity of the listener; as we have seen, the artist "must be judged according to his own laws." "He who wishes to comprehend" such art "must listen in large unities"; "only in the light of large unities do all the particulars acquire purpose and meaning. Only then does all that seemed 'cold' in itself come to life."[19] Only then does the listener discern behind the "would-be lack of feeling" a "feeling on a large scale," behind the "caprices"—logic, behind "discontinuity"—a "titanically unified design."[20]

The ears and intellects of a large proportion of audiences were schooled by performances of the "primary," musically narrative type, often in its salon manifestation. Critics of similar upbringing reacted (outside of technique) only to "musicality" or "sensitivity" of individual phrases, to the logic of the consecutive unfolding of events, and to the character of the final episode, where, in their opinion (not in the correlation of all episodes, not in the work as a whole), the interpretation of a given composition is summed up. It comes as no surprise that from such positions, Busoni's interpretations seemed incomprehensible, appeared as sometimes lovely, but meaningless "architecture in sound," a kaleidoscope of colors.

The authors of these judgments were, of course, mistaken. Busoni's musical architecture—like any architecture—contained its own expressivity, and *colors* communicated specific *ideas.*[21] He fought, in word and action, in the press and on the stage, not merely for *non legato* versus *legato,* or for "terraces" versus "waves," but first and foremost, against spiritual trivialization of performance, for the renaissance of an art of great thought and feeling, for a profound fathoming and determined incarnation of the central idea of a composition. "Busoni seeks the innermost musical vision" of the composer; "most remarkable is Busoni's ability to underscore the principal idea of the composer, to separate it from the secondary. In this regard he has no rivals."[22]

How, then, did Busoni approach a composition, how was his interpretation different from those of other pianists? Let us compare two interpretations of the same composition—Busoni and another great pianist of his time. Liszt's *Rigoletto Paraphrase* affords a convenient example.

Chapter Ten

In 1904, M. Welte, a Freiburg manufacturer, built an apparatus he called "Welte-Mignon" designed to record and reproduce piano playing by means of piano rolls.[1] This method of recording had a number of disadvantages compared to the acoustical,[2] but also some advantages; in particular, it registers various elements of the performance (such as rhythm, tempo, basic dynamics, partially even pedaling) in a manner that allows exact measurement, and, therefore, analysis.[3]

In 1905 Busoni recorded a number of piano rolls, including Liszt's *Rigoletto*. In 1906, the same composition was recorded by the famous Russian pianist Annette Essipoff (1851–1914),[4] the student and, together with Paderewski, the most typical representative of the school of Leschetitzky.

Let us compare the two versions.

On first hearing, what immediately attracts attention is the exceptional technical brilliance of Busoni's playing, much greater than Essipoff's. When it comes to the interpretation, however, the first impression leans rather against Busoni: his playing seems strange, at times even wild in comparison with the traditionally rounded, beautiful playing of the Russian lady. It is easy to understand the unknown critic who chided Busoni, writing, "having lived so long in Germany, he has forgotten how they sing in his native land. To phrase this way here (in the *Rigoletto*—G. K.) is just plain wrong; as wrong as it is to transform passionate melodies indo pianistic acrobatics. . . ."[5]

If the listener does not unquestioningly trust his first impression, but attempts to listen more deeply, to fathom Busoni's interpretation, to perform his own "half of the work," the picture gradually begins to change.

First we notice that in Essipoff's playing there are no *characters:* all the dramatis personae are alike, all of them—the Duke, Rigoletto, Maddalena, Gilda— appear to the listener as equally attractive beings, or rather, as one being, singing against a background of elegant passages a few equally pleasant melodies, which blend seamlessly one into the next. But, where there are no characters, there are no conflicts, no drama: Essipoff plays not a drama, but an elegant salon-virtuoso potpourri on the favorite opera tunes, such as were written before Liszt by Thalberg and the like.

In Busoni's interpretation, on the other hand, the characters are sharply individualized, clearly delineated. Thus, the Duke is not a romantic lover, not a Werther, not a Romeo who sings passionate melodies with sincere emotion, but a cold libertine, a professional seducer, using the same[6] standard lines to entice women:

Bella figlia dell'amore,
Schiavo son de'vezzi tuoi;
Con un detto, un detto sol tu puoi
Le mie pene, le mie pene consolar.
Vieni e senti del mio core
Il frequente palpitar, etc.[7]

These fake declarations (the experienced Maddalena "knows their worth") are given the intonation of an actor's tirade, underlined even more by the ironic-sounding ("just look at him go"[8]) triple replies of the orchestra:

Ex. 1. Verdi-Liszt, *Rigoletto-Paraphrase*, mm. 17–19, Busoni's variant

Ex. 2. Verdi-Liszt, *Rigoletto-Paraphrase*, mm. 20–21, Busoni's variant

Ex. 3. Verdi-Liszt, *Rigoletto-Paraphrase*, mm. 24–25, Busoni's variant

Busoni substitutes these close chords, borrowed from Verdi's original, for Liszt's softer arpeggios:

Ex. 4. Verdi-Liszt, *Rigoletto-Paraphrase*, mm. 17–19, Liszt's original

Ex. 5. Verdi-Liszt, *Rigoletto-Paraphrase*, mm. 20–21, Liszt's original

Ex. 6. Verdi-Liszt, *Rigoletto-Paraphrase*, mm. 24–25, Liszt's original

Following the Duke, Maddalena enters:

Ah! ah! rido ben di core,
Che tai baje costan poco[9]

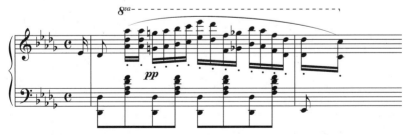

Ex. 7. Verdi-Liszt, *Rigoletto-Paraphrase*, mm. 32–34

Essipoff begins Maddalena's comment very softly, as if bringing it out of the final *ritenuto* of the Duke, and only gradually accelerates the tempo: the first two sixteenth notes of Maddalena's part:

Ex. 8. Verdi-Liszt, *Rigoletto-Paraphrase*, m. 33

are played by her in the same character and tempo (eighth note = 58) as the last Db of the Duke's part, later accelerating at the following rate (one eighth is taken as the unit of measurement): 65, 63, 69, 64, 71, 75, 80[10] (Gilda's retort is next). Thus, Essipoff conceals the transition from the Duke's lines to those of Maddalena, turns the latter's vulgar flirting into salon gracefulness, robs her first "Ha Ha!" of meaning with her slow tempo.

Busoni's tempo is the following: MM eighth note = 58 (the Duke's final Db), 96, 110, 118, 118, 118, 125, 115, 118; in other words, he makes a marked change between the two parts, takes a new, faster tempo at Maddalena's "entrance," and performs her entire statement much faster than Essipoff, with a cold, metallically bright tone.

The matters are the same in the second half of the composition, where Essipoff completely blends (partially with the aid of the pedal) the parts of Rigoletto and Gilda, depriving the former of any independent meaning, interpreting it as merely the bass line of the latter. Instead, Busoni individualizes Rigoletto's part, freeing it from the pedal captivity and emphasizes, recitative-like, its threatening undertones:

Ex. 9. Verdi-Liszt, *Rigoletto-Paraphrase*, mm. 77–78

Thus, Busoni paints the heroes of the drama more realistically, in greater relief. But another circumstance calls attention to itself here. The sensation of artificiality, of playacting is present in Busoni's interpretation not only in the parts of the Duke and Maddalena, where it is obviously warranted, but also in the parts of Gilda and Rigoletto—characters that, it would seem, demand a different approach. This lends to Busoni's entire interpretation a feeling of irony, of mockery, of "playing at emotion." As if we see in front of us—and the performers consistently emphasize that fact—no real-life drama, but a theatrical production, a play—and no more. As B. L. Yavorsky correctly summarized: "In the *Rigoletto* fantasy . . . Busoni's entire attention was directed into a remarkably faithful reproduction of a typical Italian Operatic performance, true to the genre; . . . the tenor marched victoriously, the coquette flirted, the heroine declaimed pathetically, the baritone forced his voice with ominous drama; all was prominently displayed."[11]

This interpretation of *Rigoletto* was neither Busoni's caprice nor his invention. In fact, it had a historical foundation. Even Victor Hugo himself, the author of the play that gave Verdi his subject matter, in his well-known foreword to *Cromwell* (1827) saw in every drama a mixture of the "elevated and the grotesque," a "tragedy in the guise of comedy" and proclaimed the task of art to be the "recreation of the strings by which fate directs the human puppets";[12] in the same play he declares, in the words of Cromwell's Fool that "from our places" everything "seems to be a stupid drama": "So let us watch. In front of our eyes two dozen actors will pass, some calm, some sad, some happy. And we, mute observer-philosophers, staying in the shadow, will applaud the successful numbers, laugh at the catastrophes, let Charles and Cromwell blindly fight and destroy each other for our enjoyment!"[13]

The concept of life as "stupid drama," a cruel human comedy whose heroes, like puppets pulled by strings, suffer and rejoice, love and hate, hope and perish, but not seriously, as it appears to the participants, but only for someone's "enjoyment," this concept permeated the work of Hugo and other Romantics, such as E. T. A. Hoffmann and Heine in the twenties and thirties of the past century.

Liszt was a contemporary, friend, and, in many ways, a confederate of these writers. He often read and reread Hugo, whose poetry provided the program for many of his works (*Mazeppa, Ce qu'on entend sur la montagne*[14]). He lived in Paris in 1832, the year Hugo's play *Le roi s'amuse*, which was the subject of *Rigoletto*, was produced and promptly forbidden, and the grand political scandal that ensued.[15] Liszt could not help but remember all this when, in 1851, Verdi's *Rigoletto* came out and gained great popularity. The future author of the *Mephisto Waltz* lived at the time in Weimar. Verdi's opera is mentioned often in his correspondence with Bülow; Liszt shows great interest in it. In particular, he informs Bülow that Julius Egghard[16] played him his own fantasy on *Rigoletto* and that Liszt did not like it too much; nor was he satisfied by the two later paraphrases of Bülow himself. Liszt felt that more could and should be extracted from the opera than a brilliant salon piece.

These facts, undoubtedly familiar to Busoni, throw more light on Liszt's perception of Verdi's opera as he transforms it in his paraphrase, and on Busoni's interpretation of the paraphrase. Liszt approached this work much more seriously than his youthful operatic fantasies. By 1859, when he wrote his transcription of the *Rigoletto* quartet for von Bülow's Berlin concerts, the salon-virtuoso excesses of his youth were far behind him; by this time he was already the author of two symphonies, twelve symphonic poems, both piano concertos, and the

B-Minor Sonata. In Verdi's opera he, doubtlessly, saw Hugo's play—not some banal melodrama, but literature of profound ideas and meaning. This meaning harmonized perfectly with Liszt's own feelings at this trying time in his life. His difficult renunciation of his concert career brought him to Weimar; but Weimar, too, disappointed. Heartbroken by a lengthy and vile intrigue, his conducting of Cornelius's *Barber of Baghdad* hissed by the public, Liszt immediately resigns his directorship of the opera theater to which he had dedicated ten years of his life.[17] Weary and disheartened, he prepares to leave the city in which his prolonged sojourn began and ended with heavy creative, social and personal traumas—from the defeat of the Hungarian revolt, the death of Chopin (1848–49), to the death of Liszt's twenty-year-old son after a prolonged illness at the end of that same 1859, when the *Rigoletto* paraphrase was written. Ahead looms Rome and priesthood.

During these years, filled with doubts, pondering the meaning of life, Liszt more and more often turns to the image of what seems to him must stand in the wings of the "stupid drama," pulling the "human puppets" by the strings, which sarcastically mocks their hopes and efforts, "laughs at the catastrophes"—the image of Mephistopheles. The year of *Rigoletto* is also the year of the *Mephisto Waltz,* the year of the final version of the *Totentanz;* only two years earlier, in 1857, the composer completes his *Faust Symphony,* in whose final "tableau" Mephistopheles so cruelly parodies the feelings, desires, and dreams of Faust and Gretchen.

Such is the milieu at *Rigoletto's* birth. If Mephistopheles nowhere in it actively takes the stage, his presence "in the wings" of the brilliant spectacle is palpable to a thoughtful musician. The weapon by means of which the "spirit of evil" (or "fate," its favorite Romantic pseudonym) does his work is, as is usual in such cases, the most insignificant, least conspicuous of the characters—Maddalena—for it is she who is thrown in Gilda's and Rigoletto's paths by the "backstage director," she who precipitates the shattering of Gilda's love and Rigoletto's revenge. Is this not why Liszt frames the entire fantasy with the echoes of Maddalena's laughter, insistently repeating it at the beginning and end of the piece? Does he not endow these "intonations of laughter" with a deeper, more symbolic meaning, when in the opening "prelude" he carries them unexpectedly into the low register, seemingly incompatible with the idea of an empty-headed, lighthearted coquette?

Busoni's "strange" interpretation suddenly reveals its significance. He begins the paraphrase with the ominously sardonic laughter of the "director"; the laughter sounds softer and duller each time, the director has gone backstage; and now in front of us the elegant theater glitters and shines in gold and silver; the crowd quiets down, the velvet curtain rises—and at the same moment, before the start of the "spectacle," in total silence, from afar (from the wings), but quite clearly, the half-concealed laughter is heard again, this time in the high register:

Ex. 10. Verdi-Liszt, *Rigoletto-Paraphrase*, mm. 15–17

Essipoff performs this place in the spirit of a ballade—gently, thoughtfully, not fast: the first eighth note (the A-flat in the bass, which concludes the previous passage) at quarter note = 38, then—MM quarter note = 38, 54, 47, 40, 48, 28. Busoni gives the phrase a cold metallic glint, plays it fast, as usual sharply differentiating it from the previous (and slowing it down more abruptly in the end): MM quarter note = 48 (the bass A♭), 100, 110, 80, 57, 58, 26; equally maliciously (and considerably louder than the composer's *pianissimo*) sounds the fragment of the same phrase at the end of the paraphrase—after the puppets have played out their drama:

Ex. 11. Verdi-Liszt, *Rigoletto-Paraphrase*, mm. 90–91

Only the repetition of this fragment in the next measure is played considerably softer and slower, as if moving farther away. And the listener, if he is sufficiently impressionable and sensitive, will remain, at the conclusion of the final, emphatically "indifferently" played octave passages, in a state similar to that of one listening to Chaliapin or that of patrons of Auerbach's cellar at the end of a little "meaningless" joke about a flea:

> . . . And the air is still full of the fiery thunderous voice, the mouths open in terror still have not closed, but already there is the sound of the offensive, demonically good-natured laughter: Ha-ha-ha-ha-ha-ha-ha-ha. Ha-ha-ha-ha-ha-ha-ha-ha. As if to say—"sorry, fellows, I just made a joke about a flea. Yes, just a joke—shall we have some beer: the beer is good here. Hey, barkeep!" And the

fellows, staring in disbelief, quietly searching the stranger for signs of a traitor-
ous tail, choke on their beer, smile pleasantly, creep out of the cellar one after
another, and silently slink home along the wall. And only at home, after clos-
ing the shutters and separating himself from the world by the generous body
of Frau Margarete, he whispers to her fearfully and mysteriously: "do you know
something, my dear, I think I saw the devil today."[18]

The reader can now judge the critical responses for himself, particularly of
those critics who perceived nothing in Busoni's interpretation but technique
and a "kaleidoscope" of colors. Busoni's "strange" performance of *Rigoletto* not
only clearly reveals an original and well-thought-out design, but, in addition, it
would seem, that this design is incomparably closer to that of the composer than
Essipoff's superficial and hackneyed rendition (as well as those of many other
interpreters of this popular work). It does not follow, however, that Busoni's
interpretation of the paraphrase entirely agrees with Liszt's. Busoni, without a
doubt, grasped the implications of Liszt's conception, but he went further than
Liszt, deepening, developing, and sharpening the elements present in embryo.
This deepening and development followed the same path by which Liszt himself
proceeded to evolve; but, as in Busoni's edition of *Don Juan,* it somewhat antici-
pated in the Liszt of the 1840s–1850s the attainments of the 1870s and 1880s.
Moreover, Busoni looked at *Rigoletto* with the eyes of a person who had lived
through the development and transformation of Romantic ideas brought by
the following decades. For that reason, Busoni's concept of *Rigoletto* is not only
akin to the worldview of Liszt, Hugo, and E. T. A. Hoffmann,[19] but to certain
motifs in the work of Flaubert,[20] Anatole France,[21] Henri de Régnier,[22] Romain
Rolland,[23] Rimsky-Korsakov,[24] and Rachmaninov,[25] as well as, and to an even
greater extent, to Stravinsky's *Petrushka,* to the poetry of Blok,[26] the plays of Leonid Andreyev[27] and Pirandello,[28] the "marionette theater" of Maeterlinck[29] and
Gordon Craig.[30] In other words, starting with Romanticism, coming in contact
with Realism slightly on his way, Busoni moves in his interpretation to (or almost
to) Symbolism.
    But it is too early yet to make a final evaluation of Busoni's art. Let us acquaint
ourselves with its other aspects.

Chapter Eleven

As we have already seen, while Busoni's interpretations ignited important arguments, his technique was unanimously acknowledged to be unique in the pianistic world. Therefore, familiarity with his views on this aspect of pianism, his recommendations regarding devices and methods of technical work are of great interest.

Busoni considered technique not the preeminent, but a very significant aspect of piano playing. In his article "On the Requirements Necessary for a Pianist" and in his review of Galston's *Work Book*[1] he wrote:

> No, technique is not and never will be the Alpha and Omega of piano-playing, any more than it is with any other art. Nevertheless, I certainly preach to my pupils: "provide yourselves with technique, and thoroughly, too . . . a great pianist must first of all be a great technician . . ."; "desiring to rise above virtuosity, it is necessary first to possess it. . . ." They say "thank Heaven, he is not a virtuoso." They should say: "he is not only a virtuoso, he is more than one."[2]

However, Busoni understands technique differently than it is understood "in the piano classes of all Europe."[3] ". . . Technique, which, of course, forms only a part of the pianistic art, consists not only of fingers, wrist, strength and endurance," he writes in "On the Requirements Necessary for a Pianist," "Technique in the higher sense of the word is concentrated in the mind,[4] it is composed of geometry—an estimation of distance—and wise co-ordination. Even that, however, is only a beginning, for touch also belongs to true technique as does very particularly the use of the pedals."[5]

Similar thoughts are expressed by Busoni in the preface to his edition of Liszt's *Don Juan:*

> During the lifelong course of his pianistic studies the editor has always endeavoured to simplify the mechanism of piano playing and to reduce it to what is absolutely indispensable in movement and expenditure of strength. His mature opinion is that the acquirement of a technique is nothing else than fitting a given difficulty to one's own capacities. That this will be furthered to a lesser extent through physical practising and to a greater extent through keeping an eye on the task mentally is a truth which perhaps has not been obvious to every pianoforte pedagogue, but surely it is obvious to every player

who attains his aim through self-education and reflection. It is not through attacking the difficulty repeatedly but through the analysis (Prüfung) of the problem that success in solving it is possible.[6]

The principle remains the same, but solving the difficulty demands a new adaptation, an individual nuance in every instance.[7]

The "simplification" of a difficulty as a result of "analysis," its "adaptation" to "one's own capabilities" (instead of the opposite—the adaptation of one's abilities to the given difficulty, as the task of technical work is usually understood) by "wise judgment"—all this in Busoni's "system" finds practical expression first of all in the method of *mental regrouping* or, as Busoni referred to it, "technical phrasing" of a passage.

The essence of the method is this: Busoni had noticed that the ease and speed of playing of a passage consisting of a string of sounds of equal length depends greatly on how one mentally subdivides this string, how the constituent sounds are grouped together. While Busoni voiced this observation (in the Appendix to Fugue X, Book I of his edition of the *Well-Tempered Clavier*[8]) in regard to octave passages, his performing and pedagogical practice showed that it is equally worthwhile and productive applied to other types of piano technique, and even beyond that. Imagine, for example, that your task is to pronounce rapidly the following:

ookbookbookbookbookb, and so on

It is obvious to anyone that this string consists of several repetitions of a unit of four letters, and to pronounce this tongue-twister one will mentally subdivide it:

ookb-ookb-ookb-ookb, and so on
Now try to regroup the same string of letters differently:
(ook)-book-book-book, and so on

The difficult, as if by magic, becomes easy: the ease and speed of pronunciation increase "by themselves" by at least half.

The same takes place in piano playing. Many, for instance, remember the episode that took place in the 1920s during a piano master class given by Egon Petri, Busoni's foremost student and disciple, at the Moscow Conservatory. Petri gave the participating pianists a seemingly impossible task—to play at sight, without any preparation, quickly and cleanly, a passage of broken tenths, built on the degrees of the diminished seventh chord:

Ex. 12. Broken tenths

Then, after some luckless attempts on the part of the students, Petri suggested that they mentally regroup the notes in such a way that the first note became an upbeat,[9] and the rest—a progression of broken octaves:

Ex. 13. Broken octaves

The result of the experiment astonished everyone present, according to the testimony of Grigory Prokofiev, who happened to be at the master class, the change in perception "immediately adds great speed and precision to the passage."[10]

The "magic trick" illustrated by Petri caused much commotion and discussion in its day in Moscow's pianistic circles. However, it would not have been such a novelty, had our pianists been more familiar with the thesis of "technical phrasing" published by Busoni thirty years earlier. For Petri's experiment, effective as it was, was only one application of Busoni's concept. The psychological mechanism involved is analogous to the mechanism of the pronunciation trick: the tenth for a pianist is the unwieldy *ookb,* the octave—the easy *book,* and herein lies the explanation of what happened at Petri's lesson.

So, why is a tenth an *ookb,* while an octave is a *book?* And why, in both cases, is it easier to say *book-book-book* than *ookb-ookb-ookb?*

The secret is hidden in the laws of automatization, the psychological process that lies at the root of any rapidity (pianistic, athletic, etc.), consisting of the "substitution of many single-action impulses by a few impulses directed at complex actions. . . . A number of individual intentions is replaced by one complex action which takes place automatically and unconsciously and is governed by one impulse of will."[11] The more such "individual intentions" are combined into a single "impulse of will," the fewer such impulses take place—the faster "individual actions" of the fingers (in playing the piano), of the lips and tongue (in speech), of the legs (in running) can occur.[12] So, the point is to subdivide the passage into the longest possible and the most similar as possible automatized "chains." However, in piano playing as in speech, not all "syllables" are equally convenient to pronounce, not every succession is easily automated and combined into a "single impulse." *Book,* for instance, or a broken octave, require one impulse of will, whereas *ookb,* or a broken tenth, require two (one at the beginning and one between "k" and "b"); therefore, grouping in tenths (*ookb-ookb*) necessitates twice as many impulses as grouping in octaves (*book-book*), which is why the first grouping takes twice as long to perform.

Without stopping here to analyze which "syllables," that is which successions of keys are better or worse suited to automatization, and, thus, which methods of "technical grouping" of various passages are most appropriate (the reader will find a detailed discussion of this subject, along with a number of musical examples in Chapter 27 of my aforementioned book),[13] let us consider the following very important question: is it legitimate to change, even if only mentally, the grouping indicated in the music? Certain teachers, while not denying the technical advantages of one or another regrouping, nevertheless reject it on the basis that it contradicts the composer's intended grouping, changes and distorts it. This accusation is superficial and not well-thought-out. What "composer's intended grouping" is implied? As everyone knows, notes, especially eighths, sixteenths, thirty-seconds, which comprise virtuoso passages, are not usually united into groups according to the composer's subjective will (except for rare, unusual occasions), but according to the standards, common to all composers, that require exclusively metrical clarity and uniformity: any passage, whatever its real—motivic—structure, is usually (with few exceptions) subdivided into similar groups of four, eight, sixteen (or three, six) notes, where the first note of each group falls on the strong or relatively strong, and the last—on a weak beat of the measure (*trochaic* meter). Therefore, the very grouping that we find in the score and ascribe to the composer mostly contradicts the composer's thought, distorts the melodic logic of the passage, the bar lines cutting off either the "head" or the "tail" of the component motives, forcing them into the Procrustean bed of equal metrical groups. The inexperienced student may sometimes naively equate the metrical clothing of an episode with the underlying melodic body of the passage; but no musician of any merit would ever commit such an error.[14]

Another more serious question is the relationship of technical and artistic phrasing, that which, occasionally marked with slurs in the text and sometimes not marked at all, nevertheless expresses the musical substance of the passage. Naturally, if the "phrasing" *ookb-ookb-ookb* is replaced with *book-book-book*, the meaning of the passage suffers no damage, for the phrase is meaningless. But music, real music, does possess meaning; it is not an expressionless construction such as Petri's broken tenths, it is expressive speech. And in expressive, meaningful speech, a particular "grouping" ceases to be "neutral," it becomes a factor influencing the connotation of the words. Imagine the following unfortunate reading of *Hamlet:* "To be or not?—To be!" as opposed to the real thing.[15] Does something similar not take place also in music? Does regrouping not distort its artistic logic, its emotional content? Does it not get lost in the sharp divergence between "technical" and "musical" phrasing? Do clarity, ease and speed of playing come at the price of turning musical speech into a nonsensical tongue twister?

Foreseeing these natural apprehensions, Busoni accompanied his exposition of the principles of "technical phrasing" with a special disclaimer that "musical phrasing" retains its rights, the technical subdivisions must be heard by the performer alone, and take place, in a public performance, only mentally. That this duality of thinking is possible in principle is proved by the well-known ability of the great performer to pay attention both to the metrical and to the motivic structure of a passage, despite the occasional sharp divergence between the two. But this is not achieved easily, to which the practice of Busoni and his followers testify.

In fact, consider the following curious circumstance. Upon careful study of the examples of "technical regrouping" it becomes obvious that, in the majority of cases, the beginning of the phrase is shifted to the weak, and the ending—to the strong beat of the measure, which endows the passage with a greater energy and determination. This "iambic" phrasing is especially close to the spirit of Bach and Liszt; in the music of these composers, it almost always serves to uncover the melodic subtext and the inner structure of the musical thoughts; it corresponds to artistic phrasing. Not all composers thought "iambically"; Chopin's thinking was rather "choreic." In other words, in playing his works, technical phrasing comes into conflict with the artistic. Could this be another reason why Busoni and Petri's Bach and Liszt sounded natural and convincing, while many works of Chopin, for all their technical perfection, left an impression of some sort of artificiality, inauthenticity, some violence to the composer's creative will?[16]

The conclusion suggests itself. "Technical phrasing" can be used without danger only in those—very numerous—cases, where it corresponds to artistic phrasing, or, at least, does not contradict it. In other cases, "technical phrasing" should be used—if at all—very carefully, and in small doses, as a temporary— that is, at a certain stage of work—and strictly subordinate procedure. "Technical phrasing" is not a panacea for all pianistic problems, but a working device to be used appropriately, with thought, in deciding each case individually. On the other hand, is that not the case of all pianistic devices, without exception?

Chapter Twelve

The second important link in Busoni's technical "system" is the so-called method of technical variants. Following Liszt's legacy[1] again, Busoni counsels every pianist, in working out a difficult passage, to invent textural variants for them and use these as helpful exercises and etudes. As examples, he offers his own technical variants to Preludes I, II, III, V, VI, XV, and XXI of Book I of the *Well-Tempered Clavier* of Bach,[2] to Etudes, Op. 10, nos. 1, 2, 7, 8, and 9 and to Prelude, Op. 28, no. 3 of Chopin.[3]

This method of technical work is echoed by other great pianistic authorities,[4] but is not accepted in the "piano classes in all of Europe." It demands of the students a greater than usual creative initiative and more independence of thinking; in addition, along with other aspects of Busoni's pedagogy, it demolishes the academic separation between theory and practice, between training for performance and analysis and compositional exercises.[5] For Busoni, as for Liszt, the "analysis of a problem" is the best pianistic exercise, altering the texture, transcribing is the best analysis; only by changing something do we comprehend it and only by comprehending something do we master it. "Only in the mirror of the variant are the interesting features of the original uncovered," says the epigraph to Busoni's variants to Chopin's Etudes.

As has been said before, the method of variants is not accepted by all teachers. Some rebel against it on the basis that it "distorts" the composer's text.[6] Elsewhere,[7] I have already shown how unconvincing this argument truly is. Distortion as an argument can only be applied to performance; during the learning process, it is constantly necessary to take a composition apart, to vary the tempo and dynamics, to accentuate the meter, and to otherwise "distort" the piece; in this regard, the method of technical variants does not introduce anything fundamentally new into the long-established practice of all performers and teachers in the world.

Other objections against this method are more serious. The first is concerned with the character of the variants. It is easy to see the practical value of these Busoni variants to the first and second Preludes from Book I of the *Well-Tempered Clavier:*

Ex. 14. J. S. Bach, Prelude I, WTC I, Busoni's variant

Ex. 15. J. S. Bach, Prelude II, WTC I, Busoni's variant

Ex. 16. J. S. Bach, Prelude II, WTC I, Busoni's variant

But what is the purpose of transforming the first Prelude:

Ex. 17. J. S. Bach, Prelude I, WTC I

into:

Ex. 18. J. S. Bach, Prelude I, WTC I, Busoni's variant

or:

Ex. 19. J. S. Bach, Prelude I, WTC I, Busoni's variant

So what if the variants in these examples are formally connected with the text of the original? Their texture is so far removed from it that it requires entirely different technical devices, which in no way prepare one for the performance of the real thing.

The second objection reinforces the first. Many of the variants are not only far removed from the texture of the original, they are also exceedingly difficult. Compare, for example, Prelude II:

Ex. 20. J. S. Bach, Prelude II, WTC I

with its variants:

Ex. 21. J. S. Bach, Prelude II, WTC I, Busoni's variant

Allegro moderato

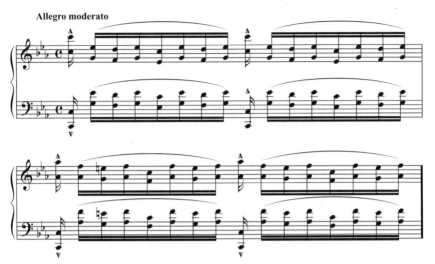

Ex. 22. J. S. Bach, Prelude II, WTC I, Busoni's variant

or Prelude III:

Ex. 23. J. S. Bach, Prelude III, WTC I

with variant:

Ex. 24. J. S. Bach, Prelude III, WTC I, Busoni's variant

or Prelude VI:

Ex. 25. J. S. Bach, Prelude VI, WTC I

with variant:

Ex. 26. J. S. Bach, Prelude VI, WTC I, Busoni's variant

Prelude XXI:

Ex. 27. J. S. Bach, Prelude XXI, WTC I

with variants:

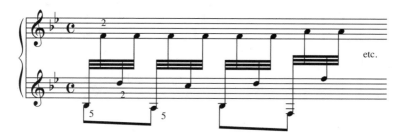

Ex. 28. J. S. Bach, Prelude XXI, WTC I, Busoni's variant

Ex. 29. J. S. Bach, Prelude XXI, WTC I, Busoni's variant

Ex. 30. J. S. Bach, Prelude XXI, WTC I, Busoni's variant

Ex. 31. J. S. Bach, Prelude XXI, WTC I, Busoni's variant

Ex. 32. J. S. Bach, Prelude XXI, WTC I, Busoni's variant

Truly, in comparing these examples, the question does occur, what exactly prepares for what: the variant for the original, or the original for the variant? But then, what is the purpose of the variants? Why master "preparatory etudes" that are much more difficult than the composition, when the latter can be mastered faster and easier without the "help" of these etudes?

And, finally, one more consideration. Let us suppose that we have found the answer to the first two questions and have convinced ourselves that the mastery of all of Busoni's variants is indeed very useful and helpful in achieving a skillful performance of the original. But the variants are quite a few in number: some of the preludes of the *Well-Tempered Clavier* are accompanied by four or five "helpful etudes" and a suggestion to the student to compose some of his own. Godowsky goes further still: he gives nine variants to Chopin's Etude Op. 25, no. 11, twenty-six to Etude Op. 25, no. 9, thirty-one to Etude Op. 10, no. 7, fifty-one to Op. 25, no. 3, and seventy-two to Op. 10, no.1! Each variant is the length of the entire Etude, and many are significantly more difficult than the already difficult original. So the third question begs itself: how long is all of this going to take?

Just how many hours, days, weeks, and months must one spend to master, say, the first Chopin Etude with its seventy-two Godowsky variants? Is this system of work rational, even on the (still questionable) condition that, in the end, one will play this Etude as perfectly as Godowsky himself? How many compositions can one manage to learn in this way during a lifetime? Does the ardent adherent of the method of technical variants not face the unenviable fate of that pedantic Swiss pianist whose anecdotal image has come down to us in the colorful depiction of the renowned musicologist W. de [*sic*] Lenz?[8] "This theme,"[9] relates Lenz,

> occupied the entire life of one artist, by the name of Werstedt, who, in 1827 was considered the best professor of the piano in Geneva. He was known to play only the first three exercises of Cramer and the A-flat Sonata of Weber. . . . The Theme and Variations from Beethoven's A-flat Sonata completed this small repertoire, which Werstedt mastered with perfection truly inimitable. . . . He saw life as a short passage, useful only for practicing a few measures of the great masters with the goal of playing them somewhat cleanly, as he would say. . . . Werstedt concluded that, following his advice, I could hope to play, in a year's time somewhat cleanly the first eight measures of the theme; the *crescendo* in the ninths (six sixteenths in unison) would require new and serious work on *crescendo* in general and on this specific one in particular; as for the second part of the theme, I should, he said, renounce the hope of playing it for the reason of the devilish trill on *d*, which he himself has never accomplished cleanly—after twenty years of work. . . . The trills with the fourth and fifth fingers in difficult circumstances, Werstedt made his life's work![10]

It would appear that the tragicomic story of the professor from Geneva, who gave his life to the study of endless variants of "*crescendo* in general" and "trills with the fourth and fifth fingers" hammers the last nail into the coffin of the method. However, one cannot avoid noting the startling difference in the results achieved, on the one hand, by the Swiss musician, and, on the other, by the previously named partisans of the method of variants. Werstedt has remained in the memory of a few specialists, mainly as a comic figure; Liszt, Busoni, Hofmann, Godowsky, and Cortot entered the history of pianism as the greatest of the great. Werstedt, slaving all his life, had acquired a repertoire of three etudes and one and a half sonatas; the great pianists each possessed a huge, unlimited repertoire, which, in addition, grew with magical speed and ease. How was that possible, then? How could Liszt and Busoni manage to learn the most difficult of pieces in a matter of just days? It would seem that we have missed something about the "method of technical variants." It would seem that its similarity to the "method" of Werstedt is deceptive, and in fact they must have some crucial difference.

Of course, the difference exists—a cardinal, decisive difference. Determining it will help us to more correctly understand the essence of the method of technical variants, and to answer the three questions that occurred to us earlier.

Werstedt's method is pyramidal: a wide base supports a narrow summit. He performs tens and hundreds of exercises to execute one passage in one work. The mountain gave birth to a mouse. Busoni's method is the exact opposite: the variants are selected with the purpose that, while working on one passage of one work, the performer would simultaneously prepare himself for future work on tens of passages in tens of pieces. "There are artists," writes Busoni in his essay, "Playing From Memory,"

who study the instrument and the musical apparatus as a whole and artists who single out separate passages and separate pieces in order to make them their own. To the latter every piece is a new problem to be solved again, laboriously from the beginning. They are obliged to construct a new key for every lock. The first named are locksmiths who, with a bundle of small picklocks and skeleton keys, can examine and overcome the difficulties of any lock. This refers to the technique as well as to the musical content and to the memory. If, for example, one has the key to Liszt's technique for passagework, to his melodic and harmonic system, to his formal structure (where does the accent lie? where the climax?) and to his style in expression of feeling, it is all the same whether one plays three or thirty of his pieces. I believe I have proved that this is no mere high-flown phrase. The new task for the memory arises—in proportion—when one is concerned with a composer, a nation, an epoch, or a direction for which one has not yet constructed a general key. This happened to me the first time I tried César Franck.[11]

Busoni returns to the same thoughts in his review of Galston's *Work Book:*

When I have said before that I do not like the concept of "repertoire pieces," I meant that, according to my criteria, a great pianist must be so well equipped, armed, and prepared, that a piece, which he has not played yet, could not present him with any novel problems. Having played twenty-five of Liszt's works, one has mastered all of them, and it is unnecessary to say that one's "repertoire" includes only those first twenty-five. In our music, which is still limited in scope, that is not even any sort of a feat of magic. Only where there is a new world—such as the harmonic world of César Franck—does a new problem arise. Then, the task is to make a key, which permits entry to this new world. And all that belongs to this world is again open to you.... The pianist who only possesses "repertoire" belongs to the second class.[12]

These citations from Busoni are in the direct path of development from Liszt, who advised his student Valerie Boissier to "grasp art in its basic principles," referring this advice also to "technique," to "chords, modulations, harmonic progressions," and so on. Liszt argued that "all possible passages can be reduced to a few basic formulas, from which flow all encountered combinations ... all traits in music, all combinations can be traced to a certain number of essential passages, which are the keys to everything"; "new combinations happen seldom, or the alterations are so small, that they do not become obstacles." Therefore, concludes Liszt, having mastered the "keys," and being well-practiced in the variants derived from "basic formulas," "one shall not meet with any difficulties in any printed music": they have all been "previously conquered," the pianist "not only accomplishes them easily," but at times even "plays everything at sight . . . with no need for practicing."[13]

Unfortunately, school pedagogy at the time bypassed these thoughts. It continued to assert that "passages change so often, and there are so many of them, that in a thousand pieces, perhaps, there are not ten even slightly similar ones."[14] But Liszt and Busoni were right, not the schoolteachers; the ensuing examples are convincing proof:

Ex. 33. Beethoven, Sonata Op. 31, No. 2 (1st mvt.). Beethoven, Sonata Op. 111 (1st mvt.)

Ex. 34. Beethoven, Sonata Op. 14 No. 2 (3rd mvt.). Beethoven, Sonata Op. 27 No. 2 (3rd mvt.). Beethoven, Sonata Op. 31 No. 2 (1st mvt.)

Ex. 35. Liszt, *Consolation* No. 4. Liszt, *Gnomenreigen*. Liszt, Polonaise in E Major. Liszt, Concerto in E-flat Major

Ex. 36. Beethoven, Sonata Op. 31, no. 2 (3rd mvt.). Chopin, Waltz Op. 64, no. 1

Ex. 37. Chopin, Etude Op. 25, no. 12. Liszt, Concerto in A Major

Ex. 38. Bach, Prelude XIV, WTC I. Liszt, *Hungarian Rhapsody* No. 13

Does it occur to a young pianist that, working on the passage from Beethoven's Sonata Op. 31, no. 2 (ex. 33), he is simultaneously studying a passage from Sonata Opus 111 of the same composer? That, while learning the arpeggios from the Chopin Etude, he is, at the same time, also "preparing" the arpeggio from Liszt's concerto (ex. 37)? That the "technical formula" of the F-sharp-Minor Bach Prelude is identical to the formula from the finale of Liszt's Thirteenth Hungarian Rhapsody (ex. 38)?

These examples (whose number can easily be multiplied) confirm the opinion of Liszt and Busoni regarding the possibility of reducing many passages to a "certain number of basic formulas," in whose "limited scope" is enclosed much of the piano literature. Thence is Busoni's conclusion that it is inefficient to study difficult sections "one at a time," "each time anew," that it is more productive to work out the "key" formulas and their main derivations. Seeing an excellent collection of these "formulas" in the first book of the *Well-Tempered Clavier*, Busoni conceived the thought of utilizing his edition of the work to "introduce and develop from it, 'as if from a tree-trunk,' the many-sided branches of modern piano technique."[15] This explains the genesis of those variants to Bach's preludes that are beyond the limits of the texture and technical problems of the preludes themselves. Busoni's variants are not destined only to aid in learning the original, they aim farther. The materials of Preludes I, VI, and XXI prepare the student for "Scarlatti technique" (exx. 28–31), for the fourth Paganini-Liszt Etude (ex. 19), for the "Grand Etudes" of Henselt, Chopin, and Liszt (exx. 26 and 32). This is the greatest advantage and justification of variants; without it, were the variants meant exclusively as an aid to the given prelude, they would risk becoming first or second cousins to Werstedt's exertions.

Of course, it would be ludicrous to suppose that mastering the "Scarlatti" or the "Paganini" variant to a Bach Prelude allows the student consequently to master Scarlatti's Sonatas and the Paganini-Liszt Etudes without any additional work, or that the motion needed to play the figuration from Chopin's twenty-fourth Etude can be directly "transplanted" into the corresponding place in Liszt's Second Concerto. Similar places in different compositions are never quite identical, always differ if not in tempo, rhythm, volume, and details of the text, then in character of sound, nuances, and functional meaning. Therefore, "transplantation" of the technical pattern to a new location is unthinkable without greater or lesser adaptation; but the same can be said of scales, which have for a long time served pianists as key formulas of piano technique. The solo part of Beethoven's C-Minor Concerto opens with a C-minor scale; naturally, the latter demands a certain amount of work and some adaptation. But how much longer this work would take, how much more difficult it would be for the performer who has never dealt with scales before!

So far, we have found the answers to the first two questions that had occurred to us in regard to the method of technical variants. Only the third remains—is it rational to dedicate so much time to the study of all possible variants?

Here, it is necessary to note that Busoni opposed "variant excesses," like those of Godowsky, who strove not to miss any of the logically conceivable possibilities of textural variation in Chopin's Etudes. In the foreword to his collection of exercises *Lo Staccato*,[16] Busoni pronounces it "cheap and irresponsible to invent technical combinations that exceed instrumental and physical capacities, and in doing so, to place insoluble problems in front of the student. This gives him a false picture of his own ineptitude and forces him to exhaustion or despair."[17] The number of variants to Bach Preludes is much smaller than the number of Godowsky's variants to Chopin Etudes; moreover, Busoni (as well as Godowsky) never considered it obligatory to master all of the variants offered. Still, learning the Bach Prelude along with the variants does take up a great deal more time than learning the same prelude by itself; but the "extra" time spent will later repay itself many times over. "Yes, the first time you may need years, but as a result of these years you will not work slower than today, but many times faster," said K. S. Stanislavsky to G. A. Tovstonogov.[18] The performer who possesses the "keys" to technique so shortens the time needed to learn new pieces that he will soon overtake one who, in the very beginning mastered the *Well-Tempered Clavier* faster, but, begrudging the time, did not obtain for himself the collection of keys, and is then obliged to learn each passage "with difficulty, and anew."

By the end of his life Busoni had compiled—first in five, later in ten books— his school of piano technique, the *Klavierübung*. It is a collection of exercises, built on typical formulas; at the end of each exercise is a list of pieces where this formula is encountered. The value of this work is immense. It is a pity that it remains unknown to most teachers and students today.

Chapter Thirteen

The technique of a great artist can never be a thing in itself, separate, independent of art as a whole; it is always closely related to that art, adapted for the expression of the creative worldview, ideas, and intentions of the artist.

At the bottom of Busoni's technical system was the same principle of thinking in "large unities," in blocks, that underlies his interpretations.[1] "Technical phrasing" subdivides a passage into groupings; Prelude XV of the first Book of the *Well-Tempered Clavier:*

Ex. 39. J. S. Bach, Prelude XV, WTC I

is turned into blocks by means of the following "technical variant":

Ex. 40. J. S. Bach, Prelude XV, WTC I, Busoni's variant

The same principle reigns in Busoni's fingering. The "three-fingered" approach of Czerny-Leschetitzky is replaced by the "five-fingered" technique of Liszt,[2] which allows an interpretation of a passage as a succession of "positions," a sequence of large chunks":

Ex. 41. Busoni, *Klavierübung*, Part I

Ex. 42. Busoni, *Klavierübung*, Part I

Ex. 43. Busoni, *Turandots Frauengemach*

Ex. 44. Liszt, *Totentanz*

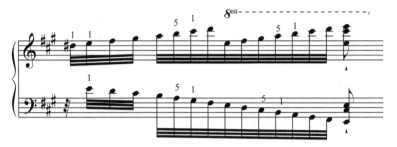

Ex. 45. Liszt, *Don Juan*

For this reason, Busoni avoids the traditional passing under of the thumb,[3] and prefers to "throw" the entire hand, and to pass the second and third fingers over the fourth and fifth:

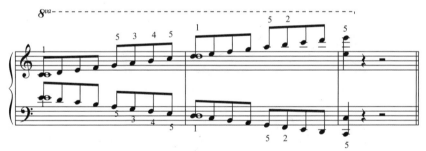

Ex. 46. Busoni, *Klavierübung,* Part I

Ex. 47. Busoni, *Klavierübung,* Part I

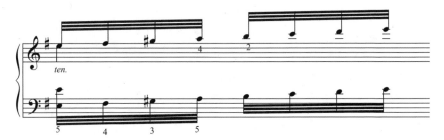

Ex. 48. J. S. Bach, Three-Part Invention No. 2

Ex. 49. Bach-Busoni, Organ Prelude in E Minor

Ex. 50. Bach-Busoni, *Chaconne*

Liszt's device of playing with one finger is also widely used:

Ex. 51. Bach-Busoni, *Chaconne*

Ex. 52. Liszt, *Don Juan*

Ex. 53. Mozart-Busoni, Concerto No. 9 (Andantino)

Another variety of the same thing is sliding from one key to the next:

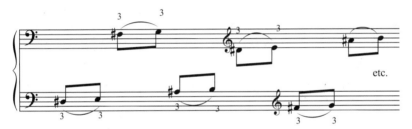

Ex. 54. Busoni, *Klavierübung*, Part I

Ex. 55. Busoni, *Klavierübung*, Part I

Ex. 56. Busoni, *Klavierübung*, Part I

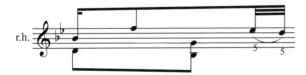

Ex. 57. Bach-Busoni, Chorale Prelude in G Minor

Busoni's fingering of double notes, particularly passages of thirds, is also unusual, though the scope of this book does not allow an in-depth discussion;[4] in chords, Busoni often placed the thumb not on the outer note, as it is normally done, but in the middle:

Ex. 58. Liszt, Sonata in B Minor

An important role in Busoni's fingering was given—again, following Liszt—to the distribution and redistribution of the passage between the two hands. This device further assists in subdividing the passage into "blocks":

Ex. 59. Busoni, *Klavierübung*, Part V

Ex. 60. Paganini-Liszt, Etude in E-flat Major

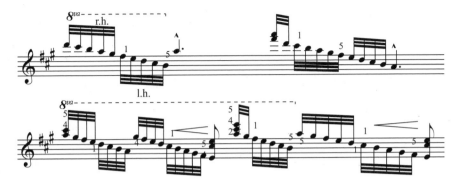

Ex. 61. Liszt, *Don Juan*

Ex. 62. Liszt, *Spanish Rhapsody*

Ex. 63. Busoni, *Turandots Frauengemach*

it also makes it possible to cleverly "avoid" a problem—for instance, to eliminate a jump:

Ex. 64. Paganini-Liszt, Etude No. 6. Top system. Liszt's original. Bottom system. Busoni's variant

Ex. 65. Paganini-Liszt, *La Campanella.* Top system. Liszt's original. Bottom system. Busoni's variant

Busoni's fingerings cannot be correctly understood and evaluated without an understanding of his principle of *non legato* playing, and of the gestures and motions typical of Busoni and his school. The softly rounded "arcs" of the Romantic pianists, the bouncing wrist of Leschetitzky is replaced with a focused gathering together of the physical apparatus, particularly vertical and horizontal movements of the arm used as a whole, with an unbending, stable wrist.[5]

In the area of hand positions, the familiar straight lines and angles carried the day; fingers were often, also against tradition, straight or almost straight—either standing like spokes, as Liszt used to say,[6] or the legs of a tripod, or, instead, flat, almost lying on the keys.[7] The former position was used by Busoni in places that demand *martellato,* fierce sound, "brass" (see exx. 51, 52, and 58); flat fingers attacking the key without the help of the wrist[8] were instrumental for achieving the famous pearly *leggiero.*

Pedaling occupied an important place in Busoni's technique; he owed to it the richness and variety of colors in his playing. In "The Requirements Necessary for a Pianist" and "The Pianoforte Should Be Esteemed," he calls the pedal a most considerable part of the "true technique," "an inimitable device, a picture of the sky, a ray of moonlight."[9] However, to characterize Busoni's manner of pedaling, to discover the "secrets" of his unusually artful pedal technique, all of these subtle, almost imperceptible "half-pedals," "quarter-pedals," "pedal tremolos," and so on is extremely difficult. It is only possible to note that Busoni's pedaling was distributed in layers: a layer of clean, pedal-less sonority[10] was followed by a layer of thick pedal, boldly mixing various harmonies like a "majestic full organ," whose mixtures "contain the fifth and the octave, and even the third and seventh of every note."[11] "Busoni," as G. P. Prokofiev justly pointed out, "uses the pedal above all else as a color. . . . The harmonic outlines are blurred, and sometimes, in breaking, create new, whimsical combinations. 'Dirty pedal,' you hear the voice of a neighbor somewhere nearby; but, fully acknowledging the justice of this comment, you want to grumble at the musical hypocrisy, the excessive strictness."[12]

Debating against this "musical hypocrisy" and academic rigorism, Busoni wrote in "The Pianoforte Should Be Esteemed": "The potential effects of the pedals are still unexhausted because they have remained the slave of a narrow-minded and senseless harmonic theory; the way in which they are used is like trying to convey the movements of air and water by geometric forms. . . . The pedal is decried. Senseless irregularities are to blame for this. Let us experiment with *sensible irregularities.*"[13]

Unfortunately, today we can have only an approximate idea of Busoni's "sensible irregularities." The few extant recorded examples of his playing did not capture its artistic essence, nor that "personal magnetism"[14] whose presence, to a decisive extent, determines the effect of the art of Busoni or any other great artist. The colors disappear; all that remains is "dirty pedal."

Chapter Fourteen

Let us now return to describing Busoni's activities after he moved from America to Europe and settled in Berlin. Piano playing, to which we have devoted so much attention on the preceding pages, was the Master's central occupation, but far from the only one during these years. He continued to devote a great deal of attention to the field of musical creation, to composition. The change that he had undergone in his artistic worldview made its mark here, too: his composing went down a new road. He ardently attempted to disavow everything he wrote earlier. ". . . In the ideal sense," he declares, "I first found my way as a composer in the Second Violin Sonata (Op. 36a),[1] which among friends I also call my Opus 1. . . . But my entire personal vision I put down at last and for the first time in the *Elegies* (finished January 1908)."[2]

The *Elegies* are a cycle of seven pieces for the piano, dedicated to Busoni's students;[3] the four piano pieces that make up the cycle *An die Jugend*[4] are dedicated to them as well.

Among Busoni's other works of the years in question, the most deserving of attention are the Fantasy for piano on themes of Bach, dedicated to the memory of Busoni's father;[5] two versions of the great *Fantasia contrappuntistica* for the piano on the theme of the unfinished fugue from Bach's *Kunst der Fuge*;[6] the first book of the *Indian Diary*[7] (four piano etudes on themes of songs and dances of North American Indians); the *Indian Fantasy* for piano and orchestra;[8] the grandiose five-movement concerto for piano, orchestra, and six-voice male chorus (on the text of the Dutch poet A. Oehlenschläger), the *Elegiac Lullaby* for orchestra,[9] dedicated to the memory of the composer's mother;[10] two suites for orchestra—*Geharnischte Suite* (the revision of the earlier second orchestral suite)[11] and *Turandot* (based on the materials of his incidental music to the famous "theatrical fairy tale" by Gozzi); the orchestral *Lustspielouvertüre* (the reworking of the second of the early *Two Happy Overtures*);[12] and the opera *Die Brautwahl* ("the fantastic musical comedy in three acts with an epilogue," on his own libretto based on the novel of E. T. A. Hoffmann), first staged in Hamburg on April 13, 1912.[13]

What is that new quality that separated these compositions from Busoni's earlier works? First, as in his piano playing, it was the break with "Academic Romanticism." This is especially evident in the area of harmony and form; the former becomes more "daring," the latter—"freer," closer to improvisation. Naturally, both elicited sharp attacks from those to whom the master referred as "lawgivers." They are not shy in their expressions of dislike: to them, Busoni's music is "formless," "curious," "comical," "real nonsense," and the like.[14]

Now, after the passage of time, after all the innovations brought to music by Prokofiev and Shostakovich, Stravinsky and Hindemith, the reactions of contemporary critics seem rather "comical" and "curious" themselves. No matter what one might think about these compositions, who among us today will be fearful of the following harmonies that so "shocked" some musicians in their day?

Ex. 66. Busoni, Concerto Op. 39 (3rd mvt.)

Ex. 67. Busoni, *Indian Diary* (Etude No. 2)

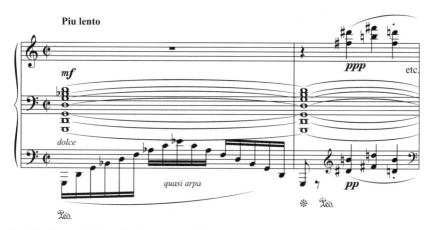

Ex. 68. Busoni, *Fantasia Contrappuntistica*

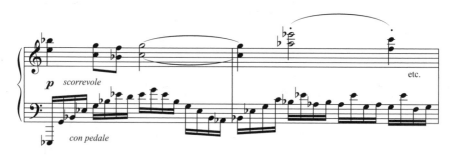

Ex. 69. Busoni, *Indian Fantasy*

However, it is necessary in all honesty to note that Busoni's works also contain harsher—and less justified—harmonic combinations, for example:

Ex. 70. Busoni, Second Sonatina

But unsuccessful experiments had their place, as we know, in the works of Mussorgsky, Prokofiev, Bartók, and many other great composers. Busoni, the same as they, should be judged on the merits of his best, not his weakest creations.[15]

Matters stand the same with Busoni's innovations in the area of structure and form. The composer rebelled against "forcing" the music into any predetermined, externally imposed schemes—be they architectonic or programmatic; but rejection of a priori schemes did not equal rejection of form. "By 'freedom of form' I never meant formlessness," he fumed in one of his "open letters";[16] he demanded, in another open letter, only that the form of a composition be determined by its content, that "every idea fashions its own form for itself."[17] "Every motive—so it seems to me—contains, like a seed, its life-germ within itself," he writes in a third place, ". . . in each motive, there lies the embryo of its fully developed form; each one must unfold itself differently, yet each obediently follows the law of eternal harmony. This form is imperishable, though each be unlike every other."[18]

Upon these principles Busoni built the form of his compositions. Although to a superficial glance it might have seemed entirely improvisatory, evolving solely through the impetus of ever-changing momentary impulses, it possessed a rigorously developed architectonic logic, illustrated visually by Busoni in the aforementioned graph to the *Fantasia contrappuntistica*.

Not everything that drove the composer in his youth had died in the mature period of his life; in particular, Busoni remained as much an enthusiast of polyphony as ever, and his mastery of this technique reached a very high level. But the polyphony of Busoni's compositions from 1900 on is different than that practiced by the adepts of the "Leipzig" school: it is melodic rather than harmonic. The composer followed to a certain extent the advice given to him by Tchaikovsky (which was mentioned in Chapter 1): the Italian, the melodist is increasingly evident in his music. In the Concerto (where the composer signs himself Ferruccio Busoni of Empoli), in "All'Italia" from the *Elegies*[19] and other works of this period many beautiful, expressive melodies can be found, for example[20]:

Ex. 71. Busoni, *All'Italia!*

Ex. 71.—*(concluded)*

From all we have said, it becomes clear that the best of Busoni's compositions of this period possess a number of merits, including—in piano works—an amazing knowledge and use of the instrument's capabilities, the capacity to "teach the pianist (if he knows how to think) more than the most musical academy in the world."[21] Nevertheless, Busoni's compositions did not achieve the sort of fame that was the fate of his playing. His music was performed and published, he had his group of admirers, who saw, in the composer of the *Fantasia contrappuntistica* and *Die Brautwahl* not just a talent, but a genius in the same category with Schoenberg and Stravinsky.[22] Outside of this narrow circle, however, Busoni's compositions were not popular; many saw him, as once Liszt had been seen, only as a genius pianist, nearly completely lacking a creative gift.

Even if this judgment is unfair, it is necessary to concede that Busoni's strengths were less convincing and powerful, and his weaknesses more apparent and consequential in his compositions than his pianism.

A much happier fate awaited Busoni's transcriptions. With the exception of a group a pianists who rejected any alteration of original text on principle,[23] the entire musical world valued Busoni's best transcriptions as the finest examples of the transcriber's art, as the most notable (after Liszt) contribution to this genre of piano literature. This is especially true of Busoni's transcriptions of the works of Bach. "In terms of 'organ-like' quality," noted a reviewer, "his transcriptions of Bach's organ compositions stand incomparably higher than all similar attempts, not excluding even those belonging to such interpreters of genius as Liszt himself."[24]

The devices worked out by the master for transcribing from organ music are systematized in the First Appendix to his edition of the *Well-Tempered Clavier.* Compared to those of the earlier epoch, Busoni's transcriptions are notable for "metricization" of rhythmically free passages, the substitution of arpeggios with blocked chords, doubling at the distance of two, rather than one, octaves (skipping the middle octave), "moving apart" the registers, again with the middle empty and other similar peculiarities. Here is an illustration, from two transcriptions of Bach's D-Minor Toccata:

Ex. 73. J. S. Bach, Toccata in D Minor. Top system. Tausig's transcription. Bottom system. Busoni's transcription

The Organ Preludes and Fugues, Chorale Preludes, and Toccatas of Bach-Busoni have already been heard consistently for more than half a century from all student and concert stages of the world; the famous *Chaconne* has become one of the most popular pieces of the piano repertoire. The fame of these transcriptions has so closely bound together the names of the composer and the transcriber, that the wife of the latter, during her sojourn in New York, was repeatedly (seriously!) addressed as Mrs. Bach-Busoni.[25]

Among Busoni's other transcriptions, the most popular are those of the piano works of Liszt (the aforementioned Spanish Rhapsody, the *Heroic March in Hungarian Style*, the Polonaise in E Major, the "Paganini" Etudes); also the Liszt Fantasy on themes of Mozart's *Marriage of Figaro*, of which an unknown and unfinished manuscript was found, completed, and first published by Busoni in 1912.

Next to the master's transcriptions are his editions. Both grew out of his performing: we have already seen how his interpretations developed into transcriptions, and the hours of preparation for performances—into textological study. During the years in question, Busoni undertook the painstaking, time-consuming labor of editing all of Liszt's piano Etudes, which took three volumes of the complete works published by the Liszt Fund, and began work on the complete keyboard works of Bach, personally editing (with detailed commentaries) nine out of twenty-five volumes of this edition, executed under his general supervision by Bruno Mugellini[26] and Egon Petri.[27]

During this period of the full blossoming of his creative powers, Busoni undertook many other musical activities. He organized, at his own expense, a series of "orchestral evenings" in Berlin, with the purpose of popularizing new and seldom performed works. From 1902 to 1909, twelve such evenings took place, which, besides works by Busoni himself, presented (some for the first time) the compositions of Sibelius (the Second Symphony and two symphonic poems), Sinding, Nielsen, Delius, Nováček, Bartók (*Scherzo*), Pfitzner, Schenker (*Syrian Dances* in Schoenberg's orchestration), Rimsky-Korsakov (*Fantasia on Serbian Themes* for violin and orchestra), Franck (the D-Minor Symphony, *Les Djinns*, *Le chasseur maudit*), Saint-Saëns, Fauré, d'Indy, Guy Ropartz, Magnard, Ysaÿe, Debussy (*The Afternoon of a Faun, Nocturnes*), and others;[28] Busoni participated not only as a pianist but also as a conductor.[29] Material difficulties prevented the continuation of these invaluable educational events; after presenting one final orchestral evening, in 1913, following a long break, Busoni handed the reins of the enterprise over to conductor Ivan Frebe.

Busoni was equally active as a pedagogue. During the summer months of 1901–2 in Weimar and 1910–12 in Basel he taught a *Meisterkurs* (an advanced class) for young pianists; during the 1907/8 school year he directed the piano class of the famous *Meisterschule* at the Vienna Conservatory;[30] in 1913/14 he was a professor and director of the Bologna Conservatory (Liceo Musicale). In all these cities as well as in Berlin, where he spent most of his time, gifted young musicians gathered around the teacher who opened new horizons for them; among them were Egon Petri, Theodore Szanto, Michael Zadora, Rudolf Ganz, Eduard Steuermann, John Hunt, Gino Tagliapietra, Leo Sirota, Grigory Beklemishev, Yosif Turchinsky, Vera Maurina-Press, Percy Grainger, Selim Palmgren, Louis-Theodore Gruenberg, Richard Zinger, Augusta Cottlow, Leo Kestenberg, Emile Blanchet, and other renowned pianists, composers, and musicians.[31]

Finally, recounting the many directions of Busoni's multifaceted activity, one must mention his literary works, already familiar to the reader from the many fragments quoted in the previous chapters of this book. During his sojourn in Berlin (1894–1915), Busoni published in various German journals and newspapers, and as forewords to his editions and transcriptions nearly fifty long and short articles on various subjects. There are reviews of a concert of the works of Schoenberg, of a book on questions of pianism, polemics on the subject of a magazine review of Busoni's Liszt *Klavierabend* or an "orchestral evening," reflections on his own work, a letter "To Youth," "Aphorisms on Mozart," musicological, bibliographic, and critical etudes on the works of Liszt, pronouncements regarding the piano ("Playing from Memory," "The Requirements Necessary for a Pianist," "The Pianoforte Should Be Esteemed," "The Pianoforte Genius"), humor ("From the Classical Valpurgian Night"), a letter about America, foreword to E. T. A. Hoffmann's *Fantastic Stories,* a speech in defense of transcriptions, methodical remarks regarding textbooks of instrumentation and harmony, discussions of "art and technique," of "routine," of "futurism in musical art," and of "the future of opera."[32]

These essays are remarkable for both their content and their style. The brilliance of the latter immediately attracted the attention of the reading public, who esteemed the breadth of the author's intellect, the power of his irony, the precision of his aphorisms; the former—the content of the writings—aroused, as did all of Busoni's activities, discussions and arguments, with which the reader is already partially familiar, and will become more familiar still in the ensuing chapters.

Even more lively were the debates provoked by Busoni's most important literary work—his short book *Entwurf einer neuen Ästhetik der Tonkunst,*[33] published in 1907 and reprinted in an expanded second edition in 1916; the first edition was translated into several languages, including Russian.[34] We have mentioned this book earlier and will continue to discuss it further.

Taking a concluding look at all that the Master did during these years—concertizing and teaching, editing and transcribing, composing and writing, and so on—it is difficult to remain unimpressed with the great intensity and broad scope of his activities. Like most great artists, Busoni possessed an unusual ability to work and an insatiable industriousness that drove him to search for ever new areas to which he could apply his inexhaustible energy; he was interested in much and could do much. And if not everything he did was fully successful, it was enough to confirm Busoni's position as "one of the most remarkable figures of the contemporary music world" and, "without a doubt, the most multifaceted musician of today," surrounded by "a halo of almost legendary fame," that could be claimed by "no virtuoso since Liszt and Rubinstein."[35] Busoni's influence was important and felt not only among his own students; also drawn into his orbit were such pianists as Vianna da Motta, James Kwast, Frieda Hoddap, M. Barinova, Schnabel, Fischer, Galston, theoreticians of pianism Elizaveta Kaland, Breihthaupt, conductors Brecher, Oscar Fried, musicologists Lessmann, Bekker, Leichtentritt, writers Wasserman, Stefan Zweig, poets Stefan George, Rainer Maria Rilke, and others.[36] Busoni's house at 11 Victoria-Louisa Platz in Berlin was the center of an international elite, the meeting place of the best minds of the artistic intelligentsia of many countries, attracted by the genius, personal charm, and intellectual breadth of the host, who was fluent in a "half-dozen languages."[37]

All this came to an end with the start of World War I; the war marked the end of the second and beginning of the third, and final period of the Master's biography.

Chapter Fifteen

We have now completed the description of Busoni's twenty-year sojourn in Berlin—the period of the greatest blossoming of his talents, the final development, full unfolding, and solidification of the most important and best aspects of his art. It is time to take stock, to analyze the nature of Busoni's pianistic and compositional endeavors and the essence of his esthetic views.[*]

The cardinal question of any esthetic is the question of the relationship of art and life. Is art a reflection and an expression of life, or is it a collection of purely formal, "unexpressive" constructions, unconnected to human thoughts and feelings?

Obviously, the first of these two points of view is that of *realism*. The acceptance of a close connection between art and life is a *necessary* prerequisite of the realistic esthetic. Necessary, but not entirely sufficient: this acceptance does not in and of itself impart a realistic inclination to a given esthetic system as a whole. However, the rejection of this connection is a true, sufficient symptom of antirealism of a given esthetic conception.

What was Busoni's position on this question?

For the answer, let us turn to his own words. In the very beginning of his primary work on esthetics we encounter the following unequivocal proclamation: "all arts, resources and forms ever aim at the one end, namely, the imitation of nature and the interpretation of human feelings."[1] Three years later, the essay "The Requirements Necessary for a Pianist" concludes with a notable warning: "But one requirement comes before all others: *Anyone who will master the language of art must have nurtured his life through the soul*."[2] This is also the topic of Busoni's later articles: "expression—this is what influences, and, in the final analysis, decides, in any work of art"; ". . . the final goal of music is the expression of human feelings . . ."; "to move—that is the quality of art, without which it descends to the level of craft,"[3] and so on.

---

[*] In the following chapters, Grigory Kogan puts forth a concerted effort to make his book acceptable for publication in the Soviet Union of 1964. Whereas in the previous chapters he merely inserts an occasional quotation or sentence of official orthodoxy, Chapters 15 to the end focus on a discussion of "realism" vs. "formalism" in Busoni's aesthetic, Busoni's own antibourgeois views, hatred of capitalism in general and American culture in particular, and his failure to participate in "social struggle" as the principal reason for his artistic failures. Readers are respectfully asked to draw their own conclusions.

BUSONI AS PIANIST 93

These lines leave no room for doubt: in the question of the relationship between art and life, Busoni occupied, at least at the start—a position of realism.[4]

The question of realism occupies a small, far from central place in Busoni's esthetic.[5] Its pathos, as well as that of Busoni's entire career, is elsewhere.

Where exactly? It is not as easy to answer this question as it might seem. A superficial glance will see this pathos in overthrowing any and all traditions, in preaching innovation at all cost, in justifying an individualistic, subjective approach to art. And in fact, Busoni's writings themselves give much evidence for this conclusion. "Everyone, who possesses a gift, which allows him to achieve outstanding results in the field of any art," he writes in a review of Breithaupt's *Die natürliche Klaviertechnik,* "achieves this goal by inventing his own theory, a theory which gives value to his individual abilities, and devaluates his short-comings. Thus the artist instinctively uses the principle of differences between people. The theoretician, instead, falls into the error of presupposing similarity between people, and attempts to use a theory derived from observing the achievements of one person, to all humanity."[6] Simply put, Busoni states the following: there are as many theories as there are people, but that is the same as saying *there is no theory.* Busoni ridicules "lawgivers" who believe in the "amazing number of analogous situations" that allow the use of the same "craftsmanlike devices"; "But I think in this way about music: that every case should be a new case, 'an exception.'"[7] "The creator," he writes elsewhere, "should take over no traditional law in blind belief, which would make him view his own creative endeavor, from the outset, as an exception contrasting with that law. For his individual case he should seek out and formulate a fitting individual law," for "he who follows . . . laws, ceases to be a creator."[8]

Building on this philosophy, Busoni protests against one-size-fits-all solutions,[9] demands individualizing the form in each composition, a personal interpretation, and so on. Ridiculing the routine that "reigns in the piano classes of all Europe," he urges "all pianists with serious intentions" to study for themselves the nature of the piano and derive their own rules for playing the instrument.[10] He presumes—together with Galston—that "almost every pianist has his own personal fingerings," and, to the question of "why isn't the fingering here more comfortable?" answers simply by saying "it is more comfortable for me," rather than referring to some "laws."[11] "Avoid routine!" he proclaims, "Let each beginning be as if none had been before! Know nothing, but rather think and feel and learn through being able to do!" . . . "There are no laws, but there are models and—generally—much too much routine!"[12]

There is a certain whiff of anarchism about these writings: it is easy to discern the musical echoes, so to speak, of a sometime fashionable theory of "the naked Man upon the naked Earth." It is true, however, that the adepts of this theory, while immolating (in words) all prejudices and traditions, "stuffed" their naked man with a fair number of both, only of a specific variety. Busoni is equally prudent. Sending the student off to seek "his own" pianistic earth, he, as we have seen, does not neglect to first seed this so-called naked earth with a decent number of examples and admonitions on performing various compositions and the technical methods of working thereon. Of course, he accompanies these admonitions with a note that they should be taken only as "guiding suggestions, and not absolute rules," merely "road signs that those who know a better way need not follow";[13] he warns that, for example, his edition of Liszt's *Don Juan* is not "the final form, "but only an "edition of the Fantasy that is satisfactory to himself . . . exclusively the fruit of his personal experiment, educational to himself."[14] But if Busoni's version of *Don Juan* is "satisfactory" only to himself, then what was the purpose, one must ask, of having it published? If "each pianist has his own fingerings," why should a student care which fingerings Busoni preferred for himself? Why should an "elegant" interpretation of Bach be seen as an "offensive error," if "there are no rules?" How must one integrate our master's theoretical analyses and other scholarly research with his motto "Know Nothing"? For all of the aforementioned "examples and suggestions" of Busoni's were published, it would seem, in the expectation that they might satisfy not just himself, but—at least to some degree—other pianists, as well. But in that case, what is left of Busoni's justifications? What is left of his "theory?"

All of the above leads to one of two possible conclusions: either the "principle of differences between people" is in need of serious corrections, or the entire pedagogical, editorial, literary (and to follow the argument to its logical end, also performing and composition) work of Busoni has no significance. Obviously, understanding this inevitability, the Master hurries to correct the situation with a new explanation. Basing himself on the reasons cited above, he points out in his review of Breithaupt's book, "it would seem that it makes no sense, then, to write any theoretical works about art. However, there are rules about what each person must avoid, and about what will benefit everyone, and this is the beginning of all theories."

What are these rules, about what is beneficial to all, and about what everyone must avoid, and how do they differ from the dogmas pushed upon "all mankind" by those "theoreticians" Busoni so dislikes? The difference—he replies—is that "theoreticians" raise to the level of "universal laws" the subjective conjectures of "particular people," whereas "real" rules are grounded in objective information—the specifics of tools and materials used in a given art, and the universal traits of human nature. "Breithaupt's book differs from other books on piano playing in that it builds its theory of technique on the only two correct postulates: on *logical thinking* and the inescapable outcomes of two *natural laws*—the law of muscle function and the law of inertia and weight."[15] "Art forms are more lasting, the more closely they adhere to the nature of their individual species of art, the purer they keep their essential means and ends."[16] Busoni underpins his pianistic and compositional recommendations with references to "naturalness," the "nature" of the piano, and the "nature" of the thematic kernel. The "singing" ideal in piano playing is detrimental because it represents an "unnatural" (from the point of view of the technical design of the piano) imitation of an "arbitrarily selected performance ideal" of an entirely different nature (such as the human voice or the violin), instead of the "innate character of the instrument"; *non legato* is preferable because it best "fits the nature of the piano."[17] "But I demand—no, *the organism of art demands*" that the form of the composition be derived from its idea; "the organism, not I" revolts against ossified architectonic schemes.[18]

Thus, it seems, Busoni does not linger long within *subjectivism;* the celebration of the latter quickly transforms into its obituary. He now shifts onto the opposite platform of *objectivism:* in his "open letter" to Paul Bekker, the Master demands a "renunciation of subjectivism," invites the young to enter the "cleansing path to objectivity."[19] "The principle of *differences* between people" recedes unnoticed into the shadows; now, instead, the aspects of *similarity* between them, the all-human laws of "logical thinking," "muscle function," and so on, are brought to the fore.

Unfortunately, the "objectivist" foundation of Busoni's esthetic proves no more solid than the "subjectivist." Perhaps if the Master had been better informed about the history of the development of sociology, he would have seen that the view of "human nature," and the "nature" of things, in general, not only is not new, but had been long discredited, especially in questions of ideology. History has shown that this "nature" (unless reduced to the thin and barren abstraction of Condorcet's thesis[20] that "humans are feeling and thinking creatures") is interpreted differently by all and leads to very different, even diametrically opposed, conclusions. "Human nature," cited by philosophers as an objective measure of all things and the highest arbiter in disputes between subjective passions, turned out to be a most subjective concept itself—remarkably similar to the "nature" of that social class to which the given philosopher belonged.[21]

An analogous picture can be observed in the history of art in general, and the history of piano playing in particular. All theoreticians claim to base their work on those "only two correct postulates." Who among them, from C. P. E. Bach (*Versuch über die wahre Art das Clavier zu spielen*, 1753) to Erwin Johannes Bach (*Perfect Piano Technique*, 1929)[22] had not derived their "natural" conclusions, following the "inescapable" laws of "logical thinking," from the innate nature of the piano and the inborn qualities of the human organism? And yet whose understanding of these basic natural laws matched those of the others? Instead, each pronounced the approaches and ideals of the others as abnormal or perverted! We have already seen how differently Busoni and Leschetizky viewed the "nature of the piano." Equally dissimilar are the "natural" techniques of Kullak and Breithaupt, Johnen and Malwine Brée.[23] The cult of the singing *legato,* which Dr. Steinhausen sees as the "natural goal" of piano playing[24] appears to Busoni to be an "unnatural prejudice." On the other hand, Josef Hofmann considers it unnatural to give preference to that very *non legato* that Busoni deems to correspond best to the "innate character of the instrument." And, just as Busoni accuses the Romantic pianistic school of imitating the voice or the violin, are woodwinds, whose sonority he instructs the pianist to emulate,[25] an any less "arbitrarily selected ideal?" Furthermore, the "nature of the piano," as Busoni sees it, seems oddly similar to the nature of the *organ!*

All this being said, one must not diminish the value of natural laws, including those of the piano, of muscle function, and so on. It is necessary and important to study these laws. However, in arguments about stylistic differences in piano playing (no more than political arguments about social systems), these laws play a no bigger role than, say, the laws of digestion in the question of why the food that reaches the stomach of a Rockefeller is different from that which reaches the stomach of a destitute unemployed American.[26] While founding their theories on the same "nature of the piano," different theoreticians and practitioners of piano playing arrive at entirely different conclusions, because they regard said nature from radically different points of view:

> *Si vous jugez de lui tout autrement que nous,*
> *C'est que nous le voyons par d'autres yeux que vous.*[27]

Thus, the issue here is not the nature of the instrument, but, rather, the social-creative nature of those movements in art that determine, among others, the understanding of the instrument's nature.

But, Busoni did not possess at his disposal a method of scholarly inquiry that would have allowed him to pose the question correctly and might have helped him to answer it. This is why the Master, for all his intellect and knowledge, remained unable to reconcile the various aspects of his own esthetic. Mentally trapped within a metaphysical problem—either the "principle of differences" or the "assumption of similarity" between people—he became lost in contradictions, turned from one extreme to another, confusing commentators and critics, some of whom[28] counted him among the subjectivists and others,[29] with equal reason (based on his writings), among the objectivists.

Matters stand much the same in the question of tradition versus innovation. In reality, Busoni was never the nihilist or the futurist that he is sometimes portrayed as being, on the basis, one must admit, of his own overblown formulations. It seems ridiculous to accuse the man who worshipped, studied, performed, and edited Bach and Mozart with great attention to each note and each rest in the text of disrespect for tradition! This was, after all, the man who, when told of Stravinsky's surprise that he, Busoni, admires the German classics, asked a mutual acquaintance to convey to the composer of the *Rite of Spring* his opinion that "if he (Stravinsky) knew the classical composers he would also value them."[30]

On the other hand, Busoni certainly was not an indiscriminate admirer of anything novel just because it is novel.[31] In a series of articles from his Berlin period, as well as the later years, he decisively separates himself from the Futurists, Expressionists, or any other "sect," declaring that he has nothing to do with "caricature-like experiments," the "spirit of contrariness and rebellion . . . or the clowning" of those "brainless innovators" who "begin with the negation and denial of the present." In his opinion, "if there is one thing which is just as bad as wishing to retard progress, it is this: forcing it stupidly." "Progress," he writes, "must mean an enrichment, not a replacement of means. . . ." "whoever strives for the new and unheard-of, overshoots his aim," "the old does not yield to the new but to the better," "the goal is Better, not Different." So he condemns those supposedly progressive critics who confuse "freedom with anarchy," and judge a composition not "according to the value . . . but according to the direction in which it moves; [they] reject good things moving in older directions, and honor bad productions with the newest tendencies"; but, the Master notes, "a piece is not good because it is new and (this is the comical thing) it is not new because it appears without form or beauty!"[32]

As these passages make clear, Busoni's aesthetic, for all of its internal confusion, differed sharply from that of the modernists. Does this mean that his esthetic worldview was therefore realistic and free from formalistic elements? We have already seen that it is not so. In the master's books and essays, much is unclear, confusing, and contradictory, and leads to opposite conclusions. It is no wonder that various musicologists came to contrary conclusions, indeed. So who among them was correct—those who saw Busoni as a destroyer or those who considered him the keeper of traditions?

To answer *both* would mean *neither.* Both sides in this argument miss seeing that, in the words of Marx, "it is necessary for the writer to differentiate between what a given author really produces and what he produces only in his own mind's eye."[33] What both groups of musicologist fail to observe is that the very concepts of "tradition," "innovation," and the support or rejection of "laws" are merely *masks* that history endows with different meaning in every instance, depending on which social or artistic group hides behind a particular mask and which specific laws are being supported or rejected. In the nineteenth century, the Romantics rebelled against Classicism under that same flag of "naturalness" and freedom from artificial rules, which was waved again in the twentieth century by the Neoclassicists in their revolt against the Romantics. For the former, this meant the destruction of structured form in the name of the poetic program; for the latter, the rejection of the poetic program in favor of structured motivic development. To miss these distinctions is to halt at the threshold of understanding. In order to understand a given artistic experience, one must lift the mask of "traditionalism" or "modernism" and look that experience straight in the face.

Chapter Sixteen

What was the nature of the "face" hiding behind the masks of Busoni's "old" and the "new" artistic principles? What was the real, as opposed to the imagined, pathos of his art?

This pathos was in his struggle against the Academic and Neoclassical Romanticism that reigned in art between the end of the nineteenth and the early years of the twentieth centuries. This was the stylistic hybrid whose self-indulgent passions swallowed and dissolved both the intense ardor of Romanticism and the joyful freshness of Classicism. Busoni was not the first among composers, but first among pianists to acutely sense the breath of imitative, derivative decadence and dissipation that wafted from the elegant lyricism of Hofmann, Essipoff, Arenski, or Massenet,[1] as well as the heavy, deceptively profound rhetoric of Reger or Glazunov, Reisenauer, or Pugno,[2] who sensed the falseness of this "style-less" style, so akin to the "overwrought Viennese palaces, and the costume dramas of Ebers and Felix Dahn, the corteges of Makart,"[3] the style in which the creative inventions of the great Classics and Romantics became mere "tricks of craftsmanship,"[4] stereotypical, mass-produced devices, death masks of once profound emotions and thoughts. With great talent and determination, especially in his playing, Busoni led an attack against all that, began the fight for a new *Rinascimento*,[5] for the rebirth of pure styles,[6] the art of great emotions, profound ideas, and impressive creative power.

Busoni understood that the "rebirth" of art is not the same as turning it back. The "Great Pan" of Romanticism had died, and could not be brought back to life. The meaningfulness, the profundity of pianism, such as Rubinstein's, can only be achieved again by leading art forward along new pathways that lead far away from the content, form, and style of "titanic Anton."[7]

Thus, Busoni's struggle against the derivative triteness of late Romanticism leads him to a break with the very foundations of the Romantic style. Hence, the banishment of Mendelssohn, Schumann, and Brahms from his repertoire; hence, the frequent failure in Chopin. Of course, Liszt remains one of the central figures of Busoni's pianistic art to the end, but not Liszt the Romantic, rather Liszt the master craftsman, the perfect genius of pianistic orchestration, Liszt the philosopher, the forerunner of Impressionism and Symbolism, Liszt of the second edition of *Don Juan*. "And right alongside the 'inimitably played Paganini-Liszt Etudes,' those pieces where Liszt's lyricism predominates, such as the A-flat Major *Sonetto*, Busoni was unconvincing. . . ."[8]

Upon what path did Busoni strive to lead music, and, particularly, the art of the piano, away from Romanticism? Of course, the evolution of any art does not take place in a vacuum; it follows the evolution of society in general. Busoni understands, or, at least, intuits this dependency. He senses the connection between the degradation of art and of the societal changes around him. While criticizing the former, he touches upon certain features of capitalist civilization. The "first and greatest obstacle" to the revival of art is the bourgeois public itself. "In theater . . . most people demand a strong human experience from the stage, no doubt because such experiences do not come into ordinary lives and also because they crave for excitement for which they lack the courage; and the stage deals out these excitements without involving the audience in the accompanying dangers and disasters and, above all, sparing them any exertion."[9] At concerts, instead of preparing to perceive art as something "solemn" and "festival-like," people "clatter in . . . during the second movement of a Ninth Symphony . . . from the street, railway train, or restaurant."[10] There is no question here of hearing large portions as part of a greater whole, or of the receiver "doing half of the work!"

In these conditions music is profaned, it becomes a servant of bourgeois daily life, "a trivial decoration for trivial occasions like, for example, a dispenser of entertainment in restaurants and inns"; the business of concerts is turned into an immoral enterprise, and schools of art are "institutions which are arranged . . . for the maintenance of teachers."[11]

The power of money is the main cause of the destruction, degeneration, and ruin of bourgeois art: "and above all it must be separated from aims of gain. A way must be found to free it from this if the next century is not to shine in history as the century without art."[12]

But how to do that? After all, the "aims of gain" did not just randomly enter art—no, they are nurtured by the laws and the spirit of bourgeois society.

Busoni understood this, too. For this reason, according to the testimony of Adolf Weissmann, he was so annoyed by the symbols of capitalist culture—the aggressiveness of businessmen, the mass-produced quality of objects, and the industrial appearance of cities.[13] "His most profound hatred was reserved for America," the classical country of overripe capitalism. Chicago's skyscrapers— "ungainly stone cubes of twenty or more stories," "obvious symbols of pedestrian thought, that rise more thickly and ever-higher to such altitudes that cannot be observed without damage to our neck vertebrae—inspire him to a philippic against that city—the material, prosaic, typical center and heart of an almost automated social mechanism," against "Americanism, which is relentlessly infiltrating the most ancient areas of our historical culture," against the "twentieth century in the New World, a century of mechanical superpower in the world of independence through capital."[14]

Thus, the contemplation of the destiny of art, the concern over its present and its future, brought Busoni to his criticism of bourgeois society. There was only one step left to take—to understand that no struggle against the degrada-tion and decay of art can possibly be successful without struggle against what gives birth to and feeds this degradation—against the bourgeois social system, against capitalism, which, in Marx's genius observation, is organically "inimical to various areas of spiritual production, such as, for example, art and poetry."

Busoni did not take this step. The Master was far removed from politics, from Marxism; he wished to live, and hoped to live in the "pure" world of art. ". . . I am first of all an artist, and, for me, artistic creation is the goal of all human striv-ing. Science, politics, religion, philosophy appear to me only as artistic images and cause me joy and worry only as such."[15] He indulges himself in a utopian idea—to "separate" art from the "aims of gain" that reign in the surrounding society. He celebrates the "Gothics of Chicago"—two scholars of polyphony (Bernhard Ziehn and Wilhelm Middelschulte[16]), who, located in the very center of the tasteless and airless "mechanistic" civilization, "in severe silence, turning their gaze inward, study and develop ancient Gothic art."[17] He himself longs to lose himself in some "cozy little house," built horizontally, not upward, or in the midst of nature, where there is "pureness and quietness in the air, something like a Sunday," where the "roar of businesslike practicality that permeates the world of culture" would disappear somewhere far off in the distance and where he might "on a quiet morning, at home . . . open a beloved score—the Finale of Act II from Mozart's *Figaro* for example—and spin . . . into its silken web."[18] "To work on his compositions in the quiet of his study, to think and to read—this was the greatest joy of the master," relates the author of one of Busoni's biographies. "He could live only within his art, his ideas, and books. He was never happier than when he could free himself of the everyday and be in solitude."[19]

This separation from society could not be beneficial to his search for an artis-tic revival. In separating himself from society, from social struggle, he denied himself the only true criterion for selecting a path toward that artistic *Rinasci-mento* for which he so strived. What to leave behind was much clearer to Busoni than where and how to go forth—hence, all the contradictions and vacillations in his art that could not have escaped the reader of the preceding chapters. In his wandering, Busoni largely meandered blindly; thanks to his genius instinct he found much, but in some things wandered further afield that necessary, "threw the baby out with the bathwater" at times, and sometimes strayed from the correct course. He followed the path of realism, but often veered off toward impressionism, symbolism and even formalism. These detours where more sig-nificant in his original compositions than in his playing; here the virtues far out-weighed the flaws.

In setting out to find the *eau vive* needed to heal decaying art, Busoni walked halfway and was approaching a historical crossroads that separated so many human destinies. The world was approaching war—a cruel and merciless test of people and ideas.

Chapter Seventeen

World War I, which began in August 1914, did not immediately bring great changes in Busoni's life. In January 1915 he undertook a long concert tour of America. However, he was unable to return home: during his absence Italy declared war on Germany, and the road to Berlin was closed to the Italian Busoni. Instead, like some other artists (d'Albert, Masereel,[1] Romain Rolland), he went to Switzerland and settled in Zurich for the remainder of the war.

The slaughter into which capitalism dragged humanity shook Busoni profoundly. To his honor, he did not succumb to the lies of the chauvinistic slogans and did not join either imperialist camp. Instead, he found the courage to polemicize openly against the "patriotic ecstasy" that the press of the warring countries attempted to use to silence "that which calls out to Heaven." The reason for Busoni's writing was the untimely death at the front of one of his friends, the young artist Boccioni.[2] The popular Italian newspaper, *Corriere della Sera,* had "honored" the memory of the artist with an obituary in which he was portrayed, in direct contradiction to his true views, as a raging nationalist who was happy to give his life for his homeland. In his letter "Der Kriegsfall Boccioni," published in the Swiss paper *Neue Züricher Zeitung,* Busoni published excerpts from Boccioni's letters, which proved the opposite, and blamed the prevailing "deliberate misrepresentation of the truth" and "ubiquitous silence about unforgivable events." "Why does this go on?" he cries at the end of the letter. "Why is the indignation that should sweep through parts of Italy not being openly expressed? . . . In Goya's series of etchings *Los desastres de la guerra,* the penultimate sheet is titled "Murió la verdad" (The truth has died); "¿Se resucitará?" (Will it live again?) is the title of the final one."[3]

It is not difficult to imagine the reaction to Busoni's actions in circles that supported the policies of imperialism. Both Italian and German "patriots," who so ardently argued their country's right to be regarded as Busoni's true motherland earlier (and later), now equally fervently distanced themselves from the "rootless" musician. Some called him a Germanized renegade, and a traitor,[4] others accused him of internationalism and of anti-German spirit. Especially fervent in this opinion was the German composer Hans Pfitzner, who not only criticized Busoni's esthetics but saw within them a manifestation of the "international Jewish movement" that had brought Germany to the "shame and crime of revolution."[5]

Obviously, attacks of this kind are honorable decorations in the Master's biography. Unfortunately, however, speaking out publicly against the war, as in the case of Boccioni, was a singular event in Busoni's life. While he hated the war, Busoni did not comprehend clearly either its causes, or, consequently, the way to struggle against these causes. It is no wonder then that he, like Romain Rolland during those years, preferred to remain *hors de combat*. But, while Romain Rolland moved further away from these illusions day by day, Busoni clung to them more desperately the more the very ground under them was being washed away. In the face of events his isolationism grew, became more pronounced, and acquired an almost pathological character. "At this time," he writes to a friend, "when people do not think, and God does not govern (and, sadder yet, if all that is going on should be considered a result of thinking and government), there is nothing to do but to curl in upon oneself like a snail inside one's own safe haven."[6] With a greater disgust than ever the Master turns away from the world, where such horrifying and appalling deeds are possible, closes the door of his Zurich home to politics and to newspapers, agrees with Boccioni that "there is only art," all else is but a "game next to a perfect brushstroke, a harmonious poem, a well constructed chord," a game that induces "contempt for everything that is not art."[7]

But Busoni attempts in vain to create for himself, amid life's roaring ocean, a blessed island, Aldington's Aeaea,[8] where he could shelter the "silken web" of his art from storms. Art cannot be separated and torn apart from reality. Its blood flows from life; the attempt to cut the connecting arteries only leaves art bloodless. Busoni's art slowly loses its vitality; formalistic tendencies, never quite absent before, gather more weight. All that is turbulent, passionate, fiery, fervent disappears almost entirely from Busoni's playing; all is squeamishly reigned in with "miserly dynamic cautiousness." Liszt's *fortissimos* become *mezzo forte, forte—piano; con strepito, con brio, con bravura, fuocoso* are transformed into *misuratamente, leggiero, con freschezza*,[9] "the fire of Liszt's style" becomes "ethereal light." The colors become "ascetic," playing is "crystallized," there is now within it a cult of the "transparent, glass-like, flesh-less,"[10] it begins to resemble some semi-mystical sound dance of all possible *fliessend, flüsternd, flimmernd, scintillante, sussurando, scorrevole, granulato, perlato*.[11]

There are parallel changes in composition, as well. The Master's attitude to Beethoven cools. Busoni faults Beethoven for possessing, in addition to a "big heart" and "golden sentiment," "a head [that is] not correspondingly disci-plined."[12] Busoni blames Beethoven, as well, for introducing into music "matters of social tendency and movements of propaganda" and "arous[ing] in his suc-cessors the ambition to put significance and depth into their work and to com-pose on a cyclopean scale."[13] As a counterweight to the "human" author or the Ninth Symphony, Busoni raises the standard of the still inadequately appreciated "divine" Mozart, the "friend of Order: miracle and sorcery preserve their sixteen and thirty-two bars."[14] "I now draw further away from the angry seriousness of the former (Beethoven—G. K.) and realize more profoundly the lofty serious-ness concealed behind the unclouded clarity of the latter (Mozart—G. K.)," we read in one of the Master's Zurich letters.[15]

There is no need to dispute Busoni's characterizations of Mozart and Beethoven in these pages, to note their accuracy of detail, but one-sidedness and incorrectness as a whole. Busoni's departure from Beethoven,[16] in addition to all we said above, completes the picture of impoverishment and decay of Busoni's pianism during the war and postwar years. Obviously, the line of demarcation is not perfectly straight. Busoni gave many more unforgettable concerts; his playing possessed many amazing qualities to the end. Still, Adolf Weissmann was correct in noting that the war had "made a breach" in Busoni's pianism: his playing grew "lifeless," and, although there remained much that was "genius," especially in Bach and Mozart, its "spiritual perfection, the reflection of internal sound process was already unrecognizable."[17]

In addition, during these years Busoni loses much of his interest in performance. He continues to concertize and teach, but the center of gravity of his activities shifts toward composition. Already in his edition of the second volume of the *Well-Tempered Clavier*, completed in the early years of the war, Busoni, in a marked departure from Volume I, "turned away from the purely pianistic side of things" and "concerned himself mainly with introducing the student to the secrets of the musical structure and the inner workings" of the composer.[18]

The final period of Busoni's life coincided with a much-increased antirealist tendency in Western music. Especially important during this period is Expressionism, a movement with which some musicologists mistakenly associate Busoni. This is incorrect.[19] Busoni did follow the *early* compositional development of Schoenberg with great interest, even publishing a "concert edition" of his Konzertstück Op. 11, no. 2.[20] The following year he published a supportive review of a Schoenberg concert.[21] But soon thereafter, he notes that Schoenberg is "beginning to turn round in a circle."[22] When Expressionism finally reached its full development, Busoni announced his criticism of this movement in a harsh "open letter" (1922), expressing many thoughts still valuable today. What Busoni sees in Expressionism is merely "hysteria and temperamental gestures," which appear as "disconnected forms of sighs and of runs, in the obstinate repetition of one or more sounds, in fading away and using the highest of the high and the deepest of the deep sounds, in the pauses and in the accumulation of different rhythms within one bar"; he attacks the "semblance of polyphony" so beloved of expressionists, by means of which "still more restlessness is imprinted," and, especially, the Expressionist harmony. In his opinion, atonality is a "system, which demands neither skill, nor imagination, nor feeling, and gives everyone the possibility of the right to stagger backwards and forwards at will." The "removal of the consonance [and] leaving the dissonance unresolved" left harmony "stunted as a means of expression" and "the individuality of the author effaced." All the harmonic constructions of the Expressionists "sound alike, whatever the composer's name may be"; in addition, "it is a characteristic that at the commencement of a piece, all means and formulas appear immediately, in full strength and are exhausted, so that every possibility for making any further stress during the course of the composition is forestalled."[23]

Busoni's attitude was similarly negative to the other fashionable modernist movements of the time—Dadaism,[24] Constructivism, and so on. Instead, he supports a new style he terms Young Classicism ("junge Klassizität"), characterized by the combination of "old and new," a cult of "the most highly developed (not the most complicated) polyphony," and, above all, "the return to melody again as the ruler of all voices and all emotions (not in the sense of a pleasing motive) and as the bearer of the idea and the begetter of harmony."[25] Busoni continues to emphasize the concept of primacy of melody in music in a number of works of the current period, beginning with the Afterword to his edition of the second volume of the *Well-Tempered Clavier* (1915), where he "proclaims the triumph of melody over all other compositional techniques," and concluding with his "Notes" (1921), where once again he asserts, "in opposition to the established point of view," that "melody . . . must govern with absolute sway" in composition.[26] He even drew up plans to develop a "system of melody,"[27] but was not able to complete the project.

As we can see, during these years Busoni expresses a number of healthy and progressive ideas on composition that continue and develop the fruitful tendencies of the earlier period in his art. Unfortunately, these thoughts, much as in the previous period, are admixed with judgments of a different sort. Both in Busoni's essays and in his compositions of this time (*Rondo Arlecchinesco, Gesang vom Reigen der Geister,*[28] *Sarabande and Cortége* for orchestra, the clarinet Concertino, Divertimento for flute, Improvisation on Bach Chorale for two pianos, piano Toccata, and a few piano Sonatinas) contain much that is contradictory; realistic features coexist with formalistic elements and mysticism, with the balance shifting to the latter.

The question of Opera takes a central place in the Master's explorations during this period. He explains his views in a series of essays. He does not join in the view that opera is dying; instead he sees a great future: "Not only do I believe that no inferior kind of music need be brought to mind by the opera, and that it will enjoy equal rights with other kinds of music . . . I expect that in the future the opera will be the chief, that is to say the universal and one form of musical expression and content."[29] However, Busoni is not thinking of an opera on a realistic verismo subject such as *La Traviata* or *Tosca:* "the sung word will always remain a convention on the stage and a hindrance to any semblance of truth; to overcome this deadlock with any success a plot would have to be made in which the singers act what is incredible, fictitious, and improbable from the very start, so that one impossibility supports the other and both become possible and acceptable. . . . It is for this reason and because it disregards this most important principle from the beginning, that I look upon the so-called Italian 'Verismo' for the musical stage as untenable." The sphere of opera, in the Master's opinion, is not the real world, but rather that of the "supernatural or unnatural . . . [where] life is reflected in either a magic or a comic mirror." In other words, it should be either a fairy tale, such as *The Magic Flute,* which "comes nearest to this ideal," or a grotesque, a play in the spirit of the old Italian commedia dell'arte. "Then it is not out of place for the singers to declare their love and unload their hate and fall into a melodic duel, and hold on to high notes in pathetic outbursts. There it is in order for them to behave intentionally in a way contrary to life, instead of turning everything upside down unintentionally (as happens in our theatres now and particularly in opera). . . . And dances and masks and apparitions should be interwoven, so that the onlooker never loses sight of the charms of pretence." [30]

In discussing the details of operatic dramaturgy, Busoni protests against episodes of "sensual" or erotic character and defends, in defiance of Wagner, the older principle of "a series of short, concise pieces" of music, and demands that the music illustrate the unseen inner workings of the personages' souls, rather than the visible events:

> When the scene presents the illusion of a thunderstorm, this is exhaustively apprehended by the eye. Nevertheless, nearly all composers strive to depict the storm in tones—which is not only a needless and feebler repetition, but likewise a failure to perform their true function. The person on the stage is either psychically influenced by the thunderstorm, or his mood, being absorbed in a train of thought of stronger influence, remains unaffected. The storm is visible and audible without aid from music; it is the invisible and inaudible, the spiritual processes of the personages portrayed, which music should render intelligible.[31]

These are the principles that underlie the three operas that were the main works of Busoni's final period of composition and the focus of most of his other compositional and literary output (orchestral studies to the operas, a series of explanatory essays, etc.). All three are based on the Master's own libretti. Two of them—the two-act *Turandot* (after Gozzi's play) and one-act "Theatrical Capriccio" *Arlecchino*—were composed in Zurich and first performed there (on the same evening) on May 11, 1917.

Turandot and *Arlecchino* are both in the style of the commedia del'arte; the music of both operas is lively, clear, and piquant. The following examples give some idea (as much as "examples" can) of its ironic character:

Ex. 74. Busoni, *Turandot*

Ex. 75: Busoni, *Arlecchino*

The first of these examples is borrowed from the final wedding march *alla Turca* from *Turandot*, the second—from a caricature military march that accompanies the entrance of Arlecchino dressed as an officer.

The final opera of the Master, *Doktor Faust*, the most substantial of Busoni's compositions, is of a very different character. The "Faust Problem" had fascinated him from as early as his youth; his unique collection of Faust literature (in several languages) was world-renowned. The libretto was written "by the first wartime Christmas,[32] as if in some frenzy, in six days."[33] The libretto is not based on Goethe's tragedy (which was, nevertheless, much revered by Busoni), but on an old German puppet show.[34] The music took much longer. Busoni worked on it for the rest of his life, but did not complete it—the final scene remained unfinished and unorchestrated. Finally completed by Busoni's student Phillip Jarnach,[35] the opera was first staged in Dresden on May 21, 1925, and made a profound impression. Since then it has been and continues to be presented mostly in German cities (Stuttgart, Hamburg, Frankfurt am Main, and others), always attracting great attention. Many prominent musicians, including B. V. Asafiev,[36] saw it as the "spiritual will and testament" of the Master.

Doktor Faust was Busoni's favorite brainchild; it was the recipient of his most sincere ambitions and aspirations. The music fascinates with its accomplishment, profundity, and individuality; while the "puppetry" carries a mystical tone.

Besides his composition, concerts, piano lessons, and dozens of new essays, Busoni finds time to do much more during his Zurich and post-Zurich years. He completes his edition of Bach's keyboard works, publishes a new, expanded version of his *Sketch of a New Esthetic of Music*, arranges the *Fantasia contrappuntistica* for two pianos, brings out his five-volume book of piano exercises, composes new transcriptions (Liszt's *Don Juan*, Paganini-Liszt Etudes, a chamber fantasy on Bizet's *Carmen*); the new admiration for Mozart finds expression in marvelous new two-piano transcriptions of the *Magic Flute* overture, Fantasy for a Barrel Organ,[37] and the Finale of the F-Major Piano Concerto[38]).

The wealth of new artistic achievements of very high quality should bring the Master joy. But "something is rotten in the state of Denmark"—not only in the world but also in Busoni's, one would think, securely "removed" and "separated" art. The artist senses this, and he grows troubled.

Chapter Eighteen

The war ended in 1918. Busoni was able to depart his Swiss confinement and resume concert tours of various countries. Europe, slowly reviving from the carnage, hastened to reclaim its surviving cultural values. Intellectual elites everywhere show the Master their respect, admiration, and love. The University of Zurich awards him an honorary doctorate. London welcomes his return to the concert stage with a series of essays by Edward Dent. The German premiere of *Turandot* and *Arlecchino* (in Frankfurt on October 15, 1918) signals the start of an energetic campaign for Busoni's repatriation to Berlin. Papers and journals, in a series of "open letters" and essays by Paul Bekker, Rudolf Kastner,[1] and other renowned musicians, persistently demand that the government and the society of the Weimar Republic invite the Master—"the pride of German musical culture"—to come back to the city in which so much of his life and work have taken place.

Finally, despite the opposition of reactionaries headed by that same Hans Pfitzner, whom we have had cause to mention earlier, this campaign was successful. In 1920, the Berlin Academy of Art elects Busoni as a member, and the new director of the Berlin Hochschule für Musik, composer Franz Schreker,[2] invites him to conduct one of the school's advanced piano classes. Busoni returns to Berlin. He is met with great honors and every manner of attention, and all his demands are met. His first concert, after a six-year absence, is nothing short of triumphant. Busoni is elected honorary chairman of the German section of the International Composers Guild. Work begins on a new instrument based on dividing the whole tone into three parts, a long-nurtured idea of his. The country undertakes a general reform of music education, based on the spirit of Busoni's ideas; his student Leo Kestenberg is appointed head of the Music Division of the Prussian Education Ministry.[3]

In 1921, Berlin celebrates Busoni's fifty-fifth birthday. *Turandot* and *Arlecchino* are staged, there is a series of concerts of Busoni's compositions,[4] and an evening of his piano duets with Egon Petri, later repeated in Paris and London.[5] Special editions of *Musikblätter des Anbruch* and *Il Pianoforte*, dedicated entirely to Busoni, come out during that year, and, slightly later, in 1922, the book by Gisella Selden-Goth,[6] as well as the collection of his essays.[7]

Still, in the midst of all this fame and recognition, the Master is not happy. Growing dissatisfaction with the world, himself and his art gnaws at him. During his very last years he sadly states that he still has not found the true path and has not reached his compositional aspirations;[8] three months before his death he confides to the celebrated Parisian professor of piano, Isidore Philipp that, unsatisfied with his piano playing, he "intends to start his work as a pianist from scratch and on a completely different basis."[9]

The intuition of a great artist does not betray Busoni: his art and his pianism, for all his mastery and for all of his professional accomplishments, lack something important, basic, and decisive. Life severely punishes those who ignore it, who attempt to scorn it as a mere "game" in comparison to art; it turns the very art into an over-refined play of masks and colors. The "safe haven" turned out unsafe—the "deadly microbes" (Weissmann) found their way in. The wrong path chosen by the Master brought him to the water not of life, but of death.

If the results of his own labors engender a vague angst within himself, Busoni's views of all that is taking place around him gives birth to confusion, abhorrence, a conscious resentment. The war is over, but the atmosphere has not cleared. Capitalism, "Americanism," the "aims of gain" rule everywhere, more powerful than ever. The illusions of a noble cooperation of intellectuals who live above the fray have been destroyed by the war. The world has decisively separated—this time not due to national, but to social factors—into two opposing, immutably hostile camps, and this division makes its mark on intelligentsia, on culture, on art. Busoni cannot find a place for himself in this new postwar world. He continues to vacillate between the two camps and becomes a little ridiculous when he insists that differences in art are only "dissimilarities of talent," and all artists "only strive for perfection"; he is sincerely shocked when his writings of an "abstract and conciliatory nature" are met with scorn, and he cannot overcome his hope that Pfitzner's attacks are caused by an honest misunderstanding; he inquires naively "can this . . . opinion be contested by honest people? Do I not much rather hold out my hands to universal understanding? Is it possible that these theories could be considered injurious and dangerous on the one side and as retrograde and compromising on the other side?"[10]

Alas, artists, just like all people in class-driven societies do not "strive" for the same thing, and do not seek "universal understanding!" Busoni's extended hand remains hanging in the air; the artist does not understand the world and the world responds in kind. Hence, a feeling of isolation seizes Busoni: he lived his last Berlin years "substantially alone, as if on an island,"[11] he traveled alienated among "alien cities and streets," remaining "alone, misunderstood, and frequently sharply condemned."[12]

As expected, all of this had to leave a mark on the Master's spiritual state. The fracture of his inner world caused by the war continues to widen and deepen; it becomes visible even externally. Photographs from the last years of Busoni's life are painful to see: some melancholy, some restless unease settle on the features of his recently handsome, chiseled face, so beautifully described by Zweig.[13]

Thus ends the process that began with the events of 1914. It becomes clear that the war not only fractured, but broke Busoni; it is not only his art that is now "dead": during the war, "Busoni in essence had died as a person."[14]

To outward appearances, however, the Master's life continues unchanged for some time longer. He continues to travel on concert tours,[15] although he finds public performance increasingly burdensome. Especially difficult for this loather of "practicality" and the "aims of gain" was the necessity to perform for a living. "As soon as I am forced to do anything with a utilitarian purpose, as soon as the subject concerns practical income, it is as if something inside me begins to bleed, I am stricken with a sort of paralysis, and do with labor and suffering what I could have done, in different circumstances, easily, happily, and better." "When I give a concert only for the sake of the fee, I always play badly, worse than the average pianist. More, I feel ashamed while playing and afterward, and this is sheer torture. . . . How revolting is this toil . . ."[16] he bitterly confesses in his letters.[17]

It is impossible to avoid pointing out that Busoni was true to his revulsion for "the aims of gain" not just in words, but in deed, as well. As opposed to Hofmann, Rachmaninov, Paderewski, and other famous artists, who died rich men, Busoni had not accumulated any wealth. His earnings went into buying books and rare editions, organizing orchestral performances, and helping young musicians. After his death, the Master's family was left without means of support and was required to gradually sell off his pianos and other possessions. The fabulous library, including the rare collection of Faust literature, was sold at auction.

As we have mentioned before, during the last years of the Master's life, his thoughts were focused primarily on issues of composition, on *Doctor Faust*. In two large-scale essays, one of which was published after his death, he develops his ideas about this opera, and the "possibilities of the opera" in general.[18] Busoni's pedagogical work at the Hochschule für Musik is also in the same sphere. He did not wish to teach piano there, and instead took the job of leading the composition class. His composition professorship there was short, but successful; among his students are famous composers such as Philipp Jarnach,[19] Wladimir Vogel, Kurt Weill (the renowned composer of *The Threepenny Opera* with Bertolt Brecht), and the famous conductor Dimitri Mitropoulos.

Busoni always worked too hard, without sparing himself. Constant fatigue combined with nervous trauma led to serious disease—myocardial dystrophy (chronic weakening of the heart muscle). From 1922 on, the disease considerably limited the Master's ability to work, forcing him, in particular, finally to stop concertizing. His last public performance took place in Berlin in May 1922, a benefit for the Berlin Philharmonic, in which he played three piano concertos, with Beethoven's E-flat Major making the greatest impression.[20]

Even during his illness the Master did not stop working. He continued to teach at the Hochschule, to work on *Doktor Faust,* and to write; his last essay, "Von Wesen der Musik," finished on June 8, 1924, was published posthumously.[21]

During the years of his illness Busoni, probably under the influence of his friend Bernard Shaw,[22] began to show increasing interest toward the new society being built in the Soviet Union. Unable to go there himself, he pressured his friends and students to do so. It is no accident that the first foreign pianists to break through the cultural blockade of the Soviet Union—Petri, Galston, Zadora, and Sirota—all belonged to Busoni's circle.

On April 1, 1924, the Master turned fifty-eight. The celebration was marred by sadness: all knew that Busoni was doomed; by this time he almost never left his bed.

On July 26, the Master lost consciousness; the next day, July 27, 1924, he was no more.

Conclusion

Busoni's place in history is based on his accomplishments during his period of artistic maturity—during the second and, partially, the third stages of his life. An artist of genius, one of the four or five greatest in the entire history of piano playing, he elevated the field of pianistic virtuosity to unseen heights, created unforgettable examples of interpreting Bach, Mozart, Beethoven, and Liszt. He enriched piano literature with wonderful editions and transcriptions, wrote a substantial amount of interesting music; his book and his many essays contain fascinating observations, interesting ideas, and valuable thoughts. And much of what he brought into piano playing, the understanding of the instrument, and the methods of technical work, have forever entered the treasury of pianistic experience.

It is Busoni's greatest historical achievement that, first among pianists, he sensed the first signs of decadence and degeneration in the art of Academic Romanticism of the end of the nineteenth and beginning of the twentieth centuries, and led the struggle against this art. But this struggle was not always based on correct positions. Failing to fully understand the social nature of the negative artistic tendencies he saw, he became confused in contradictions. Like his hero, Faust, Busoni seemingly had two souls that pulled him in opposite directions. He alternated between subjectivism and objectivism, realism and formalism, unlimited freedom and "tight reins," between richness of tonal color and asceticism, the power and truth of "great emotions" and lifeless puppetry, a reform of the tonal system and the restoration of Bach's polyphony. While striving to go forward, he often moved backward, walking toward one room, but reaching another.

The duality and self-contradictions of Busoni's art did not, of course, escape the notice of musicologists. Many among them[1] explained these by pointing out Busoni's national origins, the fact that this "half-Italian, half-German . . . combined and transformed within himself . . . the most distinct qualities of these two nationalities."[2] Understandably, this conception was most fervently embraced at the time by the Nazis,[3] but even liberal musicologists joined this point of view, disagreeing only on which of the two tendencies, the German (as argued by Bekker and Weissmann),[4] or the Italian (according to Gatti and Dent).[5] This "scholarly" argument is as fruitless as the "theory" at its core. For what mattered was not "racial differences," not biology, but, rather, sociology.

Seen this way, the duality and contradictions within Busoni's work find a much more persuasive explanation: they are a product and a mirror of the duality and ambiguity of his social position. ". . . a *petit bourgeois*," writes Marx, "deifies contradiction, because contradiction is the foundation of his being. . . . He must justify in theory that which he is in practice."[6] The duality of Busoni's social (not national) nature prevented him from understanding the dual character of the capitalist reality, which was so abhorrent to him, to find within it the fulcrum for the struggle against it, and to see the only correct door leading to the promised land of *Rinascimento*. This is why he never did find the path there, even if he found many valuable things on his journey. This is why, at the end, he only reached a crisis, a dead-end came to Craig's idea of a puppet or marionette theater.[7]

The crisis in art was a reflection and the expression of the crisis within bourgeois society. . . . The most sensitive representatives of the artistic intelligentsia observed the soullessness and the ugliness of the capitalist 'civilization,' automatism and 'mechanization' of modern life, which contributed to spiritual decay and deadening of the person, with horror and anxiety. . . . The very conception of his (Craig's—G.K.) production, this transformation of living people into a 'dead' world of 'super-marionettes,' lays bare, albeit in a foggy and veiled form, the whole process of 'dehumanization' in art, where all that is living bleeds away into death."[8]

In the end, Busoni failed to resolve his own dilemma: in attempting to pour new blood into the aging bourgeois art, he himself was bled dry as an artist by the bourgeois society. But the contribution of the great Italian pianist cannot be viewed only negatively. While we dispense with all in his esthetic that was reactionary, idealistic, formalist, we must not forget about true and meaningful realistic values and gifts with which he enriched musical art—especially during the second stage of his life, and primarily in the world of pianism. In the interest of our Soviet performing arts culture, it is necessary to study and to *critically* master Busoni's contradictory but fertile legacy.

Busoni ends his essay "Wie lange soll das gehen?" written in December 1910, on the open ocean aboard the steamship *Oceanic* with symbolic words: "Now the whistle sounds. We swim in fog—the horn has just uttered its warning cry."[9]

Busoni did not escape the fog and did not succeed in leading musical art out [of the fog] either. But he did belong among those fin–de-siècle artists who, like the late Rimsky-Korsakov and early Stravinsky, Rilke, and Blok, in the era of imitative vulgarity and self-satisfied artistic "stylelessness" understood the danger and "uttered their warning cry."

In paying attention to this cry, we will understand the nature of Busoni's art.

Annotated Discography

It is a great misfortune to generations of music lovers and historians of piano playing that Ferruccio Busoni lived during the infancy of sound recording technology. His acoustic recordings, of a few works of Bach, Beethoven, Chopin, and Liszt, total only about a half-hour of music. These have the usual shortcomings of the early seventy-eights—a great deal of noise, and an inability to record longer works without substantial cuts. There is also a fascinating amount of improvisation, great rhythmic freedom, and a certain lack of adherence to the printed page that a contemporary listener might find shocking.

In addition, Busoni recorded an impressive number of piano rolls, in addition to the *Rigoletto Paraphrase,* which is the subject of Chapter 10. A few reproducing machines capable of playing these rolls are still extant, and, with care and patience, have been coaxed by specialists into producing performances that may be the truest reproduction of the artist's playing.[1]

For the rest of us, the only practical access to Busoni's recordings is on modern CD technology. The following CD discography is incomplete by its very nature, as new recordings are produced all the time, but is offered in the hope of aiding the reader in more fully enjoying Busoni's great contribution to the history of the piano.[2]

I

ACOUSTIC RECORDINGS

The first four of the following CDs contain all of Busoni's acoustic recordings:
BACH: Prelude and Fugue No. 1 (*Well-Tempered Clavier,* Book I)
BACH/BUSONI: Chorale Prelude *Nun freut euch liebe Christen*
BEETHOVEN: *Ecossaisen*
CHOPIN: Etude Op. 25, no. 5; Prelude Op. 28, no. 7 and Etude Op. 10, no. 5 (connected by an improvisatory-modulatory passage); Etude Op. 10, no. 5; and Nocturne Op.15, no. 2.
LISZT: *Hungarian Rhapsody,* No. 13.
Because there is so little music available, each of the following CDs combines Busoni's recordings with those of his pupils and followers. Many of these pianists are mentioned or discussed in Kogan's book. In addition, each disk uses a different method of noise reduction and digital editing for a startlingly different effect.

1. PEARL GEMM CD 9347 "Ferruccio Busoni, Egon Petri" (1989)
Additional material: Egon Petri performing Busoni's compositions with Dimitri Mitropoulus conducting the Minneapolis Symphony Orchestra. This CD is the least "interventionist" in its remastering, retaining more noise, but, perhaps, more of the high frequency sounds, as well.

2. SYMPOSIUM 1145 "Busoni: Complete Recordings, Percy Grainger, Egon Petri" (1993)
Additional material: Percy Grainger playing Chopin, Sonata in B Minor, Op. 58 and Egon Petri playing Alkan's Symphony from Twelve Studies in the Minor Keys, Op. 39.

3. ARBITER 134 "Busoni And His Legacy" (2002)
Additional material: Rosamond Ley playing Franz Liszt, *Jeux d'eau a la Villa d'Este* and *Sonata après une lecture du Dante;* and Egon Petri with the Frankfurt Radio Symphony Orchestra, Hans Rosbaud, conducting, performing Liszt's *Totentanz* and Busoni's Piano Concerto, fourth movement. Arbiter employs what they call "sonic depth" technology in their restoration. This CD includes an English translation of Heinrich Neuhaus's essay on Busoni as pianist and interpreter.

4. NAXOS 8.110777 "Busoni And His Pupils (1922–1952)" (2004)
Additional material: Egon Petri, Bach-Busoni *Chaconne;* Busoni *Albumblatt* No. 3: "In der Art eines Choralvorspiels"; *Elegy* No. 2: "All'Italia! In modo napolitano." Michael van Zadora, Busoni Sonatina No. 3: *ad usum infantis;* Sonatina No. 5: *in diem nativitatis Christi;* Sonatina No. 6: *Chamber Fantasy on Themes from Bizet's Carmen.* Edward Weiss, Busoni *Indian Diary,* Book I . This recording is not sold in the United States.

5. ANDANTE 1150 "Chopin—Solo Piano Vol. 1" (2004)
   CHOPIN: Prelude Op. 28, no. 7
   CHOPIN: Etude Op. 10, no. 5
   Additional material: works for piano by Chopin, performed by Artur Rubinstein, Alfred Cortot, Arturo Benedetti Michelangeli, Vladimir Horowitz, Sergei Rachmaninov, Dinu Lipatti, Robert Casadesus, Solomon, Josef Hofmann, Raoul Koczalski, Leopold Godowsky, Ignaz Friedman, Alexander Brailowsky, Emil von Sauer, Magda Tagliaferro, Walter Gieseking, Ignaz Jan Paderewski.

II

PIANO ROLLS

Busoni made piano rolls for several companies: Welte-Mignon, Duo-Art, Ampico, Hupfeld, and Art-Echo. Since the commercial introduction of Compact Disc (CD) in the early 1980s, Busoni's piano roll recordings have appeared on the following CDs:

A. WELTE-MIGNON

1. ADES 14.108–2 "Les maitres du piano" (1987)
LISZT/BUSONI: *La campanella* (Paganini Study No. 3)
LISZT: *Feux follets* (Transcendental Study No. 5)
Additional material: performances by Alfred Cortot, Ignaz Jan Paderewski, Josef Hofmann, and Rudolf Ganz.

2. TELDEC 8.43930 ZS "Welte-Mignon 1905. Berühmte Pianisten der Jahrhundertwende spielen Chopin" (1988)
CHOPIN: Prelude Op. 28, no. 15
Additional material: performances by Alfred Reichenauer, Ignaz Jan Paderewski, Teresa Carreño, Raoul Pugno, Emil von Sauer, Eugen d'Albert, and Fanny Bloomfield-Zeisler.

3. TELDEC 8.43931 ZS "Welte-Mignon 1905 **Berühmte Kom ponisten spielen eigene Werke. Liszt-Schüler spielen Liszt**" (1988)
VERDI/LISZT: *Rigoletto Paraphrase*
LISZT/BUSONI: *La campanella* (Paganini Study No. 3)
Additional material: Claude Debussy and Enrique Granados performing their own works, Bernhard Stavenhagen, Eugen d'Albert, Emil von Sauer, and Max Reger performing the works of Franz Liszt.

4. RECORDED TREASURES CD-1 "Ferruccio Busoni Performs Franz Liszt" (1989)
MOZART/LISZT: Reminiscences de *Don Juan*
BELLINI/LISZT: Reminiscences de *Norma*
DONIZETTI/LISZT: *Valse caprice* on themes from *Lucia and Parisina*
VERDI/LISZT: *Rigoletto Paraphrase*
SCHUBERT/LISZT: Hungarian March
BEETHOVEN/LISZT: *Adelaide*
LISZT/BUSONI: *La campanella* (Paganini Study No. 3)
LISZT: Polonaise No. 2

5. INTERCORD INT 860.856 "Welte-Mignon Digital" (1989)
BELLINI/LISZT: Reminiscences de *Norma*
DONIZETTI/LISZT: *Valse caprice* on themes from *Lucia and Parisina*
VERDI/LISZT: *Rigoletto Paraphrase*
SCHUBERT/LISZT: Hungarian March
BEETHOVEN/LISZT: *Ruins of Athens* Fantasy
LISZT: Polonaise No. 2

6. DOLPHIN: FRIENDLY DOGS MUSIC GROUP TCC38-FD 198 "Rarities. Vol. 1: Early Recordings by Great Composers and Pianists"
DONIZETTI/LISZT: *Valse caprice* on themes from *Lucia and Parisina*
Additional material: Béla Bartók, Claudio Arrau, Theodor Leschetitzky, Josef Lhévinne, Cyril Scott, Percy Grainger, Ernst von Dohnanyi, and Gustav Mahler.

*7. TUDOR 7104 "Welte-Mignon Piano. Hotel Waldhaus, Sils Maria" (2001)
BELLINI/LISZT: Reminiscences de *Norma*
Additional material: Arthur Nikisch, Georg Zscherneck, Eugen d'Albert,
Fanny Davies, Raoul Pugno, Teresa Carreño, Theodore Leschetizky, Lazzaro
Uzielli, Felix Dreyschock, Josef Lhévinne, Emil von Sauer, and Artur Schnabel.

*8. WINTER & WINTER 910 067–2 "Sils Maria, Engadin. Hotel Waldhaus"
(2003)
LISZT/BUSONI: *La campanella* (Paganini Study No. 3)
Additional material: Jörg Kienberger and the Trio Farkas performing folk
music.

As is the case with the above CD, this was recorded on the player piano in the
famous Waldhaus Hotel, in the little village of Sils-Maria near St. Moritz, which
had been the favourite refuge of Hermann Hesse, Thomas Mann, Theodor
Adorno, and Claude Chabrol. Unfortunately, the instrument appears to have
more historical than practical value.

9. NAXOS 8.110679 "Welte-Mignon Piano Rolls 3" (2004)
LISZT/BUSONI: *La campanella* (Paganini Study No. 3)
Additional material: Fannie Bloomfield Zeisler, Fanny Davies, Rudolph Ganz,
Josef Hofmann, W. Krowsky, Yolanda Mero, Olga Samaroff, Wera Schapira,
Xaver Scharwenka, Carl Schmidt, Artur Schnabel.

This disk is not available for sale in the United States.

B. *DUO-ART*

*1. FONE 90F 13 CD "Great Composers at the Keyboard. Ferruccio Busoni"
(1990)
BACH/BUSONI: *Chaconne* from Violin Partita No. 2
CHOPIN: 24 Preludes, Op. 28
LISZT/BUSONI: *La chasse* (Paganini Study No. 5)
LISZT: *Feux follets* (Transcendental Study No. 5)
LISZT: Polonaise No. 2

2. BELLAPHON 690–07–019 "The Condon Collection-Busoni" (1993)
BACH/BUSONI: *Chaconne* from Violin Partita No. 2
CHOPIN: Preludes Op. 28, nos. 1–13, 15–24
LISZT/BUSONI: *La chasse* (Paganini Study No. 5)
LISZT: *Feux follets* (Transcendental Study No. 5)
LISZT: Polonaise No. 2

3. NIMBUS NI 8801 "The Grand Piano Era" (1997)
BACH/BUSONI: *Chaconne* from Violin Partita No. 2
Additional material: Ignaz Friedman, Frederic Lamond, Harold Bauer, Niko-
lai Medtner, Ignaz Jan Paderewski, Percy Grainger, and Josef Hofmann.

4. NIMBUS NI 8810 "Ferruccio Busoni" (1997)
BACH/BUSONI: *Chaconne* from Violin Partita No. 2
CHOPIN: Preludes Op. 28, nos. 1–7, 9–11, 14–16, 20, 23
LISZT/BUSONI: *La campanella* (Paganini Study No. 3)
LISZT/BUSONI: *La chasse* (Paganini Study No. 5)
LISZT: *Feux follets* (Transcendental Study No. 5)
LISZT: Polonaise No. 2
This CD contains the complete set of Duo-Art rolls.

5. DAL SEGNO DSPRCD 019 "Masters of the Piano Roll—Ferruccio Busoni" (2005)
BACH/BUSONI: *Chaconne* from Violin Partita No. 2
CHOPIN: Preludes Op. 28, nos. 1–13, 15–24
LISZT/BUSONI: *La chasse* (Paganini Study No. 5)
LISZT: *Feux follets* (Transcendental Study No. 5)
LISZT: Polonaise No. 2

6. DAL SEGNO DSPRCD 032 "J. S. Bach: The Original Piano Roll Recordings" (2007)
BACH/BUSONI: *Chaconne* from Violin Partita No. 2
Additional material: piano roll recordings of Bach's music by Alfred Cortot, Eugen d'Albert, Myra Hess, Harold Bauer, Vladimir de Pachmann, and Ignaz Friedman.

7. DAL SEGNO DSPRCD 033 "Franz Liszt: The Original Piano Roll Recordings" (2007)
LISZT/BUSONI: *La chasse* (Paganini Study No. 5)
Additional material: piano roll recordings of Liszt's music by Alfred Cortot, Guiomar Novaes, Rudolph Ganz, Josef Hofmann, Arthur Friedheim, Harold Bauer, Ignaz Friedman, and Vladimir de Pachmann.

C. *AMPICO*

1. ANDANTE 1190 "Chopin—Solo Piano, Vol. 2" (2005)
CHOPIN: Nocturne Op. 15, no. 2
Additional material: piano works by Chopin performed by Edward Kilenyi, Ignaz Jan Paderewski, Alexander Brailowsky, Francis Planté, Jeanne-Marie Darré, Vladimir Sofronitzki, Alfred Cortot, Raoul von Koczalski, Emil von Sauer, Artur Rubinstein, Dinu Lipatti, Maryla Jonas, Ignaz Friedman, Vladimir Horowitz, and William Kapell.

2. DABRINGHAUS UND GRIMM MDG 645 1402–2 "Player Piano 2. Chopin: Famous Pianists Around 1900" (2006)
CHOPIN: Ballade No. 1, Op. 23

Additional material: Eugen d'Albert, Alfred Reisenauer, Moriz Rosenthal, Mischa Levitzki, Mieczyslaw Munz, Alfred Mirovitch, Leopold Godowsky, and Leo Ornstein.

(*) In these recordings either the piano roll or the apparatus used for playing the piano roll is highly problematic. Among others, it fails to reproduce the sustaining pedal. Thus, the playing appears to be what Egon Petri calls "a travesty of Busoni's playing" (see Larry Sitsky, *Busoni and the Piano* [Westport, Conn.: Greenwood Press, 1986], 329).

Notes

Preface

1.   Dent freely admits the need for a separate volume in the preface to his biography of Busoni. See E. J. Dent, *Ferruccio Busoni* (London: Oxford University Press, 1933), vii. Other major biographical works on Busoni include: Hugo Leichtentritt, *Ferruccio Busoni* (Leipzig: Breitkopf und Härtel, 1916); Jean Chantavoine, "Ferruccio Busoni," *La Revue musicale* 11 (October 1924): 235–43; H. H. Stuckenschmidt, *Ferruccio Busoni: Chronicle of a European* (Zurich: Atlantis, 1967); and Antony Beaumont, *Busoni the Composer* (Bloomington: Indiana University Press, 1985). Larry Sitsky's very important study of Busoni is more of a catalogue of Busoni's piano compositions, transcriptions and recordings than an in-depth look at technique, sound production, and other aspects of piano playing. Larry Sitsky, *Busoni and the Piano* (Westport, CT: Greenwood Press, 1986).

2.   Important sources of biographical information about Grigory Kogan include the following: Viktor Abramovich Tsukkerman, Preface to Grigory Kogan, *Izbrannye stat'i* [Selected Essays], (Moscow: Sovetskii kompozitor, 1985), Dmitry Bashkirov, Preface to G. Kogan "Vidennoe i slyshannoe," [Seen and Heard], *Sovetskaia muzyka* 8 (1980): 95–96. In addition, Nina Svetlanova graciously shared personal recollections.

3.   Heinrich Neuhaus, Foreword to G. Kogan, *U vrat masterstva* [At the Gates of Mastery] (Moscow: Muzgiz, 1958), 3.

4.   Peter Gay, *Modernism: The Lure of Heresy* (New York: Norton, 2008), 429–30. Russell's prescience is extraordinary, for, at the time, he had only the example of the French Revolution to guide him. Today, with the names of Stalin, Mao, and Pol Pot fresh in our minds, we have far more solid evidence that violent socialist revolutions seem to follow a similar path.

5.   Solomon Volkov and Antonina W. Bouis, *Shostakovich and Stalin: The Extraordinary Relationship between the Great Composer and the Brutal Dictator* (New York: Knopf, 2004), 54. (Solomon Volkov and Vladimir Spivakov, *Shostakovich i Stalin: khudozhnik i tsar'* (Moskow: EKSMO, 2006).

6.   Isaiah Berlin and Henry Hardy, *The Soviet Mind: Russian Culture Under Communism* (Washington, DC: Brookings Institution Press, 2004), 4. The clear-sighted and sharp-tongued Berlin, part of the British Embassy to the Soviet Union, was a native Russian speaker, and a man neither courted by nor infatuated with Stalin. As such, he was in a unique position to observe and comment on events.

7.   Anna Ferenc, "Music in the Socialist State," in *Soviet Music and Society Under Lenin and Stalin: The Baton and Sickle*, ed. Neil Edmunds (New York: RoutledgeCurzon, 2004), 11.

8.   Shock the middle class.

9.   Faced with extensive devastation and widespread starvation, Lenin loosened Marxist principles to allow some degree of private enterprise, especially in agriculture.

10.   Berlin and Hardy, *The Soviet Mind*, 53.

11.   Frederick W. Sternfeld, *Music in the Modern Age. A History of Western Music* (New York: Praeger, 1973), 35.

12.   Berlin and Hardy, *The Soviet Mind*, 138.

13.   Nadezhda Mandelshtam, *Hope Against Hope: A Memoir* (New York: Atheneum, 1970), 168.

14.   For more on this fascinating time, see Vladimir N. Brovkin, *Russia After Lenin: Politics, Culture and Society, 1921–1929* (London: Routledge, 1998).

15.   Berlin and Hardy, *The Soviet Mind,* 4.

16.   V. I. Lenin, *Polnoe sobranie sochinenii,* 5th ed., 55 vols. (Moscow, 1958–65). Lenin, *Collected Works* (45 vols.) (Moscow: Progress Publishers, 1960s). Quoted in Roy Medvedev, *Let History Judge: The Origins and Consequences of Stalinism* (New York: Columbia University Press, 1989), 626.

17.   In a letter to Myasnikov, August 1921. Quoted in Medvedev, *Let History Judge,* 626.

18.   Medvedev, *Let History Judge,* 626–27.

19.   Andrei Artizov and Oleg Naumov, comps., *Vlast´ i khudozhestvennaia intelligentsia. Dokumenty TsK RKP(b), VChK-OGPU-NKVD o kul'turnoi politike. 1917–1953 gg.* [Government and the Artistic Intelligentsia. The Documents of the TsK RKP(b), VChK-OGPU-NKVD Regarding Cultural Politics. 1917–1953] (Moscow: Mezhdunarodnyi fond Demokratiia, 1999), 6–7.

20.   In his article "Party Organization and Party Literature."

21.   Volkov and Bouis, *Shostakovich and Stalin,* 48.

22.   April 23, 1932, Party resolution "On the Reformation of Literary and Artistic Organizations." Quoted in Ferenc, "Music in the Socialist State," 12–13.

23.   *Pervyi Vsesoiuznyi s´ezd sovetskikh pisatelei. Stenograficheskii otchet* [First All-Union Congress of Soviet Writers. Minutes.] (Moscow, 1934), 716. Quoted in Volkov and Bouis, *Shostakovich and Stalin,* 16. Volkov also points out a chilling parallel: "The essence of socialist realism was formulated much more frankly and accurately, albeit more cynically, a hundred years earlier by [tsar] Nicholas I's chief of Gendarmes, Benckendorff: 'Russia's past was amazing, its present more than magnificent, and as for its future, it is better than what the most heated imagination can picture; that is the point of view from which Russian history must be examined and written.'" M. Lemke, *Nikolaevskie zhandarmy i literatura 1826–1855 gg.* [Nicholas's Gendarmes and Literature 1826–1855] (St. Petersburg: Izd-vo. S. V. Bunina, 1908), 411.

24.   Early in Stalin's reign, there were attempts to mitigate the effects of governmental control. For example, the June 1925 resolution of the Central Committee recommended that literary matters be handled with "great tact, caution, and patience, banishing the tone of literary command, all pretentious, semi-literate and complacent Communist [meddling] . . . the party must utterly extirpate attempts at crude, incompetent administrative interference in literary matters." *O partiinoi i sovetskoi pechati. Sbornik dokumentov* [On Matters of Party and the Soviet Press. Collected Documents] (Moscow, 1954), 346–47. Quoted in Medvedev, *Let History Judge,* 831.

25.   Vladimir Mayakovsky, *Literaturnoe nasledstvo,* vol. 65: *Novoe o Maiakovskom* [New About Mayakovsky], comp. V. V. Vinogradov (Moscow: Izd-vo. Akademii nauk SSSR, 1988), 562. Quoted in Volkov and Bouis, *Shostakovich and Stalin,* 55.

26.   Evgenii Zamiatin [Yevgeny Zamyatin], *Sochineniia* [Works] (Moscow, 1988), 562. Quoted in Volkov and Bouis, *Shostakovich and Stalin,* 67.

27.   Iurii [Yuri] Annenkov, *Dnevnik moikh vstrech. Tsikl tragedii,* vol. 1 [Diary of My Encounters. The Cycle of Tragedy] (New York: Mezhdunarodnoe literaturnoe sodruzhestvo, 1966), 207.

28.   Artizov and Naumov, comps., *Vlast´ i khudozhestvennaia intelligentsia,* 6. Quoted in Volkov and Bouis, *Shostakovich and Stalin,* 63.

29.   Berlin and Hardy, *The Soviet Mind,* xii.

30.   "The Great Famine (Holodomor) of 1932–33—a man-made demographic catastrophe unprecedented in peacetime. Of the estimated six to eight million people who died

in the Soviet Union, about four to five million were Ukrainians. . . . Its deliberate nature is underscored by the fact that no physical basis for famine existed in Ukraine. . . . Soviet authorities set requisition quotas for Ukraine at an impossibly high level. Brigades of special agents were dispatched to Ukraine to assist in procurement, and homes were routinely searched and foodstuffs confiscated. . . . The rural population was left with insufficient food to feed itself." *Encyclopaedia Britannica,* "The Famine of 1932–33."

31. *Vechernyaya Moskva,* August 1, 1930.

32. *Pechat´ i revoliutsiia,* 1 (1930): 85–86.

33. Grigory Kogan, "Marksizm i iskusstvo," *Muzyka* 4 (1924). The academy was dissolved and reformed in 1931. Kogan left when the academy moved to Leningrad in 1932. The history of the purges within the academy is described in Russian in U. N. Iakimenko, "Iz istorii 'chistok apparata': Akademia Khudozhestvennykh Nauk v 1929–1932," *Novyi istoricheskii vestnik,* no. 1/12 (2005), www.nivestnik.ru/2005_1/11.shtml.

34. Boris Schwarz, *Music and Musical Life in Soviet Russia, 1917–1981* (Bloomington: Indiana University Press, 1983), 114. It may not be immediately obvious to a Western observer how music might promote "the development of a Marxist-Leninist musicology," or, in fact, why music of any type needs to be opposed ideologically. Isaiah Berlin, again, explains it best: "Stalin firmly grasped a truth which perhaps Napoleon was the first among secular rulers fully to realize and act upon, namely that discussion of ideas—disputes about issues apparently remote from politics, such as metaphysics or logic or aesthetics—was, by promoting the critical spirit, in principle more dangerous to despotic regimes engaged in a struggle for power than belief in any form of authoritarianism. . . . The very notion that there was an area of permissible disagreement about the interpretation of even unquestioned dogma created the possibility of insubordination; this, beginning indeed in spheres remote from the centres of power—say musical criticism or linguistics—might spread to more politically sensitive areas and so weaken the drive for economic and military power for which no sacrifice was too great or too immoral." Berlin and Hardy, *The Soviet Mind,* 143–44.

35. While Gorky lived (he died in 1935), at least a few interesting writers enjoyed at least a little protection from persecution. He seems to have had few illusions about the situation in which he found himself. The writer Kornei Chukovsky quotes Gorky in his diary: "I never bent the truth before, but now with our regime I have to bend the truth, lie, and pretend. I know that it can be no other way" (K. Chukovksii, *Dnevnik, 1901–1929* [Moscow, 1991], 148. In English, see Chukovsky, *Diary, 1901–1969* [New Haven: Yale University Press, 2005].) And when reminded about the brutality of the Soviet regime, his response was: "They have very large goals. And that justifies everything for me." E. Zamiatin, *Sochineniia* (Munich: Neimanis, 1986), 355.

36. A year earlier, Osip Mandelstam wrote a satirical anti-Stalin poem, which he unwisely allowed to circulate. He was arrested on the night of May 13, 1934, and charged with committing a terrorist act against the Beloved Leader. In Mandelshtam's often-quoted words—"only here is poetry respected—here they kill over it." A few years later, he would have been killed, but in 1934 his punishment was only exile.

37. *Vlast´,* 233. Quoted in Volkov and Bouis, *Shostakovich and Stalin,* 90.

38. Ibid., 277. Quoted in Volkov and Bouis, *Shostakovich and Stalin,* 90.

39. Volkov and Bouis, *Shostakovich and Stalin,* 82. Shaw became a professed Communist in the 1930s. He went on a nine-day visit to the Soviet Union on the invitation of Stalin himself in 1932, at the height of the famine in Ukraine, and, upon coming home, proclaimed, "Hunger in Russia? Nonsense. I've never been fed as well anywhere as in Moscow." Quoted in Helen Rappaport, *Joseph Stalin: A Biographical Companion* (Santa Barbara,

Calif.: ABC-CLIO, 1999), 88. In his own "Letter to the Editor: Social Conditions in Russia by George Bernard Shaw," *Manchester Guardian,* March 2, 1933, Shaw dismisses stories of the famine as slanderous. As Will Bennet, the *Telegraph* art sales correspondent wrote on June 18, 2003, an "extraordinary document" was going to be auctioned at Sotheby's in London, a series or hand- and type-written responses by Shaw to a questionnaire sent to him by the journalist Dorothy Royal upon his return from his Moscow trip. The answers provide a "shocking insight into the naivety of Soviet sympathisers."

40. Berlin and Hardy, *The Soviet Mind,* 6–7.

41. Schwarz, *Music and Musical Life,* 119.

42. Ferenc, "Music in the Socialist State," 4.

43. See more about this in Volkov and Bouis, *Shostakovich and Stalin,* 109.

44. Volkov and Bouis, *Shostakovich and Stalin,* 92.

45. Sternfeld, *Music in the Modern Age,* 37.

46. Glenn Gould, "Music in the Soviet Union," *The Glenn Gould Reader* (New York: Knopf, 1984).

47. The musicologist Richard Taruskin thinks that "Shostakovich was singled out for attack not because his works gave particular offense, but because of his preeminence among the Soviet composers of his generation. If Shostakovich could be summarily silenced and brought low, then nobody was safe." Richard Taruskin, *The Oxford History of Western Music,* vol. 4 (Oxford: Oxford University Press, 2005), 791.

48. Medvedev, *Let History Judge,* 832.

49. *Pravda,* March 3, 1936, and *Literaturnaya gazeta,* March 10, 1936. Quoted in Volkov and Bouis, *Shostakovich and Stalin,*113.

50. Medvedev, *Let History Judge,* 446–48.

51. In 1956, after Meyerhold's rehabilitation, at a meeting of the All-Russia Theatrical Society, Ilya Ehrenburg read the text of Meyerhold's final statement before the closed NKVD court that condemned him. "He . . . renounced all testimony he had given during the investigation, since it had been forced out of him by torture (Medvedev, *Let History Judge,* 448).

52. Berlin and Hardy, *The Soviet Mind,* 75.

53. Ibid., 75.

54. Ol´ga Vsevolodovna Ivinskaia, *V plenu vremeni: gody s Borisom Pasternakom* (Paris: Fayard, 1978). In English, see Olga Vsevolodovna Ivinskaya, *A Captive of Time: My Years with Pasternak: The Memoirs of Olga Ivinskaya,* trans. Max Hayward (London: Collins, 1978).

55. Lazar Fleishman, *Boris Pasternak v tridtsatye gody* [Pasternak in the 30s]. (Jerusalem: Magnes Press, Hebrew University, 1984), 423. Quoted in Volkov and Bouis, *Shostakovich and Stalin,* 147.

56. Some of the fellow travelers did, eventually, come to see the truth. Their confessions are collected in Arthur Koestler and R. H. S. Crossman, *The God That Failed* (New York: Harper, 1949).

57. Of course, Shaw did not believe in the German death camps, either. Emrys Hughes, *Bernard Shou* (Moscow: Molodaia gvardiia, 1966), 272. A willful refusal to see anything contrary to one's beliefs must make life much more comfortable. Like the Holocaust denial of later generations, the denial of Stalin's crimes has spawned somewhat of a cottage industry outside of the USSR. See, for example, the whitewash, the apologia and the justifications of journalists Michael Sayers and Albert Kahn (*The Great Conspiracy against Russia* [New York: Boni & Gaer, 1946]). This book was quickly translated into Russian, Croatian, Czech, and Japanese for propaganda purposes. American political scientist Frederick Schuman dismissed reports of the Gulag labor camps for the very good reason that, since each critic gave a different number of victims, the critics must be anti-Communist zealots and the camps

themselves simply their invention. Frederick Lewis Schuman, *Soviet Politics at Home and Abroad* (New York: Knopf, 1946). For a more in-depth discussion, see Gay, *Modernism: The Lure of Heresy*, 430.

58. Volkov and Bouis, *Shostakovich and Stalin*, 83.

59. Medvedev, *Let History Judge*, 476.

60. *Novy mir*, no. 1 (1966): 233–35. Quoted in Medvedev, *Let History Judge*, 476.

61. Medvedev, *Let History Judge*, 475–76.

62. Volkov and Bouis, *Shostakovich and Stalin*, 83.

63. Lion Feuchtwanger and Irene Josephy, *Moscow, 1937: My Visit Described for My Friends* (New York: Viking Press, 1937).

64. In 1949, during the campaign against "cosmopolitanism," Feuchtwanger fell out of favor and was called a "literary huckster." In better times, his novels were published again. I, along with the rest of my generation, grew up reading *The Judean War* and the *Spanish Ballad*.

65. Medvedev, *Let History Judge*, 475–76.

66. Ibid., 476.

67. Gay, *Modernism: The Lure of Heresy*, 426.

68. The policy that emerged was named *zhdanovshchina*, after him.

69. *Pravda*, August 21, 1946.

70. Lydia Chukovskaya, *Zapiski ob Anne Akhmatovoi*, vol. 2, iii. Quoted in Volkov and Bouis, *Shostakovich and Stalin*, 207. In English, see Lydia Chukovskaya, *The Akhmatova Journals*, trans. Milena Michalski, Peter Norman, and Sylva Rubashova (Evanston, IL: Northwestern University Press, 2002).

71. *Doklad t. Zhdanova o zhurnalakh "Zvezda" i "Leningrad"* (Moscow, 1946).

72. Volkov and Bouis, *Shostakovich and Stalin*, 208.

73. Berlin and Hardy, *The Soviet Mind*, 16–17.

74. Volkov and Bouis, *Shostakovich and Stalin*, 217–18.

75. *Pravda*, February 11, 1948.

76. *Sovetskaia muzyka* 2 (1948): 35, 45. Quoted in Volkov and Bouis, *Shostakovich and Stalin*, 228.

77. Volkov retells an anecdote about this "education" that would be comical were it not heartbreaking: "A wave of public gatherings, organized from above and widely reported in the mass media, rolled across the country. In accordance with the prepared rituals, they hailed the 'historic resolution' and viciously attacked the 'anti-people formalists.' Carefully vetted 'representatives of the people' were given the opportunity to lecture and teach common sense to world-acclaimed composers. Typical was a letter published in a newspaper (and servilely reprinted by the magazine *Sovetskaia muzyka*) from a comrade Zagoruiko, foreman of a foundry in a machine-building plant in the town of Nalchik. 'The resolution is correct, it will bring music closer to the people. . . . Some Soviet composers, for whom the people created all the conditions they need to work, write music that you can't even listen to. No rhyme or reason—just a wild whirlwind of sounds.'" *Sovetskaia muzyka* 1 (1948): 117. Quoted in Volkov and Bouis, *Shostakovich and Stalin*, 229.

78. Ferenc, "Music in the Socialist State," 16. Obviously, writing about Busoni would have been out of the question—a musician with a very brief and unsuccessful career in Russia, and no great historical or philosophical ties to the Soviet Union is not appropriate subject matter for a good Soviet scholar.

79. Unwilling to institute a cult of himself, but needing a substitute immaculate and infallible authority, Khrushchev introduced a vigorous cult of Lenin, as an image of absolute wisdom and goodness and moral guidance in all things. This explains the need to

insert quotations from Lenin's writings in literature on any subject, including musicology, no matter how gratuitous, as Kogan does in his book.

80.   Italian Communist leader Palmiro Togliatti expressed thoughts that must have troubled many at the time: "Previously all the good was due to the superhuman qualities of one man; now all the evil is attributed to his equally exceptional and shocking defects . . . the real problems are skipped over—how and why Soviet society . . . could and did depart from the self-chosen path of democracy and legality to the point of degeneration." Quoted in Mark Frankland, *Khrushchev*, intro. Harry Schwartz (New York: Stein and Day, 1967), 124.

81.   According to Shostakovich: "the historic resolution correcting the historic resolution." Quoted in Volkov and Bouis, *Shostakovich and Stalin*, 262.

82.   *Pravda*, October 26, 1958.

Introduction

1.   [Ferruccio Busoni, "On the Future of Opera," in *The Essence of Music*, trans. Rosamond Ley (New York: Dover, 1965), 4. —Trans.].

Hans Pfitzner, "Futuristengefahr" and "Die neue Äesthetic der musikalischen Impotenz," in *Gesammelte Schriften* (Augsburg: Filser, 1926), vol. 1, 185–223 and vol. 2, 99–203; Paul Bekker, "Futuristengefahr" and "Impotenz oder Potenz?" in *Kritische Zeitbilder* (Berlin: Schuster und Loeffler, 1921), 265–70, 310–27; Feruccio Busoni, "Offener Brief an Hans Pfitzner" and "Junge Klassizität," *Von der Einheit der Musik* (Berlin: Max Hesses, 1922). [In English, see Ferruccio Busoni, "Open Letter to Hans Pfitzner" and "Young Classicism," in *The Essence of Music*, trans. Rosamond Ley (New York: Dover, 1965), 17–19 and 19–23. —Trans.]

2.   Karl Thiessen, "Busoni als Erfinder einer neuen Notenschrift," *Signale für die musikalische Welt* [hereafter *Signale*] 45 (1910): 1685–88; *Signale* 47 (1910) s.v. "Neue Notensysteme": 1771–72; *Die Musik* X/7, 10 (1910).

3.   Albert Gutmann, "Eingesandt 'Wie lange soll das gehen?'" *Signale* 3 (1911): 88–89; August Spanuth, "Der verdächtigte Busoni," *Signale* 9 (1911): 327–28; *New York Tribune*, 1911.

4.   Busoni's Concerto for Piano, Orchestra and Chorus, Op. 39. First performance took place on October 23, 1904, in Berlin, Busoni at the piano, Carl Muck conducting.

5.   That is, a work worthy of a place together with Beethoven's nine symphonies.

6.   Philomele (pseud.), "Muzyka za granitsei" [Music Abroad], *Russkaia muzykal'naia gazeta* 4 (1904): 1061–63.

7.   [Isai Moiseevich] Knorozovsky, "Muzykalnye zametki" [Music Notes], *Teatr i iskusstvo* 47 (1912): 915–16.

8.   See numerous reviews, including: Otto Lessmann, *Allgemeine Musikzeitung* [hereafter *Allgemeine*] 45 (November 10, 1911): 1154; Georg Schünemann, *Allgemeine* 48 (December 1, 1911): 1238; Lessmann, in *Allgemeine* 51/52 (December 22, 1911): 1325–26; *Signale* 45 (1911) s.v. "Busoni's Liszt-Feier": 1566–67. Also, *Die Musik* XI/4, 5, 6, 7 (1911); *Allgemeine* 44, 47 (1911); *Signale* 46, 47, 51 (1911).

9.   [Otto Lessmann (1844–1918), German pianist and critic. Lessmann had been the owner and editor of the *Allgemeine Musikzeitung* from 1882 to 1907. —Trans.]

10.   Otto Lessmann, "Gibt es noch eine weitere Entwickelung des Klavierspiels? Betrachtungen nach dem jüngsten Busoni Clavierabend," *Allgemeine* 1 (January 1910): 6–7.

11.   [Boleslav Leopoldovich Yavorsky (1877–1942), a student of Taneyev at the Moscow Conservatory, eventually taught at the Kiev and Moscow Conservatories together with

Kogan. His theory of "modal rhythm" influenced generations of Soviet musicologists, but is largely unknown in the West. —Trans.]

12.   B. Yavorsky, "Posle moskovskikh kontsertov Feruchcho Buzoni" [After the Moscow Concerts of Ferruccio Busoni], *Muzyka* 104, 105 (1912).

13.   August Spanuth, review of January 6 concert, in *Signale* 2 (1909): 51–52; Ferruccio Busoni, "Letter to the Editor," *Signale* 4 (1909): 125; Arthur Friedheim, "Busoni und Liszt-Interpretation," *Signale* 6 (1909): 202–3.

14.   Lessmann,"Gibt es noch"; Adolf Weissmann, "Busoni," in *Der Virtuose* (Berlin: Paul Cassirer, 1918), 136 and in *Die Musik* 16 (1924): 887; Paul Bekker, "Busoni," in *Klang und Eros* (Berlin: Deutsche, 1922), 83–87, and *25 Jahre neuer Musik* ([N.p.]: Universal, 1926); Adolf Martienssen, *Die individuelle Klaviertechnik [auf] der Grundlage des schöpferischen Klangwillens* (Leipzig: Breitkopf und Härtel, 1930); Alfred Cortot, *Cours d'interpretation* (Paris: Legouix, 1934); Edwin Fischer, "Schuler und Meister," in *Von den Aufgaben des Musikers* (Weisbaden: Insel, 1960), 43. Numerous reviews, including Paul Schwers, "Aus den Berliner Konzertzälen," *Allgemeine* 3 (January 1909): 53; Georg Schünemann, "Aus den Berliner Konzertzälen," *Allgemeine* 6 (February 1909): 119; *Allgemeine* 44 (1910); Lessman, review in *Allgemeine* 45 (1911): 1154; Hermann Wetzel, "Kritik-Konzert," *Die Musik* VIII/9 (1908–9): 188; reviews in *Signale* 44 (1910) and 51 (1911), and others.

15.   Jean Chantavoine, "Ferruccio Busoni," *La Revue Musicale*, October 1924: 242.

16.   F. Busoni, *Sketch of a New Aesthetic of Music*, trans. T. Baker (New York: Schirmer, 1911).

17.   Grigorii Prokofiev, "Konzerti v Moskve" [Concerts in Moscow], *Russkaia muzikal'naia gazeta* 50 (1913): 1166–69; *Muzyka* 101 (1912) and 158 (1913).

18.   See Arno Nadel, "Arnold Schönberg," *Die Musik* XI/18 (1912): 356–57; Adolf Weissmann, ["Ferruccio Busoni,"] *Die Musik* XVI/12; Paul Bekker, *Die Musik* XX/3, and *Musikblätter des Anbruch* (October 1924); Edwin Fischer and Richard Schpecht, *Die Musik* XX/7; Ziegfried Günter, *Die Musik* XX/10; Robert Prechtl, ["Zweig auf Busonis Grab,"] *Melos* 4, no. 2; Chantavoine, "Ferruccio Busoni," *La Revue Musicale* (October 1923): 243; R. Faber, *Zhizn' iskusstva* 33/1007 (1924).

19.   See Pfitzner, "Futuristengefahr"; Walter Nieman, *Meister des Klaviers* (Berlin: Schuster und Loeffler, 1919); Paul Moose, *Die Philosophie der Musik* (Stuttgart: [N.p.], 1922); articles and reviews of various authors in the journals and newspapers of those years (*Die Musik* VII/12, X/11, XIII/9, XIII/14; *Russkaia muzykal'naia gazeta* 45 (1904), 48 and 49 (1912), 47 and 48 (1913); *Muzyka* (1912) 101; *Teatr i iskusstvo* (1913) 48; *Golos Moskvy* 252 (1913); *Russkie vedomosti* 273 (1913); *Den´* 310 (1913); *Rech´* 313 (1913); *Novoe vremia* 13535 (1913).

20.   *The Complete Works of Heinrich Heine*, vol. 11 (St. Petersburg: M. O. Wolf, 1900), 308–9.

21.   *Vechernee vremia* 279 (1912).

22.   See *Allgemeine* 1 and 44 (1910); *Russkaia muzykal'naia gazeta* 48 (1912) and 50 (1913); *Rech'* 286 and 293 (1912); *Den'* 18 and 26 (1912), 315 (1913); *Golos Moskvy* 235 and 252 (1912) and 272 (1913); *Utro Rossii* 272 (1913); *Birzhevye vedomosti* [evening edition] 13883 (1913); *Obozrenie teatrov* 2269 (1913) and others.

23.   [Viktor] Kolomiytsev, *Den'* 26 (1912).

24.   [Adolf Weissmann (1873–1929), an important German writer on music. He was the critic for *Berliner-Zeitung am Mittag* and the *Berliner Tegeblatt*, as well as for German music magazines. —Trans.]

25.   Adolf Weissmann, "Die Music der Weltstadt," *Die Music* X/13 (1911): 41; *Die Musik* XVI/12.

26.   G. Prokofiev, "Kontserty v Moskve," *Russkaia muzykal'naia gazeta* 48 (1912).

27.   G. Prokofiev, *Russkie vedomosti* 274 (1913).

Chapter 1

1.   This circumstance became the subject of various jokes. When asked about the date of his first stage appearance, he answered: "Eight days before my birth." Gerda Busoni, *Erinnerungen an Ferruccio Busoni* (Berlin: AFAS Musik, 1958), 21.

2.   F. Busoni, "Zwei autobiographische Fragmente. Mitgeteilt von Friedrich Schnapp," *Die Musik* 21 (October 1929): 1.

3.   Ibid.

4.   Ibid., 3.

5.   Ibid., 6.

6.   Ibid., 1.

7.   F. Busoni, "Selbst-Rezension," in *Von der Einheit der Musik,* 177. [In English, see "Self-Criticism," in *The Essence of Music,* 48. —Trans.]

8.   [Friedrich] Schnapp, "Busonis musikalisches Schaffen," *Zeitschrift für Musik* 12 (December 1932): 1045–46.

9.   [Friedrich] Schnapp, "Busonis persönaliche Beziehungen [zu] Anton Rubinstein," *Zeitschrift für Musik* 12 (December 1932): 1053–54. Rubinstein's recommendation is dated February 6, 1876, not 1879, as Schnapp mistakenly indicates, as a result of illegibility or a mistake in the original.

10.   [Edward J. Dent gives 1834 as the year of Mayer's birth (*Ferruccio Busoni: A Biography* [London: Eulenburg Books, 1974]). The *New Grove* agrees with Kogan's date. —Trans.]

11.   [E. N. von Reznicek (1860–1945), Austrian composer and conductor. (Paul) Felix von Weingartner (1863–1942), celebrated Austrian conductor, composer, and author. Wilhelm Kienzl (1857–1941), Austrian composer. —Trans.]

12.   F. Busoni, "Nachruf für Dr. W. Mayer," in *Von der Einheit der Musik.* [This obituary is not included in the English edition. —Trans.]

13.   Schnapp, "Busonis persönaliche Beziehungen [zu] Anton Rubinstein," 1053–54.

14.   Ibid., 1056–57.

15.   F. Busoni, "Bemerkungen über die Reihenfolge der Opuszahlen meiner Werke," in *Von der Einheit der Musik,* 96. ["Remarks about the Proper Order of the Opus Numbers of My Works," in *The Essence of Music,* 77. —Trans.]

16.   An opera of Peter Cornelius.

17.   Melanie Prelinger, "Erinnerungen und Briefe aus Ferruccio Busonis Jugendzeit," *Neue Musikzeitung* (1926/1927).

18.   [Egon Petri began as a violinist. His piano talent was recognized and encouraged by Busoni, whose most important student he eventually became. Petri performed together with Busoni in four-hand concerts and assisted the latter with his editions of Bach. In his own right, Egon Petri was renowned for his interpretations of Bach and Liszt. —Trans.]

19.   P. I. Chaikovskii [Tchaikovsky], *Muzykal´no-kriticheskie stat´i* [Musical-Critical Writings] (Moscow: Muzgiz, 1953): 353–55.

Chapter 2

1.   A reflection of this new influence is a small collection of four-hand piano pieces—*Finnländische Volksweisen* [Finnish Folk-Tunes] Op. 27.

2.   [Martin Wegelius (1846–1906), founder of the Helsinki Music Institute, now Sibelius Academy. Robert Kajanus (1856–1933), the most prominent Finnish composer

of his day, founder of the Helsinki Philharmonic Society, which later became the Finnish National Orchestra. Armas Järnefelt (1869–1958), Sibelius's brother-in-law, the first Finnish composer to conduct the operas of Richard Wagner in Finland. —Trans.]

3.   [Present-day Helsinki. —Trans.]

4.   [Carl Eneas Sjöstrand (1828–1906). —Trans.]

5.   The well-known transcription of Beethoven's Ecossaises by Busoni, which came out the same year, is dedicated to her.

6.   For the story of this courtship and marriage, see Gerda Busoni, *Erinnerungen an Ferruccio Busoni* (Berlin: AFAS Musik, 1958).

7.   [Finland was a Russian Grand Duchy from 1809 until 1917. Rather than being directly annexed, Russified, and absorbed, as were Russia's many other conquests, Finland was allowed to retain its traditions and its forms of government, but with the person of the tsar replacing the Swedish king as sovereign. —Trans.]

8.   See *Rules of the International Competition for the Musical Prizes of Anton Rubinstein*, comp. N. M. Lisovski (St. Petersburg: M. Bernard, 1889), 81–84.

9.   [Dubasov is heard from again in 1914, when, as a jury member, he "vehemently protests" Prokofiev's victory of the composition prize in the same competition. For details, see Israel Nestyev, *Sergei Prokofiev: His Musical Life*, trans. Rose Prokofieva (New York: Knopf, 1946), 33. —Trans.]

10.   *Novoe vremia*, August 18, 1890.

11.   *Novoe vremia*, August 18, 1890; *Peterburgskaia gazeta*, August 19, 1890; *Bayan* 9 (1890).

12.   Rubinstein gave Busoni 3½ points each (out of 5) for his performances of Bach, Mozart, and Beethoven; Dubasov received 4½ for the same composers. Both contestants got 4 points for Schumann, 4½ points for Chopin, and 5 points for the Liszt Etude. L. Barenboim, *Anton Grigor´evich Rubinshtein*, vol. 2 (Leningrad: Muzgiz, 1962), 444.

13.   *Peterburgskaia gazeta*, August 18, 1890.

14.   *Peterburgskaia gazeta*, September 7, 1890; *Bayan* 9 (1890).

15.   *Novoe vremia*, August 16, 1890; *Peterburgskaia gazeta*, August 16, 1890; *Novosti*, August 17, 1890. [Napoleone Cesi (1867–1961) was, in fact, the son of Beniamino Cesi (1845–1907), a much-respected pianist invited by Anton Rubinstein to direct the piano schools in St. Petersburg. Napoleone became a respected composer in his day. —Trans.]

16.   *Novoe vremia*, August 18, 1890; *Peterburgskaia gazeta*, August 18, 1890.

17.   [In the novel, Busoni appears under the name Bernard. —Trans.]

18.   Busoni's edition of Bach's *Well-Tempered Clavier.*

19.   A. Levitin [A. M. Schepelevski], three quotations from the short novel "V muzykal´noi burse" [In a Music School], *Sovetskaia muzyka* 2 (1936): 49–50.

20.   *Muzyka* 101 (1912).

21.   [Vasilii Il´ich Safonov (1852–1918) was the teacher of some of the best Russian pianists and composers, including Scriabin and Medtner and, eventually, a well-respected conductor, one of the first to never use a baton. —Trans.]

22.   F. Busoni, "Wert der Bearbeitung," in *Von der Einheit der Musik*, 147. ["Value of the Transcription," in *The Essence of Music*, 86. —Trans.]

23.   Edward J. Dent, "Ferruccio Busoni 'Italiano,'" *La Rassegna Musicale* 1 (January 1930).

24.   Busoni, "Wert der Bearbeitung," 147. ["Value of the Transcription," 85. —Trans.]

25.   Johann Sebastian Bach, *The Well-Tempered Clavier,* with a Foreword, Notes, and Exercises by Ferruccio Busoni, vol. I.

Chapter 3

1.   An amusing incident is connected with Busoni's Canadian trip. During one of his visits there, the artist was taken to court for giving a concert on a Sunday, thereby violating the sanctity of the Sabbath. However, upon hearing a number of witnesses, including a policeman, who testified that nothing unwholesome went on, except that "one person constantly played on the piano" ("too loudly," in the policeman's opinion), the judge found the defendant not guilty. See the details of this episode in *Zeitschrift für Musik* (February 1926) and *Muzyka i oktiabr´* 3 (1926).

2.   See more about this "war" in Chapter 5 and the Introduction by this author to Josef Hofmann's *Fortepiannaia igra* [*otvety na voprosy o fortepiannoi igre*] [Piano Playing: Answers to Questions about Playing the Piano] (Moscow: Muzgiz, 1961), 15–21.

3.   These were preceded by two other Liszt cycles (of two and three *Klavierabends*), given in 1904–5 (in Berlin, Paris, and London) and in 1909 (in Berlin).

4.   The following sources that describe Busoni's playing are quoted here and later: Books: Adolf Weissmann, *Berlin als Musikstadt* (Berlin: Schuster und Loeffler, 1911); Hugo Leichtentritt, *Ferruccio Busoni* (Leipzig: Breitkopf und Härtel, 1916); Walter Niemann, *Meister des Klaviers*, vol. 8 (Berlin: Schuster und Loeffler, 1919); Adolf Weissmann, *Der Virtuose*, vol. 2 (Berlin: Paul Cassirer, 1920); A. Dandelot, *Francis Planté* (Paris: Dupont, 1920); Gisella Selden-Goth, *Ferruccio Busoni* [*Der Versuch eines Porträts*] (Leipzig: E. P. Tal, 1922); Paul Bekker, *Klang und Eros* (Stuttgart: Deutsche Verlags-Anstalt, 1922); *25 Jahre neue Musik*, Jahrbuch der Universal-Edition (Vienna: Universal, 1926); Grigorii Prokofiev, *Igra na fortepiano* (Moscow: Muzsektor Gosizdata, 1928); Carl Adolf Martienssen, *Die individuelle Klaviertechnik auf der Grundlage des schöpferischen Klangwillens* (Leipzig: Breitkopf und Härtel, 1930); Siegfried Nadel, *Ferruccio Busoni* (Leipzig: Breitkopf und Härtel, 1931); Edward J. Dent, *Ferruccio Busoni* [*A Biography*] (London: Oxford University Press, 1933); Alfred Cortot, *Cours d'interprétation* (Paris: Legouix, 1934); Emil Debusmann, *Ferruccio Busoni* (Wiesbaden: Brucknerverlag, 1949); Stefan Zweig, *Begegnungen mit Menschen, Büchern, Städten*, vol. 2 (Berlin: S. Fischer, 1956); Carl Flesch, *The Memoirs of Carl Flesch* (London: Rockliff, 1957); Edwin Fischer, *Von den Aufgaben des Musikers* (Weisbaden: Insel, 1960); Artur Schnabel, *My Life and Music* (London: Longmans, 1961). Journals: *Die Musik* II/3, IV/10, V/6, 11, VI/10, VIII/9, IX/6, X/11, 13, XI/1, 4, 5, XII/7, XIII/11, XVI/12, XIX/11; *Neue Musikzeitung* XXIX/11; *Allgemeine Musikzeitung* 3, 6 (1909), 1, 44 (1910), 44, 45, 48 (1911); *Signale für die musikalische Welt* 2, 6 (1909), 44 (1910), 45, 51 (1911), 21 (1913); *Melos* (September 1924); *Musikblätter des Anbruch* (October 1924); *La Revue Musicale* (October 1924); *Le Courrier musical et théatral* (November 15, 1927); *Le Ménestrel* 35 (1931); *Russkaia muzykal´naia gazeta*, 7–8 (1903), 3–4, 7 (1905), 9 (1906), 2 (1910), 40, 45, 46, 48 (1912), 50 (1913); *Muzyka* 101, 105 (1912), 158 (1913); *Rampa i zhizn´* 43, 44, 48 (1912), 47, 48 (1913); *Teatr i iskusstvo* 44, 47 (1912), 47, 48 (1913); *Obozrenie teatrov* 1884, 1888, 1896, 1904 (1912), 2269, 2280 (1913); *Muzykal´naia kultura* 2 (1924); *Zhizn´ iskusstva* 33/1007 (1924). Newspapers: *Golos Moskvy*, October 12, 20, 21, November 1, 6, 7, 1912; November 26, 28, 1913; *Russkoe slovo*, October 12, November 6, 1912, November 27, 28, 1913; *Russkie vedomosti*, October 13, 20, 21, 2, 9, November 20, 1912; November 9, 28, 1913; *Moskauer Deutsche Zeitung*, October 14, 24, November 4, 1912; November 29, 1913; *Vechernee vremia*, October 18, 21, 24, 30, 31, November 7, 1912; November 14, 19, 30, 1913; *Rech,´* October 2, 8, 18, 25, 30, 1912; November 20, 28, 1913; *Birzhevie vedomosti* [evening edition], October 18, 30, 31, November 7, 1912; November 19, 30, 1913; *Novoe vremia*, October 19, 25, November 9, 1912; November 20, 1913; *Den´*, October 19, 27, 31, November 8, 11, 1912; November 20, December 1, 1913; *Utro Rossii*, October 21, 23, November 2, 1912, November 26, 1913; *Izvestiya*, August 12, 1924.

5.   [For the sources of the above quotes, the reader must refer to note 4. —Trans.]

6.   [The Chaconne from Bach's Partita for Unaccompanied Violin in D minor, BWV 1004. —Trans.]

7.   At that time, Rachmaninov limited himself primarily to the performance of his own compositions.

Chapter 4

1.   [Yuly Dmitrievich Engel (1868–1927), Russian critic, composer, and folklorist, student of Taneyev and Ippolitov-Ivanov. Among his accomplishments was the translation to the Russian of Hugo Riemann's *Musik-Lexikon*. —Trans.]

2.   Some idea of Busoni's octave technique can be acquired from his recording (on a roll produced by Welte-Mignon) of Liszt's "Reminiscences of Bellini's *Norma*."

3.   "Once," relates Martienssen, "Busoni, for a joke, broke a lump of sugar with one powerful stroke of the fourth finger." Martienssen, *Die individuelle Klaviertechnik*, 180.

4.   Julius Meyer-Greffe, *The Impressionists* (Moscow: [N.p].., 1913), 136–37.

5.   At Busoni's recitals, an unusually large number of professional pianists were always present, pencil and score in hand, in an attempt to discover and determine the "secrets" of his mastery. *Signale* 44 (1910); Weissmann, *Der Virtuose*, 136; Selden-Goth, *Fer-ruccio Busoni*, 31. "You had to watch how our pianists followed Busoni's playing with bated breath." *Rampa i zhizn* 43 (1912).

6.   *Jeu perlé* (Fr.)—"pearly playing." This term designates a specific, softly detached ("pearls on velvet," according to M. Glinka) manner of performing piano passages. John Field (1982–1837) was particularly renowned for it.

7.   Martienssen, *Die individuelle Klaviertechnik*, 116.

8.   [The sources for these quotes are listed in Chapter 3, note 4. —Trans.]

9.   [Alexander Sergeyevich Pushkin (1799–1837), universally considered to be the greatest of Russian poets. Music's debt to him includes the story of Tchaikovsky's *Eugene Onegin*, as well as the lyrics of numerous Russian art songs. —Trans.]

10.   [Alexander Bestuzhev (1797–1837), Russian poet, writer, and Decembrist. —Trans.]

11.   See epigraph [to the Introduction in this book].

Chapter 5

1.   [D'Albert's next paragraph is even more disturbing to the modern ear: "Bach knew nothing about the subtleties of passion, sorrow, and love, and he never thought to express them in music." One cannot help but wonder how much of this attitude was due to the expectations of the audience, and how much more to the sort of performance of this music the public would be likely to hear at that time. See a fascinating discussion of the topic in Richard Taruskin, *Text and Act* (New York: Oxford University Press, 1995), 142–43. Here is another instructive contemporary reaction to a Baroque performance, by Rimsky-Korsakov: "This evening, together with Glazunov, I listened to the Johannes Passion [St. John Passion of Bach] at the Lutheran Church. Beautiful music, but it is music of an altogether different age and to sit through an entire oratorio at the present time is impossible. I am convinced that not only I am bored, but everyone is, and if they say they enjoyed it then they're just lying through their teeth." Mark Iankovskii

et al., eds., *Rimskii-Korsakov: issledovaniia, materialy, pis'ma,* vol. 2 (Moscow: Izadatel'stvo Akademii nauk SSSR, 1954), 16–17. —Trans.]

2.   [Emil von Sauer (1862–1942) was a prolific composer, but is mainly remembered as one of the pianistic Titans of his generation. Eduard Schutt (1856–1933) is forgotten both as a composer and as a pianist today. The piano Etudes and a few encore-type works of Moritz Moszkowski (1854–1925) are still heard on the concert stage today. Ignaz Paderewski (1860–1941), the great pianist, editor, and politician, is currently enjoying somewhat of a revival as a composer. —Trans.]

3.   See St. Petersburg and Moscow newspapers and magazines of 1912: *Golos Moskvy,* October 21; *Rech',* November 2; *Rampa i zhizn'* 48; *Russkaia muzikal'naia gazeta* 48; *Moskauer Deutsche Zeitung* 244, and others.

4.   "She feels best in a turbulent sea, among raging waves, under rain and wind, in stormy weather, . . ." wrote Rudolf Breithaupt about Teresa Carreño (*Die Musik* 3/15). See also his article on d'Albert (*Die Musik* 3/18).

5.   [Rudolf Breithaupt (1873–1945), German pianist and author. His writings on the subject of pianism include his book *Die natürliche Klaviertechnik,* and several essays. —Trans.]

6.   Rudolf M. Breithaupt, "Alfred Reisenauer," *Die Musik* 3/8.

7.   See Busoni's foreword to Book I of the *Well-Tempered Clavier* of Bach, his *Sketch of a New Aesthetic* (p. 15 of the Russian edition), his "Aus der klassischen Walpurgisnacht," in *Von der Einheit der Musik,* 89–94, and others. [F. Busoni, *Sketch of a New Esthetic of Music,* trans. T. Baker (New York: Schirmer, 1911), 8. —Trans.]

8.   [From *Venezia e Napoli.* —Trans.]

9.   With this program Busoni began his 1912 *Klavierabends* in Moscow (October 19) and St. Petersburg (October 23). "The program of the first evening was of remarkable monumentality," noted the *Golos Moskvy* critic (October 20, 1912).

Chapter 6

1.   [The sources for these and the following quotes are listed in Chapter 3, note 4. —Trans.]

2.   [Felix Blumenfeld (1863–1931), noted pianist, professor of the St. Petersburg Conservatory, and teacher of, among others, Vladimir Horowitz and Heinrich Neuhaus. Mikhail Fabianovich Gnessin (1993–1957), composer and founder of the eponymous State Musical College. Boleslav Leopoldovich Yavorsky (1877–1942), Russian pianist, administrator, and musicologist. —Trans.]

3.   [That is, pre-1917. —Trans.]

4.   Textural changes (always stipulated) infiltrated Busoni's editions, as well. For example, note the change in the time signature of Fugue XXIV of Book I of Bach's *Well-Tempered Clavier,* the substitution of two fugues from Book I for two fugues from Book II, and so on.

5.   F. Busoni, *Von der Einheit der Musik,* 54. Busoni, *Briefe an seine Frau* (Zurich: Rotapfel, 1935), 21–22. [In English, see "The Requirements Necessary for a Pianist," and "Rules for Practicing the Piano," in *The Essence of Music,* 80–81. —Trans.]

6.   To the end of his days A. B. Goldenweiser could not forget the "silver trumpet," suddenly piercing the sonority of the Chorale Preludes in E-flat Major ("Wachet auf, ruft uns die Stimme") and G Major ("Nun freut euch, lieben Christen"). [Alexander Borisovich Goldenweiser (1875–1961), Soviet pianist, teacher, writer, and composer, student of

Ziloti, Pabst, Arensky, Ippolitov-Ivanov, and Taneyev, was noted for his academic playing—precise technique and fidelity to the text. As a professor at the Moscow Conservatory, he was the teacher of such prominent pianists as Bashkirov, Tatiana Nikolaeva, and Dmitry Kabalevsky. —Trans.]

7. According to Otto Klemperer, the performance of this sonata was "the most remarkable" of Busoni's interpretations. Otto Klemperer, *Erinnerungen an Gustav Mahler* [*und andere autobiographische Skizzen*] (Zurich: Atlantis, 1960), 46.

Chapter 7

1. F. Busoni, "Selbst-Rezension," *Von der Einheit der Musik*, 175. [In English, see Busoni, "Self-Criticism," in *The Essence of Music*, 46. —Trans.]

2. Busoni, *Entwurf einer neuen Ästhetik der Tonkunst*, 7. [In English, see Busoni, *Sketch of a New Esthetic of Music*, 4 (footnote). —Trans.]

3. [The scene to which Busoni and Kogan allude is found in the lesser-known third act of Goethe's *Faust* (III/ii). Here Faust has brought back to life and fathered a son upon Helen of Troy, the most beautiful of women. Euphorion, this son, who represents the spirit of Romantic poetry, senses the suffering of battling armies across the sea and feels an irresistible longing for death. He throws himself into the air and falls to earth, his body disappearing and his soul rising skyward like a comet, but his clothes and his lyre remain on the ground. Helen rushes to embrace her fallen son's garments and likewise disappears, also leaving her clothes behind. Unlike Euphorion's, though, her clothing turns into clouds, which carry Faust away. At this point, Forkiada (or Phorkyas, depending on the translation), who has previously been masquerading as a family friend, reveals himself to be Mephisto and offers the above-cited commentary. Goethe, *Faust*, trans. Walter Kaufmann (Garden City, N.Y.: Doubleday, 1961), 41. —Trans.]

4. Busoni, *Entwurf einer neuen Ästhetik der Tonkunst*, 10. [Busoni, *Sketch*, 7. Translation of the poem is borrowed from T. Baker's translation of the *Sketch*. —Trans.]

5. F. Busoni, "Routine," in *Von der Einheit der Musik*, 168. [Busoni, "Routine," in *The Essence of Music*, 185. —Trans.]

6. Even such an orthodox representative of musical academism as A. B. Goldenweiser admits this: "A musical composition created by the composer is recorded by him, in a more or less approximate form, on paper with the aid of musical notation. . . . It is not a painting." A. Goldenweiser, "On Musical Performance," in *Voprosy muzykal′nogo iskusstva* [Questions of Musical Art] (Moscow: Muzgiz, 1958), 3.

7. See Alexander Ziloti, *Moi vospominaniia o F. Liste* [My Reminiscences of F. Liszt] (St. Petersburg: N.p., 1911), 30.

8. "A piece of music is always many-faceted: today it is one way, tomorrow—another, like the sea," insisted Scriabin. "On a clear day, play it like this, but if it rains play it differently," Rubinstein advised Hofmann. Josef Hofmann, *Fortepiannaia igra*, 69.

9. Busoni, *Entwurf einer neuen Ästhetik*, 20–22. [Busoni, *Sketch*, 15–17. —Trans.]

10. Busoni, "Wert der Bearbeitung," in *Von der Einheit der Musik*, 150. [Busoni, "Value of the Transcription," in *The Essence of Music*, 88. —Trans.]

11. Hofmann, *Fortepiannaia igra*, 67.

12. Specifically, Rubinstein was faulted for changing the author's nuances and tempos, "abrupt changes of tempo" in the first movement of Beethoven's Sonata Op. 53, and so on.

13. See *Signale* 6 (1909), *Allgemeine Muzikzeitung* 1 (1910), and others.

14. Bernard Gavoty, *Alfred Cortot* (Geneva: Kister, 1955), 12.

15.   [Pablo Casals (1876–1973), the famous cellist. —Trans.]

16.   H. M. Korredor [J. M. Corredor], *Besedy s Pablo Kazal'som* [Conversations with Pablo Casals] (Leningrad: Muzgiz, 1960), 251–55.

17.   [Carl Flesch (1873–1944), great violinist and teacher, author of pedagogical books, in which he argued the violinist must be an artist, rather than merely a virtuoso. —Trans.]

18.   See Carl Flesch, *The Memoirs of Carl Flesch* (London: Rockliff, 1957), 80.

19.   [Lev Lebedinsky (1904–92), Russian musicologist, a fascinating figure, known as both a friend of Dmitry Shostakovich and an agent of the Cheka, the Bolshevik secret police, as well as a leader of the Russian Association of Proletarian Musicians, which officially opposed Shostakovich!—Trans.]

20.   [Feodor Ivanovich Chaliapin (1873–1938), the legendary Russian bass. —Trans.]

21.   See *Sovetskaia muzyka* 3 (1959), 35–37. Also [Emanuil] Kaplan, "Working on *Aleko*," *Sovetskaia muzyka* 2 (1963), 84–85. The above applies not only to musical performers. I am not just talking about V. E. Meyerhold, whose artistic principles had much in common with Busoni's, but even those actors who seemingly belonged to the opposing camp. Thus, V. I. Kachalov was once asked if he has the right to substitute one word for another in the text. "I do it," the actor replied, "sometimes I suffer for it, but, nevertheless, I still don't think that the text is an unbreakable law for the reader." As an example, Kachalov mentions his performance of Bagritsky's *Duma pro Opanasa:* "I omitted several episodes, moved the epilogue, put the words of one personage into the mouth of another, and, in my opinion, the poem became more dramatic, more convincing." *Sovetskoe iskusstvo,* December 5, 1935. [Vsevolod Emilevich Meyerhold (1874–1940) was one of the seminal figures in the world of Russian theater, a leader of the experimental, innovative, and avant-garde movement. In the 1930s, when Joseph Stalin began his campaign of assuming complete control of the arts, Meyerhold's works were proclaimed alien to the Soviet people, he was arrested and brutally tortured, and executed by firing squad. Kogan is able to mention Meyerhold in a complimentary way, however, since in 1955 he was cleared of all charges during the wave of de-Stalinization. Vasily Kachalov (1875–1948) was an outstanding stage and film actor, whose career spanned both the prerevolutionary and the Soviet periods. Eduard Bagritsky (1895–1934) was a poet of revolutionary ardor, whose lines were required study for generations of Soviet school children. His *Duma pro Opanasa* (Lay of Opanas), a folk epic about a peasant in the Russian Civil War, was proclaimed a masterpiece of revolutionary Romanticism. In retrospect, however, this attempt to combine Romantic concepts of freedom and nature with Soviet Realism was not wholly successful. One cannot help but wonder whether Kachalov's "liberties" with this text might not in fact have been artistically necessary. There are no reports of any textual "liberties" in Kachalov's extremely successful appearances as Hamlet. —Trans.]

22.   [Czerny's many "sins" in this edition, such as changed notes and the famous added measure in the C-Major Prelude are far too well documented to discuss in detail here. Hans von Bülow described it as "an adulteration of spiritual nourishment." Nevertheless, one simply must point out that Czerny's was the very first published edition of the Preludes and Fugues! In addition, according to Czerny himself, his editing represents the way Beethoven supposedly played them. There is undeniable historical value and curiosity here. What is equally curious and inexplicable is that Czerny's edition is still published by Schirmer today and used by unsuspecting pianists. In my own pedagogical practice, I have found myself, more than once, having to explain to new undergraduate students that it would behoove them to relegate their copy to the farthest reaches of their bookshelf and relearn their Preludes and Fugues from a different edition!—Trans.]

23.   Busoni, *Entwurf einer neuen Ästhetik,* 31. [Busoni, *Sketch,* 22. —Trans.]

24.   *Zeitschrift für Musik* 12 (1932), 1058.

25.   Busoni, *Von der Einheit der Musik*, 348. [Busoni, "Concerning Harmony," in *The Essence of Music*, 27. —Trans.]

26.   Korredor, *Besedy s Pablo Kazal´som*, 254.

27.   F. Busoni, Foreword to his edition of the *Well-Tempered Clavier*, Book I.

28.   See Foreword to Busoni's edition of J. S. Bach's Inventions; note to Two-Part Invention no. 3; notes to Three-Part Inventions no. 1 (note 3), no. 2 (note 3), no. 4 (note 2), no. 6 (note 7), and no. 15 (note 1); notes to Prelude I (note 1) and Fugue V (note 2) of Book I of the *Well-Tempered Clavier;* note to the transcription of the E-Minor Organ Fugue (second supplement to Book I of *Well-Tempered Clavier* in Busoni's edition).

Chapter 8

1.   It is necessary to mention that this review was written after that comparatively unsuccessful concert during which Busoni (as previously noted in Chapter 6), apparently played "without enthusiasm"; during other concerts, according to this and many other critics, "enthusiasm" and "pathos" were fully present. Nevertheless, as the following citations illustrate, the reviewers of these concerts, too, often agree with the main point of this article. [As in the previous chapters, the sources for quotations describing Busoni's playing are listed in Chapter 3, note 4. —Trans.]

2.   In all fairness, it is necessary to remark that opinions on the subject of the "thunderousness" of Busoni's sound were not unanimous. Certain critics insisted that, on the contrary, Busoni possesses "huge," "unbelievable" power of attack, surpasses Hofmann in "massiveness," "organ-like resonance" of sonority. L. Sabaneev explained this impression by the artistry of the pianist, his ability to create an *illusion* of power: "Busoni has a magic gift that compels one to believe in its power, even if it is not there." [Leonid Leonidovich Sabaneev (1881–1968), the Russian musicologist and composer, student of Taneyev, was an ardent follower of contemporary trends, a champion of Scriabin. He worked as a correspondent and critic for many Russian and foreign periodicals. Trained as a mathematician, Sabaneev probed the more scientific aspects of music, such as harmony, rhythm, pitch, and the relationship of sound and color. —Trans.]

3.   [F. Busoni, "Letter to the Editor," *Signale* 4 (January 1909): 125. —Trans.]

4.   "Ah, tender hearts!" Busoni writes elsewhere, "Any charlatan can move them to tears." F. Busoni, *Von der Einheit der Musik*, 224. Heine comes to mind: "That dramatic writer is praised who can evoke tears from the public. He shares this talent with a simple onion."

5.   Busoni, *Von der Einheit der Musik*, 99–101. [In English, see F. Busoni, "Open Reply," in *The Essence of Music*, 179. —Trans.]

6.   See Foreword to Book I of the *Well-Tempered Clavier*, Busoni's edition. Compare Liszt's complaints regarding "effeminacy and sentimentality" in piano playing, "agreeable" poetry, "having a sedating effect on the listener." P. D. Seletskii, *Zapiski* [Notes] (Kiev: N.p., 1884), 91.

7.   Rimsky-Korsakov's word (in a letter to [Anatoly] Liadov).

8.   Note 1 to Prelude X of Book I, *Well-Tempered Clavier.*

9.   "Emotionthought," according to the later terminology of Y. B. Vakhtangov. [Yevgeny Bagrationovich Vakhtangov (1883–1922), the renowned Russian director, was one of Konstantin Stanislavsky's most prominent students, and a practitioner of The Method. He was also greatly influenced by the work of Vsevolod Meyerhold (see more in Chapter 7), but his style combined the avant-garde approach of the former with a more naturalistic

approach. Vakhtangov died of tuberculosis in 1922 and thus was spared Stalin's purges and repression of the arts. —Trans.]

10.   Romain Rolland (in Book IV, Volume 1 of *The Enchanted Soul*) gives the following description of the "enervating sweetness of life" of the contemporary society: "Kindness, sweetness, dissolution—the aroma of water lilies. . . . People found pleasure in this heavy, soft, warm, nauseating atmosphere of beautiful apples rotting in the basement. . . . They called themselves 'Tolstovtsi' and savored the overwrought language of Scriabin and the flexible entrechats of the hermaphrodite Nijinsky." *The Collected Works of Romain Rolland*, vol. 8, *Enchanted Soul* (Leningrad: Vremya, 1933), 253. [Romain Rolland (1866–1944), French writer, winner of the Nobel Prize for Literature and an ardent Communist, was a complex figure. He viewed Communism as an almost spiritual movement, and was unable to reconcile this with the reality of historical events. Although he called Stalin the greatest man alive, acted as the Soviet Union's public defender and unofficial ambassador, and visited Moscow on Maxim Gorky's invitation in 1935, at the height of Stalin's purge trials, Rolland eventually became uncomfortable with Stalin's repressions. The seven-novel cycle *The Enchanted Soul* (1922–33) centers on a character that becomes disillusioned with material possessions and struggles to find her spiritual freedom, eventually becoming active in defending the Soviet Union. "Tolstovtsi" were followers of Leo Tolstoy's (the author of *War and Peace*) spiritual and religious principles, which were an impossible blend of Christianity and Buddhism. Vaslav Nijinsky (1890–1950) was the greatest male dancer of the twentieth century, and ballet's first modernist choreographer. He pioneered the leading roles in *Petrouchka, Rite of Spring, Afternoon of a Faun*, and many more. Nijinsky was noted, among many things, for the intense eroticism of his dancing. Why Rolland slurs him as "hermaphroditical" is unclear to this writer. —Trans.]

11.   Notes to Prelude XVI of the *Well-Tempered Clavier*, Book I.

12.   Foreword to the Little Preludes, Inventions, Book I of the *Well-Tempered Clavier;* notes to Two-Part Inventions, no. 6, Three-Part Inventions, nos. 7, 11, 15, Preludes X, XI, XVI, XXIII and Fugues III, XI, XVII of the *Well-Tempered Clavier*, Book I; the first appendix to the same volume (Russian edition, p. 203).

13.   Pensively, but not sluggishly; softly, but seriously; with a somewhat severe feeling, seriously, sternly, decisively, resolutely, energetically, boldly, with firmness, robustly, lively, freshly (German and Italian).

14.   Auguste Boissier, *Liszt-pédagogue* (Paris: Honoré Champion, 1927), 38, 49, 78.

15.   "I, too, if I wanted to, could play with such velvety paws." W. Lenz, *Die grossen Pianoforte-Virtuosen unserer Zeit aus persönlicher Bekanntschaft* (Berlin: [N.p.], 1872), 104; V. V. Stasov, "Liszt, Schumann and Berlioz in Russia," edition of *Russkaia muzykal'naia gazeta*, n.d.: 27.

16.   [Louis Spohr (1784–1859) was a leading violin virtuoso, composer, and conductor. Very little of his prolific output is still played today, with the notable exception of his fifteen violin concertos, which are still the mainstay of the pedagogical repertoire. —Trans.]

17.   See note to Prelude VI of Book I of the *Well-Tempered Clavier.*

18.   J. S. Bach, *Well-Tempered Clavier*, Book I, ed. Busoni (Moscow: Muzgiz, 1941), 35–36, 203; see also Busoni's Preface to the Bach Inventions.

19.   From which it does not at all follow that Busoni, as some think, never resorted to "singing on the piano." Granted, in the well-known note to Prelude VIII of Book I, *Well-Tempered Clavier*, he remarks that "performance on piano of sustained melodies is not only difficult, but actually unnatural" because the "nature" of the piano does not allow sustaining of sound in the way of voice or violin. However, these difficulties," continues the same note, "may be partially overcome, partially smoothed-out," which is the task of the "touch"; the author goes on to suggest how. Nevertheless, he suggests as models neither the

human voice nor the violin, but, instead, the "softer wind instruments" and "soft organ registers." Note to Prelude XXIII and the First Appendix to the same volume.

20.   Malwine Brée, *Die Grundlage der Methode Leschetizky* (Mainz: B. Schott's Söhne, 1903), 20.

21.   Bach, *Well-Tempered Clavier,* Book I, 67.

22.   Busoni convincingly reinforces his position with a reference to the later two-piano version of the same fantasy, which "comes closer to Mozart's original in its transparency, spontaneity, and avoidance of the pathetic."

23.   See notes 3, 30, 32, and 40.

24.   "The playing of Liszt's students does not paint a clear picture of the manner of his own playing. His playing, as witnessed by the contemporaries, was remarkable for its radiance, which illuminated all around it. It was, so to speak, penetrating. Perhaps, Busoni's playing most resembled it." Alfred Cortot, *Cours d'interprétation* (Paris: Legouix, 1934), 154.

25.   Artur Schnabel, *My Life and Music* (London: Longmans, 1961), 64.

26.   *Signale* 21 (1913).

27.   Nikolai Gogol, *The Marriage,* trans. Eric Bentley, in *The Modern Theater,* vol. 5 (Garden City, NY: Doubleday, 1957), 35.

Chapter 9

1.   From which it does not follow that Busoni never used "wavy" phrasing and nuances. He did use them—as much as he used *legato, cantabile,* and so on; but he used them much more seldom than other pianists, and not as the guiding principle.

2.   Among "expressions of questionable taste" such as arpeggiated chords, Busoni also names another of Leschetizky's favorite devices—bass notes played slightly before the melody. [Modern performance practice scholarship does not completely agree with Busoni on the subject of arpeggiated chords. Donnington, for one, considers the "degree of (arpeggiation) so general" in Baroque music as to need no further discussion. Other authorities, on the other hand, ascribe the prevalence of "broken-textured" or *brisé* style to the peculiarities of lute and harpsichord technique, which required spreading, or prolongation of sound on longer notes, which would otherwise fade out too quickly, something that is not necessary on the modern piano. Another possible consideration in Busoni's defense is that our contemporary knowledge of Baroque performance practice is based primarily on the evidence of four great books: Johann Joachim Quantz's *Versuch einer Anweisung die Flöte traversiere zu spielen* (1752), C. P. E. Bach's *Versuch über die wahre Art das Clavier zu spielen* (1753), L. Mozart's *Versuch einer gründlichen violinschule* (1756), and J. F. Agricola's *Anleitung zur Singekust* (1757), books that might reflect either their authors' Baroque training, or the new Rococo influences of their milieu. For detailed information, see Robert Donnington, *The Interpretation of Early Music* (New York: Norton, 1992), 277–80; Peter Williams, "Keyboards," in *Performance Practice: Music After 1600,* ed. Howard Mayer Brown and Stanley Sadie (New York: Norton, 1990), 30–32. —Trans.]

3.   Very measured, without expression and any freedom; rather quickly, but measured; with measured motion, phrasing clearly; rather quickly, with rhythmic accent; quietly, quietly animated, in equal motion, equally, measured, rhythmically, articulately, markedly, well in tempo, with firm rhythm, with precise touch, together, not arpeggiated, no acceleration (do not hurry), no deceleration (do not drag!). The frequency of *negative* commands (*ma, non*) is especially striking, both here and in Busoni's other notes. The polemical intent against the prevailing performance practice of his day is palpable.

4.   See Busoni's editions of the Little Preludes (foreword), Two-Part Inventions (Foreword, Inventions, nos. 1, 2, 4, 5, 6, 7, 9, 11, 12, 14), Three-Part Inventions (nos. 2, 15), Book I of the *Well-Tempered Clavier* (Preludes I, II, IV, V, X, XI, XVI; Fugues V, XIII, XX, XXIV; First Appendix) of Bach, and of Liszt's *Don Juan* (notes 3, 50); Busoni's transcriptions of the E-Minor Organ Fugue and the C-Major Organ Toccata of Bach and the Paganini-Liszt Etudes, nos. 5 and 6 (Variations 3, 5, 8).

5.   See Busoni's editions of the Two-Part Inventions (nos. 1, 4, 12), Three-Part Inventions (nos. 1, 8, 10, 11, 13, 14), and Book I of the *Well-Tempered Clavier* of Bach (Preludes III, X, XIV, Fugues V, IX, XI, XIII, XVII, XXI).

6.   Notes to Three-Part Invention, no. 11 and to Prelude VIII from Book I of the *Well-Tempered Clavier* of Bach and the First Appendix to the latter volume (Muzgiz edition, pp. 168 and 203).

7.   Without getting louder, without getting softer, suddenly softer, suddenly louder, softer without transition (Italian and German).

8.   For example, the Bach scholar Albert Schweitzer seconds Busoni in protesting against "garish dynamics," "wavy movement of emotion," "continual *crescendos*" peppering Czerny's edition of the *Well-Tempered Clavier*, "countless" *pianissimos, pianos, mezzo fortes, fortes, crescendos, decrescendos* "reinforcing" the usual performance of Bach's music, the "final *diminuendo*," which is played "everywhere out of habit" and is "one of the greatest enemies of stylistic performance of Bach." In the works of this master, he writes, repeating Busoni nearly verbatim, "*piano* and *forte* never blend seamlessly. A certain volume prevails during an entire segment, from which the next one will clearly differ, illuminated by a distinct sonority. . . . The attempt to finish with a *diminuendo* a cadence that concludes a *forte* episode, or to increase a section in *piano* in order to smoothly pass into a *forte* constitutes a false modernization. The gradations of power would not then be arranged, as necessary, in terraces, and the whole fabric of the structure would be destroyed." Albert Schweitzer, *J. S. Bach* (Moscow: Muzgiz, 1934), 118–22, 130. In recent years, pianists, including an interpreter of Bach as great as Glenn Gould, again tend toward a more "expressive" interpretation, based, however, on subtle development of very different aspects (agogics, intonation) than those emphasized in the time of Leschetitzky. [Some of Glenn Gould's comments, one must admit, are rather "Leschetitzkian" in nature. The five-voice Fugue in C-sharp Minor (Book I, *Well-Tempered Clavier*) is a "melancholic rumination" preceded by "its languorous and wistful Prelude." One of the Goldberg Variations possesses a "languorous atmosphere of an almost Chopinesque mood piece." The proof of the pudding is, however, in the eating, and Gould's playing is far removed from the excesses of the past generation. Glenn Gould, *The Glenn Gould Reader*, ed. and with a foreword by Tim Page (New York: Knopf, 1984), 21, 27. —Trans.]

9.   Busoni's note to Prelude XXIII of Book I of the *Well-Tempered Clavier*.

10.   The habit, much loved by the "academicians," of bringing out now this voice, now another, so warmly—and so justly—condemned by Schweitzer, [Wanda] Landowska, and other musicians, does not solve, and even accentuates this defect: like knolls on the surface of a swamp.

11.   See my article "Pianisticheskii put´ Lista" [Liszt's Pianistic Path], *Sovetskaia muzyka* 9 (1956) and my book *Rabota pianista* [The Pianist's Work] (Moscow: Muzgiz, 1963), 65–67.

12.   Curiously, more nuances become available, not fewer, as it seemed to the critics; in this, as in many other cases, Goethe's famous aphorism comes to mind: *mastery* arises from *limitations*.

13.   [As in the previous chapters, the sources of quotes describing Busoni's playing are listed in Chapter 3, note 4. —Trans.]

14. [Maria Barinova, pianist and composer, was a professor at St. Petersburg's conservatory, and a student of Hoffman, Rimsky-Korsakov, and Busoni. —Trans.]

15. M. N. Barinova, *Vospominaniia o Gofmane i Busoni* [Reminiscences of Hofmann and Busoni] (Moscow: Muzyka, 1964), 63, 81.

16. That painting and sculpture were close to the artist is confirmed by the fact that he was, according to Weissman, "at home in the visual arts" (*Die Musik* 12/XVI); wrote articles on architecture ("Gedanken über den Ausdruck in der Architektur"); drew caricatures, sketches of decorations and scenic constructions (some have been published in *Von der Einheit der Musik* . . .); and supplied his editions of others' and his own compositions with explanatory drawings (see, for example, the graphs and pictures to the Little Prelude No. 3 and Fugue I from Book I of the *Well-Tempered Clavier* of Bach and his own *Fantasia contrappuntistica*). By the way, one of Busoni's two sons—Rafaello—is a noted artist.

17. [Mikhail Fabianovich Gnessin (1883–1957), the Russian composer, musicologist, and teacher, student of Rimsky-Korsakov and Liadov. As the director of the Gnessin State Institute for Musical Education in Moscow, he taught Khachaturian and Khrennikov. Gnessin's affiliations were with the Russian symbolist movement. —Trans.]

18. *Muzykal'nyi sovremennik* (November 1915).

19. Martienssen, *Die individuelle Klaviertechnik*, 116.

20. "It is easy to accuse Rimsky-Korsakov of "mosaic-like" construction, of a lack of dialectical development and other such sins," writes B. Zukkerman in his article "On the Story and Musical Language of the Opera *Sadko*," "but it would also be necessary to explain how it is that the music of *Sadko*, garishly motley-colored, often obviously sewn together with white thread, sometimes put together out of small bits . . . how this music does not disturb the unity of the musical impression, and even, on the contrary, often possesses captivating smoothness and continuity." *Sovetskaia muzyka* 3 (1933): 66.

21. The architectural approach to music should not be mistaken for "empty form." That would be the Formalist position. The task is not, as many essays still do, to contrast "picturesqueness" to "activity," "sculptural clarity"—to "expressivity," "colors"—to "ideas," but to view the former as expressions of the latter, as shapes that embody the content. [The dreaded word "Formalist" makes its first appearance. No work of musical history, criticism, or musicology of the period, of course, would be complete without an impassioned defense of the subject from the very suggestion of this taint. See the Preface to this book for a detailed discussion of the term's meaning and history. —Trans.]

22. This was the quality that attracted those listeners to the Italian pianist who demanded something more of art than touching elegies or empty noise; this was the very reason why, according to M. I. Ulyanova, Lenin spoke so enthusiastically about Busoni. Vladimir Ilyich, who we know disliked both sentimental "sighing" and "external bravura," perfectly perceived and deeply felt not only the intellectual, but also the emotional "charge" of Busoni's playing, which was distinguished by "some special loftiness and boiling inspiration," that had a great effect on Lenin: "When I heard Busoni," he says, "I was so moved that, believe me, I slept poorly that night. . . ." *Pravda Ukrainy*, April 21, 1961. [Maria Ulyanova was one of V. I. Lenin's sisters, an early partner in his revolutionary activities and an important figure in Soviet affairs, especially after Lenin's death. This is the first of those paragraphs Kogan inserts into the book in order to please the censor. The personal esthetic views of the Glorious Leader are, obviously, the greatest and the final arbiter of artistic worth. A few years earlier, the Glorious Leader quoted would have been Stalin. Now, the Soviet author must find a more uncontroversial source of approval for his subject. —Trans.]

Chapter 10

1.   [The invention of recording and reproduction by means of piano rolls by Edwin Welte and Karl Bockisch was perfected by 1903. The Welte method of reproduction is vastly different from the regular foot-operated player piano, which merely plays a string of notes punched into a player roll, assigning the operator full control of dynamics and tempo. The Welte-Mignon Reproducing Piano is electrically operated, recreating the actual touch, tone color, and expression of the pianist. Despite the high prices of the player apparatus and the individual rolls, they were extremely popular, and attracted the greatest artists of the day. Among those who recorded for Welte-Mignon were d'Albert, Carreño, Debussy, Dohnanyi, de Falla, Glazunov, Granados, Grieg, Landowska, Lesche-tizky, Lhevinne, Mahler, Paderewski, Ravel, Schnabel, Scriabin, and many others. Arthur Ord-Hume, *Player Piano* (New York: A. S. Barnes, 1970); Harvey Roehl, *Player Piano Treasury* (N.p.: Vestal Press, 1973. —Trans.]

2.   Acoustical recording, even today, can give only an approximate impression of a pianist's playing, much inferior to the impression of the same performer in a concert hall. This is especially true in regard to those artists whose playing—due to the qualities of the individual psyche, techniques of sound production, or heavy, saturated pedaling—is, so to speak, "unphonogenic."

3.   [Welte's recording methods are shrouded in mystery. Welte himself, appar-ently always claimed that his recording system was fully automatic. The recording piano had a trough of mercury placed beneath the keyboard, into which a light carbon prong suspended from the bottom of each key would dip as the key was being pressed. That enabled the recording of exact force and duration of each note. The resulting piano roll would then activate the recreating apparatus placed directly over the keyboard of a piano, and the recorded composition would be played by "the Phantom Hands of a thousand immortal pianists." Ord-Hume, *Player Piano*, 96–97. —Trans.]

4.   [Annette Essipoff, or Anna Esipova, was, by all accounts, a remarkable pianist, one of the greatest of her day, and, in the opinion of many critics, second only to Liszt. She married Leschetizky in 1880 and separated from him in 1893, but they seemed to have remained friends and he continued to support her career. —Trans.]

5.   *Novoe vremia*, November 9, 1912. Nevertheless, not everyone concurred with this verdict; in the opinion of another reviewer, Busoni played this piece "so that it seemed as though one heard not just a pianist, but a magnificent orchestra and a singer." *Obozrenie teatrov* 2280 (1913).

6.   "This is how he swore his love to me, too!" sings Gilda, hearing the Duke's "decla-rations of love" to Maddalena.

7.   Love's beautiful maiden / I am a slave to your charms; / With one, just one word you can / Soothe my sufferings. / Come hear how quickly / Beats my heart.

8.   In Stanislavsky's words. *Besedi K. S. Stanislavskogo* [The Lectures of K. S. Stanislav-sky], 2d ed. (Moscow: VTO, 1947), 105. [This, of course, is the great Konstantin Stanislav-sky, the theater director whose ideas about acting are still at the core of actor training today. —Trans.]

9.   Ha, Ha, I laugh from the heart / That lying costs you so little.

10.   All measurements of the Welte-Mignon rolls used in this chapter were made in 1940 at my request by Professor S. S. Skrebkov of the Moscow Conservatory with the aid of M. M. Gurovich, then a research assistant in the Department of History and Theory of Pianism at the Conservatory.

11.   *Muzyka* 105 (1912).

12. Victor Hugo, *Cromwell* (Paris: J. Hetzel, n.d.), Foreword, 29, 43.

13. Ibid., Act III, 186.

14. [*Mazeppa*, Etude d'exécution transcendante No. 4, also the symphonic poem of the same name. The symphonic poem *Ce qu'on entend sur la montagne*, also known as the *Mountain Symphony* or *Bergsymphonie*, 1948. —Trans.]

15. [The play describes the adventures of the French king Francis I. However, the censors suspected that it also contained insults directed at the current king, Louis-Philippe, and banned it after one performance. Hugo instigated a lawsuit to permit performances and lost, but gained much celebrity as the defender of the freedom of speech. The play was banned for another fifty years. —Trans.]

16. This anagrammatic pseudonym concealed the somewhat successful Hungarian pianist and salon composer Count Hardegen (1834–67).

17. December 15, 1858.

18. Leonid Andreyev, "F. I. Chaliapin," *Complete Works* (St. Petersburg: A. F. Marks, 1913), vol. 6, 245–46. [Kogan quotes Feodor Chaliapin's reminiscences of his incomparable performance of Mussorgsky's *Song of the Flea*. More correctly titled *Mephistopheles's Song in Auerbach's Cellar*, the text of the song comes from the Second Act of Goethe's *Faust*. In the scene, Mephistopheles tells the drunken patrons the story of a king who raised a flea to the status of a favorite, forcing all to obey and genuflect before it. —Trans.]

19. E. T. A. Hoffmann was one of Busoni's favorite authors. His opera *Die Brautwahl* is based on one of Hoffmann's novels; Busoni also wrote an introduction to Hoffmann's *Fantastic Stories*, reprinted in *Von der Einheit der Musik*. [*Die Brautwahl* (1908–10) was first performed in Hamburg on April 12, 1912. The essay is reprinted in English as the "Introduction to E. T. A. Hoffmann's *Phantastische Geschichten*," in *The Essence of Music*, 186. —Trans.]

20. "I adore the grotesque . . . above the totality of seriousness, comedy reigns," he writes. *The Collected Works* of *Gustav Flaubert*, vol. 7 (Moscow: Goslitizdat, 1937), 174.

21. "Life is a burlesque catastrophe, the horrible in the guise of the comic, a carnival mask on bloodied cheeks." Anatole France, *Histoire comique* (Paris: Calmann-Lévy, n.d.), 81.

22. "This impression of automatism that the sight of M. de Bligneul causes in me has gradually extended to everything around me. The town of P . . . appears to me entirely like one of those large toy boxes given as gifts to children, which contain houses, trees, people, animals. . . . My aunt Chaltray strikes me as an old doll, found at the bottom of an armoire in a little town store. Mariette also seems to me a droll grotesque. Other people, equally clowns! I see their uneven, angular, illogical movements of mannequins and marionettes." (Henri de Régnier, *Provintsial'noe razvlechenie* (N.p.: Mysl,' 1926), 127–28. [The translation from the French is mine. There is no published English version. The original is *Le Divertissement Provincial* (Paris: Paul Dupont, 1925), 201. —Trans.]

23. "All human speech, all wisdom is no more than the theater of mechanical puppets." *The Complete Works of Romain Rolland*, vol. 1, *Jean Cristoff*, book 1, *Morning* (Leningrad: Vremya, 1930), 150.

24. "Only I and the Tsaritsa were real here," sings the Astrologer at the end of *The Golden Cockerel* [i.e. Rimsky-Korsakov's fairy-tale opera. —Trans.].

25. I mean the progression in his work that leads from *Polichinelle* through the *Rat-Catcher* to the *Symphonic Dances*. [*Polichinelle*, from *Morceaux de Fantasie*, Op. 3, 1892; *Krisolov*, Op. 38, 1916; *Symphonic Dances*, Op. 45, 1940. The three are among Rachmaninov's most interesting masterpieces. Instead of sweeping Romantic melodicity, there is profound tragedy and drama concealed in grotesquerie, in addition to symbolist poetry in the song *Krisolov* (*The Rat-Catcher*, or *Pied Piper*). —Trans.]

26.   [Aleksandr Aleksandrovich Blok (1880–1921) was one of Russia's greatest poets, often compared with Alexander Sergeyevich Pushkin. He developed his own symbolist style, which had a profound influence on the next generation of Russian poets. —Trans.]

27.   [Leonid Andreyev (1871–1919), Expressionist and Symbolist playwright, was discovered by Maxim Gorky and hailed as a new star in Russia. However, unlike Gorky or Blok, he could not accept the Revolution and left. He wrote little after 1914, which may be why his name remained acceptable under the Soviet regime. —Trans.]

28.   "That other masquerade, perpetual, unstoppable, diurnal, in which we, involuntary *pagliacci*, unknowingly, costume ourselves in what we appear to be." *Enrico IV*, III. "The *pagliaccio* got up—the little face, the porcelain hands—it was a pity to look at what became of them: hands without fingers, face without the nose, all cracked, all shattered, the broken bellows in the chest pierced the red satin blouse and popped out" (*Each in His Own Way*, II). See Luigi Pirandello, *Obnazhennye maski* [Naked Masks] (Moscow: Akademiia, 1932), 350, 569.

29.   [Maurice Maeterlinck (1862–1949), Belgian playwright and poet, is best known to musicians today as the writer of *Pelléas and Mélisande*, a work of mysticism and symbolism on which Debussy's opera is based. Later in his life Maeterlinck began to gravitate toward marionette theater in his search to give perfect expression to the symbolic static nature of his drama, which live actors, in his view, could not possibly do. —Trans.]

30.   [Edward Gordon Craig (1872–1966), actor, director and set designer, was the leader of the modernist movement in theater. Like Maeterlinck, he began to gravitate toward using puppets instead of actors, to achieve the greatest possible control of his productions. In his 1910 article "A Note on Masks" he writes, "There is only one actor—nay one man (*sic*) who has the soul of the dramatic poet, and who has ever served as the true and loyal interpreter of the poet. This is the marionette." J. M. Walton, *Craig on Theatre* (London: Methuen, 1983). —Trans.]

Chapter 11

1.   [Gottfried Galston (1879–1950), a pupil of Leschetizky, was considered a player of keen analytical powers and intellectual grasp. Busoni and Galston met often during their careers and formed something of a mentor–protégé relationship. Galston lived in Berlin between 1921 and 1927, while Busoni returned there in 1920 until his death in 1924. During these years in Berlin, Busoni and Galston became so close that Galston is said to have visited Busoni almost every day during his final illness. Galston compiled a large collection of Busoni memorabilia, including letters, manuscripts, photographs, and plastic casts of his hands, now known as the Galston-Busoni Archive, currently at the University of Tennessee in Knoxville. —Trans.]

2.   F. Busoni, *Von der Einheit der Musik*, 137, 144. [F. Busoni, "The Requirements Necessary for a Pianist," in *The Essence of Music*, 80. The review of Galston's book is not included in the English edition. —Trans.]

3.   F. Busoni, review of R. M. Breithaupt, "Die natürliche Klaviertechnik," *Die Musik* 22/IV: 281.

4.   Here, again, Busoni follows in the footsteps of Liszt.

5.   Busoni, *Von der Einheit der Musik*, 137. [Busoni, "The Requirements Necessary for a Pianist," 80. —Trans.]

6.   "Liszt," says Madame Boissier, "does not repeat ad nauseam the piece he wants to learn, but studies it contemplatively. . . . He examines, analyzes." Auguste Boissier, Liszt-pédagogue, 16–17, 27.

7.   Busoni, *Von der Einheit der Musik,* 262–63. [Busoni, "Mozart's *Don Giovanni* and Liszt's *Don Juan Fantasy,*" in *The Essence of Music,* 94. —Trans.]

8.   J. S. Bach, *Well-Tempered Clavier,* ed. F. Busoni, Book I (Moscow: Muzgiz, 1941), 70–71. See also F. Busoni, "On Piano Mastery: Selected sayings," vol. 1, in *The Performing Art of Foreign Countries,* ed. Georgiy Edelman (Moscow: Muzgiz, 1962), 171–73.

9.   Much as we moved the syllable *ook* out of the tongue-twister above.

10.   [Grigory] Prokofiev, *Igra na Fortepiano* [Piano-Playing] (Moscow: Muzsector Gosizdata, 1928), 79.

11.   V. Bardas, *The Psychology of Piano Technique* (Moscow: Muzsector Gosizdata, 1928), 61, 66.

12.   For more details on automation see my book: G. Kogan, *Rabota Pianista* [Pianist's Work] (Moscow: Muzgiz, 1963), 81–86.

13.   Ibid., 117–24.

14.   [This principle is widely accepted among the major pedagogues of the contemporary pianistic world. In the piano classes of Leon Fleisher, for one, students are taught to regroup sixteenth-note passages into various four-note units, avoiding the visually obvious one-two-three-four. Artistic and technical considerations usually favor the other possibilities, such as two-three-four-*one, three-four*-one-two, and four-*one-two-three.* The fascinating study editions of Alfred Cortot suggest that the pianist try every possible rhythmic grouping for various technical purposes. One of these is generally remarkably easier than all the others. It is impossible to avoid thinking that this would be exactly the one the composer had in mind! As every experienced pianist knows, difficult passagework, especially in the works of great pianist-composers, frequently "suggests," even "demands" its own grouping, which will, in turn, determine the entire choreography of finger and wrist motions and considerably simplifies performance. —Trans.]

15.   [Kogan lists a number of funny and interesting examples in Russian, entirely untranslatable, unfortunately. Here is another example in the English language: "A woman without her man is nothing" versus "A woman—without her, man is nothing." The meaning is profoundly changed by the emphasis, naturally. —Trans.]

16.   Listen, for example, to Egon Petri's emphatic ends of passages in Etudes, Op. 25, no. 6 and Op. 25, no. 9. [A discography of Egon Petri's recordings can be found in Sitsky, "Busoni and the Piano," 347–51. However, the only recording of a Chopin Etude mentioned there is Op. 25, no. 4, on a roll for Hupfeld, catalogue no. 53190. —Trans.]

Chapter 12

1.   See, for example, Auguste Boissier, *Liszt-pédagogue,* 511, 64, 68, 69, 82, 91, 96, and others.

2.   Bach, *Well-Tempered Clavier,* ed. F. Busoni, Book I (Moscow: Muzgiz, 1941), 1–2, 7–10, 16–17, 29, 35–37, 93, 135, 138–40.

3.   Ferruccio Busoni, *Klavierübung,* vol. 5 (N.p.: Breitkopf und Härtel, n.d.), 23–31. [The most accessible modern edition of the *Klavierübung* is the Russian, which includes the volumes themselves, Busoni's Foreword and excellent commentary by Y. Milstein. Busoni, *Put' k fortepiannomu masterstvu* (Moscow: Muzyka, 1968 and 1973). —Trans.]

4.   "Play good pieces and construct your own technical exercises out of them. . . . I always recommend to the advanced pianists to construct their exercises out of material that they obtain from parts of the works they study." Josef Hofmann, *Fortepiannaia igra: otvety na voprosy o fortepiannoi igre* [Piano Playing: Answers to Questions About Playing the Piano]

(Moscow: Muzgiz, 1961), 49, 162. See the numerous variants of Chopin Etudes with which Godowsky prefaces his transcriptions (Leopold Godowsky, *Studien über die Etuden von Chopin* [Berlin: Schlesinger, 1914]), the variants to selected passages of Chopin's compositions in the "working editions" of Cortot (Alfred Cortot, *Éditions de travail* [Paris: Maurice Senart, various dates]), and others. Liszt's views have been mentioned earlier.

5.   Among the latter are also those transcriptions at sight of Bach's organ works, which Busoni demanded of "any pianist with serious intentions" (foreword to his edition of the *Well-Tempered Clavier*).

6.   See the introduction of A. Nikolaev to the collection *Mastera sovetskoi pianisticheskoi shkoly* [Masters of the Soviet Pianistic School] (Moscow: Muzgiz, 1954), 38.

7.   Kogan, *Rabota pianista*, 197–200.

8.   [Wilhelm von Lenz (1809–1883), the Russian pianist and writer on music, student of Liszt and Moscheles. His book, *Beethoven et ses trois styles* (Paris: N.p., 1855), introduced and elaborated on the idea of dividing Beethoven's works into three periods. —Trans.]

9.   Theme and Variations, the first movement of Beethoven's Sonata, Op. 26; this is the movement that young Lenz played for Werstedt when he applied to study with him.

10.   W. von Lenz, *Beethoven et ses trois styles*, vol. 1 (St. Petersburg: Calvocoress, 1906), 151–53.

11.   F. Busoni, *Von der Einheit der Musik*, 82–83. [Busoni, "Playing from Memory," in *The Essence of Music*, 85. —Trans.]

12.   Busoni, *Von der Einheit der Musik*, 143. [This review is not included in the English edition. —Trans.]

13.   Boissier, *Liszt-pédagogue*, 49–52, 66–69, 78, 82, 91, 97. Liszt's "magical" ability to astonish his contemporaries by playing at sight with such "speed, ease, and perfection," "as if he had memorized them," is mentioned often. M. I. Glinka, *Zapiski* [Notes] (Moscow: Akademiia, 1930), 267; von Lenz, *Beethoven et ses trois styles*, vol. 1, 154–55; Boissier, *Liszt-pédagogue*, 45, 78, 91, 93; F. Hiller, *Felix Mendelssohn-Bartholdy* (Cologne: N.p., 1874) and others. Busoni, in his "Foreword to the Studies by Liszt" quotes the story of a witness about how "Liszt, inventing some cadenza, sat at the piano and tries out, that is played smoothly, three or four dozen variations, until he could make his choice." Busoni, *Von der Einheit*, 108. [Busoni, "Foreword to the Studies by Liszt," in *The Essence of Music*, 154. —Trans.]

14.   K. Ed. Weber, *Putevoditel´ pri obuchenii igre na fortepiano* [Guide to Teaching the Piano] (Moscow: Jurgenson, 1885), 51.

15.   Foreword to Book I of the *Well-Tempered Clavier* (Muzgiz edition, pp. XIV–XV).

16.   Busoni, *Klavierübung*, Book III.

17.   Busoni, *Von der Einheit*, 281. ["Lo Staccato" is not included in the English edition. —Trans.]

18.   [Konstantin Stanislavsky and Georgy Alexandrovich Tovstonogov (1916–89), the most famous of Russian theater directors. —Trans.]

Chapter 13

1.   This thought was advanced and developed in detail by Martienssen, in the nineteenth chapter of his often-mentioned book. [*Die individuelle Klaviertechnik auf der Grundlage des schöpferischen Klangwillens* (Individual Piano Technique on the Basis of the Creative Sound Will), published in Leipiz in 1930, and in Moscow in 1966. Carl Adolf Martienssen (1881–1955), who was a respected German musicologist and pedagogue, taught at the Leipzig Conservatory, the Musical Institute for Foreigners in Berlin, and the Hoschschule für Musik in East Berlin; he prepared Urtext Editions of Haydn, Mozart, and Beethoven

piano sonatas. His book stresses the need to shift piano pedagogy from its primarily physiological focus to the psychological. Trans.]

2.   [That is, the three interior fingers are given a much greater role than the shorter outer ones. This is an outgrowth of a much earlier Baroque keyboard practice. It still shocks the modern pianist that our illustrious predecessors preferred to cross and skip fingers rather than to use their thumbs and little fingers! This approach, naturally, made smooth legato, connected double notes, and so on, entirely impossible, and by the time of the full flowering of late Baroque harpsichord technique, the reforms of Couperin and others were beginning to replace the older system of fingering. Carl Philipp Emanuel Bach makes reference to his father's fingering approach in his treatise *Versuch über die wahre Art das Clavier zu spielen:* "My deceased father told me that in his youth he used to hear great men who employed their thumbs only when large stretches made it necessary. Because he lived at a time when a gradual but striking change in musical taste was taking place, he was obliged to devise a far more comprehensive fingering and especially to enlarge the role of the thumbs and use them as nature intended." C. P. E. Bach, *Essay on the True Art of Playing Keyboard Instruments,* trans. and ed. by William J. Mitchell (New York: Norton, 1949), 42. By the early Romantic period, the thumb, especially, but also the fifth finger, had come into use, although never on black keys. Czerny, in many ways the founder of modern piano technique and the bane of so many generations of piano students, is one of the fathers of what we now teach as "standard" fingering for scales, arpeggios, and the like. Liszt, on the other hand, deviated from the standard freely. "Liszt's playing a scale with all fingers in succession—12345, 12345—enabled him to reach extraordinary velocity, a smear like a glissando: the trick consists of a rapid shift of the hand at the end of each group of five between the fifth finger and the thumb on the next note. It was the variety of touch that Liszt extended." Charles Rosen, *The Romantic Generation* [Cambridge, Mass.: Harvard University Press, 1995], 508. A fascinating look at the history of fingering can be found in Athina Fytika, "A Historical Overview of the Philosophy Behind Keyboard Fingering Instruction from the Sixteenth Century to the Present," an electronic treatise available from Florida State University School of Music. —Trans.]

3.   Foreword to Busoni's second edition of the Bach Inventions.

4.   See more about this in my previously mentioned book, *Rabota pianista,* 149–51, and in the collection *Ispolnitel'skoe iskusstvo zarubezhnikh stran,* vol. 1, 164–69.

5.   This is how, against all tradition, Busoni and his student Petri played the fugato from the B-Minor Sonata of Liszt, attaining with this "wrong" technique, to the consternation of professionals, an unheard-of speed and steel-like sharpness of *staccato.* "The lightness and dexterity of the arm are amazing," remarked Yavorsky in *Muzyka* 105 (1912); see also the testimony of Weissmann in *Die Musik* 12/XVI, Breithaupt in his book *Die natürliche Klaviertechnik* (Leipzig: Kahnt, 1927), 113, and Martienssen in *Die individuelle Klaviertechnik,* 120–21. Curiously, the celebrated violinist Henryk Wieniawski used to amaze observers with a similar technical approach.

6.   Boissier, *Liszt-pédagogue,* 83.

7.   Playing with extended, flat fingers, forbidden by school rules, was practiced successfully by such pianists as Liszt, Cortot, and others, besides Busoni. See Boissier, *Liszt-pédagogue,* pp. 16, 48, 51, 57, 59, 67, 78, 90; Bernard Gavoty, *Alfred Cortot* (Geneva: René Kister, 1955), 6, and others.

8.   Notes to Preludes III and VI, Book I, *Well-Tempered Clavier.*

9.   Busoni, *Von der Einheit der Musik,* 137, 139. [Busoni, "The Pianoforte Should Be Esteemed," and "The Requirements Necessary for a Pianist," in *The Essence of Music,* 79, 80. —Trans.]

10.   "Not using the pedal is often its best use," remarks Busoni in the first Appendix to Book I of the *Well-Tempered Clavier* (Muzgiz edition, 197).

11.   Ibid.

12.   *Russkie vedomosti,* November 28, 1913.

13.   Busoni, *Von der Einheit der Musik,* 139–40. [Busoni, "The Pianoforte Should Be Esteemed," 79. —Trans.]

14.   Ibid., 138. [Busoni, "The Requirements Necessary for a Pianist," in *The Essence of Music,* 80. —Trans.]

Chapter 14

1.   Composed in 1901.

2.   F. Busoni, "Bemerkungen über die Reihenfolge der Opuszahlen meiner Werke," in *Von der Einheit der Musik,* 97. [Busoni, "Remarks About the Proper Order of the Opus Numbers of My Works," in *The Essence of Music,* 78. —Trans.]

3.   The fourth work in this cycle, "Turandots Frauengemach," is familiar to Soviet listeners in the interpretations of E. Petri, M. Zadora (to whom it is dedicated), and J. Ogdon; it is a transcription of the fifth movement of the orchestral suite of *Turandot.* Of the three remaining parts, "Nach der Wendung" is dedicated to Gottfried Galston, "All'Italia," to Egon Petri, and "Meine Seele bangt und hofft zu dir," to Grigory Beklemishev.

4.   [Composed in 1909. —Trans.]

5.   Busoni's father died on May 12, 1909.

6.   [The first and second versions were composed in 1910. Another version was completed in 1912. —Trans.]

7.   [*Indianisches Tagebuch,* Bk. 1, 1915. —Trans.]

8.   [*Indianische Fantasie,* 1913. —Trans.]

9.   [*Berceuse élégiaque (des Mannes Wiegenlied am Sarge seiner Mutter),* Op. 42, 1909. —Trans.]

10.   Busoni's mother died soon after her husband—on October 3 of the same year, 1909.

11.   [The original version, Opus 34a dates from 1895, the revision—from 1903. —Trans.]

12.   [The original version dates from 1897, the revision—from 1904. —Trans.]

13.   *Die Brautwahl* is Busoni's second opera; the first—*Sigune, oder Das vergessene Dorf,* composed in his youth (1888)—remained unperformed and unpublished.

14.   See, for example, *Die Musik* VII/12, X/11, X/19, XIII/14; *Russkaia muzykal'naia gazeta* 48, 49 (1912); *Teatr i iskusstvo* 48 (1913); *Novoe vremia,* and *Rech,'* November 15, 1913; *Russkie vedomosti,* November 27, 1913; Walter Niemann, *Meister des Klaviers,* and many others.

15.   Among Busoni's experiments that did not prove to be viable we must also consider his attempt to reform our tonal system: to divide the whole tone into three (and six) parts, rather than the customary two.

16.   Busoni, "Offener Musikbrief," in *Von der Einheit der Musik,* 347–48. [Busoni, "Concerning Harmony," in *The Essence of Music,* 27. —Trans.]

17.   Ibid., 249. [Busoni, "Open Letter to Hans Pfitzner," in *The Essence of Music,* 18. —Trans.]

18.   Busoni, *Entwurf einer neuen Ästhetik der Tonkunst,* 9–14. [Busoni, *Sketch of a New Esthetic of Music,* 10–11. —Trans.]

19.   Dedicated to Busoni's favorite student and disciple, Egon Petri.

20. The beautiful melody from *Turandot:*

Ex. 72. Busoni, *Turandots Frauengemach*

is not original. This is the theme of an ancient English folk song *Greensleeves.*

21. *Obozrenie teatrov* 2264 (1913).

22. See, for example, *Neue Musikzeitung* XXIX/11; *Allgemeine Musikzeitung* 43 (1910); *Die Musik* II/4, XI/10, 17, 18; *Zeitschrift für Musik* 99/12; Hugo Leichtentritt, *Ferruccio Busoni;* Gisella Selden-Goth, *Ferruccio Busoni;* Edward J. Dent, *Ferruccio Busoni,* and others.

23. Busoni renounces this point of view in his essay "Wert der Bearbeitung," reprinted in *Von der Einheit der Musik.* [Busoni, "Value of the Transcription," in *The Essence of Music,* 85. —Trans.]

24. *Golos Moskvy,* November 1, 1912.

25. See *Zeitschrift für Musik* 12 (1932): 1095. Of course, such quid pro quos testify to the cultural level of the heroes of the anecdote as much as to the popularity of Busoni's transcriptions.

26. [Bruno Mugellini (1871–1912), Italian pianist and composer, was a professor of piano at the Bologna Liceo Musicale, and later its director. —Trans.]

27.   Of the nine volumes edited by Busoni himself, three (the first book of the *Well-Tempered Clavier,* the Two-Part Inventions, and the Three-Part Inventions) are reprints of his earlier works. The complete project was finished in 1923.

28.   [These composers were well known in their day. Among those whose popularity has more or less waned are Christian Sinding (1856–1941), once considered second only to Grieg in his native Norway; Carl Nielsen (1865–1931), an important Danish composer and conductor; Frederick Delius (1862–1934), composer of intensely lyrical music championed by Sir Thomas Beecham; Ottokar Nováček (1866–1900), Czech-American violinist and composer; Hans Pfitzner (1869–1949), eminent Russian-born German composer and conductor, regarded by contemporaries as a follower of Strauss, who unfortunately became a Nazi and came to a miserable end after the war, his music forgotten; Heinrich Schenker (1868–1935), known better for his innovative approach to musical analysis; Guy Ropartz (1864–1955), French conductor, teacher, and composer, a student of Franck; and Albéric Magnard (1865–1914), distinguished French composer, killed by Nazi soldiers in his own house. —Trans.]

29.   [These programs took place in the Beethovensaal, giving the critics an added opportunity to express their disapproval: "Another of those outrages on good taste; an insult that such music should be played in a concert-hall which bears the sacred name of Beethoven." This was in response to the very last concert, in January 1909, where Béla Bartók conducted the aforementioned Scherzo from his *Orchestral Suite,* Op. 4. Among other works that were critically abused with especial enthusiasm were the *Prelude and Angel's Farewell* from Elgar's *Dream of Gerontius,* and Delius's *Paris;* the *Berliner Neueste Nachrichten* called them "particularly barren music-fabrication." Albert Petrak, *Busoni: His Life and Times,* www.rprf.org/PDF/Busoni_Bio.pdf. —Trans.]

30.   On the circumstances of his leaving the school (together with most of the students), see *Wiener Zeitschrift für Musik* 5 (1908). Busoni's predecessor at this post was Emile Sauer, and his successor—Leopold Godowski.

31.   [Michael Zadora (1882–1946) and Rudolph Ganz (1877–1972) studied with Busoni, and became important American musicians; Gino Tagliapietra (1887–1954) was an Italian pianist, teacher, and composer; Percy Grainger (1882–1961) was a celebrated Australian-born pianist; Selim Palmgren (1878–1951) became an eminent Finnish composer; Louis-Theodore Gruenberg (1884–1964), Russian-born American composer, organized the League of Composers; Augusta Cottlow (1878–1954) achieved renown in America as a pianist and pedagogue; Leo Kestenberg (1882–1962) was responsible for organizing the system of musical education in Prussia before World War II and afterward for founding Israel's first college for music teachers. Leo Sirota (1895–1965), born in Ukraine, studied with Busoni in Vienna; his debut there featured Busoni on the second piano and as a conductor. After years of living in Japan, he moved to St. Louis. Grigory Beklemishev (1881–1935) was one of the most prominent pianists and professors in Kiev. Emile-Robert Blanchet (1877–1943) was a Swiss pianist and composer, and director of the Lausanne Conservatory. —Trans.]

32.   [These essays can be found in *The Essence of Music.* —Trans.]

33.   [*Sketch of a New Esthetic of Music.* —Trans.]

34.   F. Busoni, *Eskiz novoi estetiki muzykal'nogo iskusstva,* trans. [Viktor] Kolomiytsev (St. Petersburg: Andrei Diderichs, 1912). [The original English translation, *Sketch of a New Esthetic of Music,* by T. Baker was published by G. Schirmer in 1911. There are two more current editions: by Schirmer in 1978 and by University Microfilms International (Ann Arbor, Mich.) in 1980. In addition, the earlier edition is available for free download at various Web sites. —Trans.]

35.   *Pravda,* August 10, 1924; *Zhizn´ iskusstva* 33/1007 (1924).

36.   [José Vianna da Motta (1868–1948), Portuguese pianist and student of Liszt and von Bülow, was esteemed as an interpreter of Bach and Beethoven; James Kwast (1852–1927), famous German pianist and pedagogue taught Grainger and Pfitzner; Frieda Hoddap (1880–1949), a pianist in her own right, was his second wife; Maria Barinova (1880–?) was a professor at the St. Petersburg Conservatory; Artur Schnabel (1882–1951) and Edwin Fischer (1886–1960) hardly need an introduction—both were among the greatest pianists of the century; Gottfried Galston (1879–1950), Austrian-American pianist, published the *Studienbuch* that attracted Busoni's attention. Rudolf Breithaupt (1873–1945), German pianist, pedagogue, and scholar published invaluable studies on piano playing; Gustav Brecher (1879–1940) conducted the premiere of Busoni's *Die Brautwahl* and directed the Leipzig Opera from 1923 to 1932; Oskar Fried (1871–1941), German Jewish conductor, was the first foreign conductor to be invited to the Soviet Union in 1922 and was met at the train station by Lenin himself; despite his fame and success in Berlin, Fried was forced to flee Germany in 1934 and ended up a Soviet citizen; Paul Bekker (1882–1937) wrote music criticism for important German papers; Hugo Leichtentritt (1874–1951) became one of Busoni's biographers. Otto Lessman (1844–1918) also wrote about Busoni. Jakob Wassermann (1873–1934), a Jewish German writer, had the distinction of having his books banned in Germany in 1933. Stefan Zweig (1881–1942), Austrian Jewish author, was a leading figure, together with Romain Rolland, in the pacifist movement during World War I. He left Austria for England, America, and finally, Brazil, where he committed suicide in 1942 in despair over the state of the world. Stefan George (1880–1934) was an important Symbolist and Expressionist poet. Finally, Rainer Maria Rilke (1875–1926) is, of course, one of Germany's greatest twentieth-century poets. —Trans.]

37.   Leichtentritt, *Ferruccio Busoni,* 16. A lively description of daily life in the Busoni household can be found in M. N. Barinova, *Vospominaniia o I. Gofmane i F. Buzoni,* 68–70.

Chapter 15

1.   F. Busoni, *Entwurf einer neuen Ästhetik der Tonkunst,* 8. [Busoni, *Sketch of a New Esthetic of Music,* 3. —Trans.]

2.   F. Busoni, "Über die Anforderungen an den Pianisten," in *Von der Einheit der Musik,* 138. [Busoni, "The Requirements Necessary for a Pianist," in *The Essence of Music,* 81. —Trans.].

3.   Ibid., "Conclusio zu des wohltemperirten Klavieres II. Teil," 211; "Gedanken über den Ausdruck in der Architektur," 231; and "Was gab uns Beethoven?" 294. [Only "What Did Beethoven Give Us?" is included in the English edition. —Trans.]

4.   A few years ago, there was an attempt to prove that Busoni's views were, in fact, the opposite, belonging in the antirealistic camp. Here is what A. Nikolaev had to say in his essay "On Questions of the Esthetic of Soviet Music Performance": "The view of music as an art capable of expressing the wide world of human feelings, as an art whose content is a creatively-emotional reflection of life's events, is directly opposed to the formalistic aesthetic of contemporary bourgeois artists. The capitalist world attempts with all its might to separate art from life, to instill the thought that art cannot and must not have content. 'Music consists of a progression of sounds, sound forms that have no meaning outside of themselves,' wrote E. Hanslick in 1854. This erroneous view of music was reflected even in such an outstanding musician as F. Busoni, who wrote in one of his essays: 'Music is a form-play without poetic program, in which the form is intended to have the leading part.'" A.

Nikolaev, "On Questions of the Esthetic of Soviet Music Performance," in *O muzykal'nom ispolnitel'stve* [On Musical Performance] (Moscow: Muzgiz, 1954), 148. Nikolaev quotes Busoni's book (not an essay) *Sketch of a New Esthetic of Music* (Russian edition, p. 12). This citation, obviously, is rather incriminating. Had it been correct, Busoni truly would have to be placed in the ranks of those who reject expressive content in music and its ability to reflect the world of human feelings. However, as V. Gorodinskii has already shown in his essay "The Vulgarization of the History of Pianism," *Sovetskaia muzyka* 12 (1956): 76–77, the given quote is not correct: it is used to imply a meaning opposite to that of Busoni's context. The author of the *Sketch* does not state his opinion here, but, rather, characterizes the point of view of the proponents of so-called absolute music—a point of view that he immediately rejects and ridicules. See *Sketch*, pp. 12–13, Russian edition. [Busoni, *Sketch of a New Esthetic of Music*, 5–6. —Trans.] It is left up to the reader to decide the merits of this method of quoting. Busoni, naturally, has nothing to do with it. [Aleksandr Aleksandrovich Nikolaev (1903–80) was an important music historian, and Kogan's own student at the Moscow Conservatory. He wrote extensively on questions of piano playing and pedagogy. Generations of Russian and, increasingly, European and American pianists have grown up with his beginner method books, the wonderful *School of Piano Playing* (available in English from Boosey & Hawkes). Viktor Markovitch Gorodinskii (1902–59) was a pianist and musicologist, prolific author and editor at Muzgiz, the Soviet music publisher. —Trans.]

5.   [It seems unlikely indeed that Busoni gave more than a passing thought to the question of formalism vs. realism. To Grigory Kogan, however, the question is not simply academic, but a matter of career, even livelihood. To admire, study, and perform a "formalist" composer is to invite professional death. Kogan must, therefore, defend Busoni at all costs. —Trans.]

6.   *Die Musik* IV/22: 281. It is important, however, to note that Busoni did not include this review in his collection *Von der Einheit der Musik*.

7.   F. Busoni, "Routine," in *Von der Einheit der Musik*, 167. [Busoni, "Routine," in *The Essence of Music*, 184–85. —Trans.]

8.   F. Busoni, *Entwurf einer neuen Ästhetik der Tonkunst*, 31. [Busoni, *Sketch of a New Esthetic of Music*, 22. —Trans.]

9.   Note to Fugue XIV in Book I of the *Well-Tempered Clavier.*

10.   Foreword and First Appendix in Book I of the *Well-Tempered Clavier.*

11.   F. Busoni, "Galstons Studienbuch," in *Von der Einheit der Musik*, 141. [This review is not included in the English edition. —Trans.]

12.   F. Busoni, "Wert der Bearbeitung," and "Routine," in *Von der Einheit der Musik*, 153, 168. [Busoni, "Value of the Transcription," and "Routine," in *The Essence of Music*, 89, 185. —Trans.]

13.   Foreword to the second edition of Bach's Inventions; note to Prelude IV in Book I of the *Well-Tempered Clavier.*

14.   Foreword to the edition of Liszt's *Don Juan.*

15.   Aforementioned review.

16.   Busoni, *Entwurf einer neuen Ästhetik der Tonkunst*, 6. [Busoni, *Sketch of a New Esthetic of Music*, 2. —Trans.]

17.   Notes to Preludes VI and VIII in Book I of the *Well-Tempered Clavier.*

18.   F. Busoni, "Offener Brief an Hans Pfitzner," in *Von der Einheit der Musik*, 249. [Busoni, "Open Letter to Hans Pfitzner," in *The Essence of Music*, 18. —Trans.]

19.   Ibid., 248.

20.   [Marie Jean Antoine Nicolas de Caritat, marquis de Condorcet (1743–94), one of the great thinkers of the Enlightenment, a mathematician and political scientist, was a

believer in the perfectibility of man and society; he was a proponent of equal rights for women, equality of all races, education for all, and a liberal economy. Naturally, he was persecuted by the French revolutionary authorities and died a mysterious death in prison. —Trans.]

21. See more on this subject in N. Beltov (G. V. Plekhanov), *K voprosu o razvitii monisticheskogo vzgliada na istoriiu* [The Question of the Monistic View of History] (St. Petersburg: IV, 1906), 21, 24–29, 32–27, 98, 108, 288–97. [Georgi Plekhanov (1856–1918, was Russia's first Marxist and the founder of the Social-Democratic movement. Although Plekhanov broke with the Bolsheviks and left Russia after the October Revolution, he, unusually, remained respected and widely read in the Soviet Union. The book Kogan quotes was published in English as *The Development of the Monist View of History* (London: Lawrence & Wishart, 1947). It is a classic of Marxist thought. —Trans.]

22. [Erwin Johannes Bach, *Die vollendete Klaviertechnik* (Berlin: Wölbing, 1929). Although Kogan obviously picks this book for the author's name, it was a well-respected work, which was reprinted again in 1960 by Breitkopf und Härtel. —Trans.]

23. [Adolf] Kullak, *Die Ästhetik des Klavierspiels* (Leipzig: C. F. Kahnt Nachfolger, 1905); Malwine Brée, *Die Grundlage der Methode Leschetizky* (Mainz: B. Schott's Söhne, 1903); Rudolf M. Breithaupt, *Die natürliche Klaviertechnik* (Leipzig: C. F. Kahnt Nachfolger, 1927); Kurt Johnen, *Neue Wege zur Energetik des Klavierspiels* (Amsterdam: [N.p.], 1928). [Adolf Kullak (1823–62), music writer, composer, teacher, and founder of his own music academy, was also a noted critic in Berlin. The famous book on piano playing is one of the first to contain few finger studies and more discussions about the aesthetics involved. Rudolf Breithaupt (1873–1945), German pianist and pedagogue, is remembered primarily for his studies on piano playing. Josef Hofmann (1876–1957), the great Polish/American pianist and author of the widely read *Piano Playing*, was the first head of the piano department at the Curtis Institute. Kurt Johnen (1884–1965) has more to recommend him than just his book. He invented a curious, yet fascinating device designed to aid the student pianist. Here is a caption from a 1929 newspaper article, accompanying a picture of said invention: "A NEW device has been patented by Dr. Kurt Johnen, Berlin piano pedagogue, which records the motions and bodily reactions of a piano player to determine if the selection is being properly interpreted. A lady is pictured being examined by the device. A pneumatic belt records the change of the circumference of the chest, pneumatic cuffs about the upper arms control the changes of muscle tension, through a hose is recorded the rhythms of respiration and another hose transfers the strength of touch. Dr. Johnen expects this device will aid him in instructing his pupils in interpretation" (*Modern Mechanix* [November 1929]; available at http://blog.modernmechanix/ category/entertainment/music/page/3/). Malwine Brée was Leschetizky's student and longtime assistant. Her fascinating book about the Leschetizky Method, written with his approval, includes dozens of photographs of his hands, and has been recently reissued in English in a Dover edition. —Trans.]

24. F. A. Steinhausen, *Die physiologischen Fehler und die Umgestaltung der Klaviertechnik* (Leipzig: Breitkopf und Härtel, 1913).

25. Note to Prelude XXIII in Book I of the *Well-Tempered Clavier.*

26. [The translator simply must point out the cleverness of this paragraph, as an example of Kogan's inventiveness in pleasing the censor. —Trans.]

27. You judge him differently than we do / Because you see him with different eyes. (Molière, *Les Femmes savantes.*)

28. Hans Pfitzner, "Futuristengefahr. [Bei Gelegenheit von Busonis Ästhetick]," in *Gesammelte Schriften* (Augsburg: Filser-Verlag, 1926)]; Paul Moos, *Die Philosophie der Musik*

[*von Kant bis Eduard von Hartmann; ein Jahrhundert deutscher Geistesarbeit* (Stuttgart: Deutsche Verlags-Anstalt, 1922]).

29. Martienssen, *Die individuelle Klaviertechnik*, 114.

30. F. Busoni, "Offener Musikbrief," in *Von der Einheit der Musik*, 346. [Busoni, "Concerning Harmony," in *The Essence of Music*, 26. —Trans.]

31. V. I. Lenin, *Lenin o kulture i iskusstve* [Lenin on Culture and Art] (Moscow: N.P., 1938), 298–99. [Surely a similar quote can be found in dozens (hundreds?) of books. Perhaps the idea is so commonplace that no citation is needed? No doubt, but no book can be published without its obligatory homage to Lenin's wisdom and erudition on any and all subjects. —Trans.]

32. Busoni, *Von der Einheit der Musik*, 144, 180, 247–48, 344–48, 354–55. Bruno Goetz, "Erinnerungen an Busoni," in *Die Schlapperklange* (Donaueschingen: A. Meder, n.d.). Especially notable here is the closeness of Busoni's opinions to the familiar sayings of V. Lenin (in his conversation with Clara Zetkin). [Review of Galston's book, not included in the English edition; Busoni, "Self-Criticism," "Open Letter to Hans Pfitzner," "Concerning Harmony," "Report on the Division of the Whole Tone into Three Parts," in *The Essence of Music*, 17, 25–27, 29, 50. Lenin's correspondent, Clara Zetkin (1857–1943) was the important German socialist, feminist, and Comintern leader. When the Communist party was banned in Germany in 1933, she moved to the Soviet Union, where she died. —Trans.]

33. Karl Marx, "Letter to M. M. Kovalevsky from April 1879." In K. Marx and F. Engels, *Works*, vol. 27 ([N.p.]: Partizdat, 1935), 29.

Chapter 16

1. [Josef Hofmann, thought by many to be the greatest pianist who ever lived, composed over 100 works in his youth under the name Michel Dvorsky. These are reminiscent of Chopin, and quite forgotten today. Annette Essipoff, whose fame and importance as a pianist are indisputable, has left no legacy as a composer at all. All of her works are out of print. Anton Stepanovich Arenski (1861–1906) studied composition with Rimsky-Korsakov. There is a pronounced salon feeling to many of his piano compositions, for which reason Rimsky-Korsakov prophesied his works' oblivion. However, there is a joyous delight in the instrument in his several compositions for piano ensemble, and these are still enthusiastically performed. Jules Massenet (1842–1912) was the most celebrated French opera composer of his day. His music has largely fallen out of fashion, with the exception of the opera *Manon,* and, of course, that mainstay of student recitals, the Meditation from *Thaïs.* —Trans.]

2. [Max Reger (1873–1916) was a German composer whose style combines complex counterpoint with Romantic harmony, largely absent from current concert programs. Alexander Glazunov (1865–1936), important Russian composer and conductor, and director of the Saint Petersburg Conservatory. While heir to the nationalist style of his predecessors, his music combines many cosmopolitan influences, but lacks an individual voice. Only a few works from a voluminous output are still in the repertoire. Alfred Reisenauer (1863–1907), student of Liszt and a highly successful pianist, did not leave a lasting contribution to the repertoire. Raoul Pugno (1852–1914), French pianist and composer, was one of the first pianists of international stature to record, leaving behind a fascinating view of fin-de-siècle pianistic style. Few of his works are still performed. —Trans.]

3.   F. Busoni, *Von der Einheit der Musik*, 134, 276. [Busoni, "Young Classicism," in *The Essence of Music*, 20. "Die 'Gotiker' von Chicago, Illinois" is not included in the English edition. —Trans.] Curiously, it was these same pompous pictures of Makart to which Breithaupt likens Reisenauer's playing (*Die Musik* III/8). Compare also the characterization of the decadent architecture of that epoch in the essay by academic A. V. Shchusev, "Nashi arkhitekturnie raznoglasiia" ["Our Architectural Disagreements"]: "The representative buildings of the second half of the nineteenth century are a vivid example of that artistic and cultural degradation. . . . Various monsters of bourgeois tastelessness combined together . . . in the eclectic diversity of component parts. These 'stylistic' features were especially widely used in the seventies and eighties of the past century. By the end of the nineteenth century this eclectic development in architecture climaxed into the opulent blossoming of the so-called Decadent Style. . . . All areas of fine arts and architecture of the period were dominated by examples of cheap derivative taste and eclectic stylelessness" (*Sovetskoe iskusstvo,* January 5, 1935). An analogous situation prevailed, as we know, in painting, dramaturgy and so on, of the "timeless" eighties–nineties. [Georg Ebers (1837–98) was a prolific German author and Egyptologist. His scholarly historical novels were meant to popularize Egyptian history. Felix Dahn (1834–1912) was another writer of the so-called professorial novel, with a particular interest in early German history. Hans Makart (1840–84) was the acknowledged leader of the artistic life of Vienna, painter, decorator, costume designer, and the inspiration for a whole generation, particularly Gustav Klimt. —Trans.]

4.   Busoni, *Von der Einheit der Musik*, 167. [Busoni, "Routine," in *The Essence of Music*, 184.

5.   Renaissance.

6.   Busoni, *Von der Einheit der Musik*, 134, 158. [Busoni, "How Long Will It Go On," in *The Essence of Music*, 181. "Die 'Gotiker' von Chicago, Illinois" is not included in the English edition. —Trans.]

7.   That is, Anton Rubinstein.

8.   *Russkie vedomosti*, November 28, 1913; see also the discussion about Busoni and his interpretations of Liszt in *Signale* 2, 4, 6 (1909).

9.   Busoni, *Von der Einheit der Musik*, 191–92. [Busoni, "The Future of Opera," in *The Essence of Music*, 41. —Trans.]

10.   Busoni, *Von der Einheit der Musik*, 154–56. [Busoni, "How Long Will It Go On?" in *The Essence of Music*, 182. —Trans.]

11.   Busoni, *Von der Einheit der Musik*, 154–58, 168. [Busoni, "How Long Will It Go On?" in *The Essence of Music*, 182–83, and "Routine," 185. —Trans.]

12.   Busoni, *Von der Einheit der Musik*, 156–58. [Busoni, "How Long Will It Go On?" in *The Essence of Music*, 184. —Trans.]

13.   Adolf Weissmann, *Der Virtuose*, 135 ff; Bruno Goetz, "Erinnerungen an Busoni," in *Die Schlapperklange*.

14.   F. Busoni, "Die 'Gotiker' von Chicago, Illinois" in *Von der Einheit der Musik*, 132–33. [The reason for the exclusion of this essay from the English edition seems quite clear. —Trans.]

15.   F. Busoni, "Selbst-Rezension," in *Von der Einheit der Musik*, 177–78. [Busoni, "Self-Criticism," in *The Essence of Music*, 48–49. —Trans.]

16.   [Bernhard Ziehn (1845–1912) and his student Wilhelm Middelschulte (1863–1943) were both German-born music theorists, who made Chicago their home. Ziehn's major contributions to the study of counterpoint were his *Canonic Studies* (New York: Crescendo, 1977), an analysis of double and triple canons at every interval from the unison to

the major seventh, and his symmetrical inversion theory, which allowed new and fascinating combinations of tones to make a usable chord. As Kyle Gann, composer, author, and music critic, writes in program notes to his *Chicago Spiral*, "His obsessive musical mind has been forgotten because he lived in Chicago, wrote in German, and was just too far ahead of his time. Chicago's early modernism (Ruth Crawford, John Becker) was permeated by Ziehn's bustling, fanatical, contrapuntal spirit. What would Chicago new music be like today if the scene hadn't been dissipated by the Depression?" Both Ziehn and Middelschulte worked with Busoni to help him solve the problematic combination of subjects in the final, uncompleted fugue from Bach's *Art of the Fugue*. This work was the inspiration, as well, for Busoni's *Fantasia contrappuntistica*. It is important to point out here that Kogan mentions Ziehn and Middelschulte, but carefully avoids elaborating anything about their work, outside of simply referring to polyphony. It seems rather clear that their music is the very definition of Formalism!—Trans.]

17.   Busoni, "Die 'Gotiker' von Chicago, Illinois," 132–33.

18.   Busoni, *Von der Einheit der Musik*, 154, 236, 237. [Busoni, "How Long Will It Go On?" in *The Essence of Music*, 182. "Gedanken über den Ausdruck in der Architektur" is not included in the English edition. —Trans.]

19.   Militza V. Witt, "Aus Briefen Busonis," *Deutsche Allgemeine Zeitung*, May 8, 1931.

Chapter 17

1.   [Frans Masereel (1889–1972) was a Flemish painter and woodcut artist, famous for his wordless graphic novels. —Trans.]

2.   [Umberto Boccioni (1882–1916), a painter and sculptor, was a leader and theorist of the Futuristic movement in art. He was conscripted into the army at the start of the war and died in a tragic accident, trampled after being thrown from his horse during an exercise. —Trans.]

3.   F. Busoni, *Von der Einheit der Musik*, 244. ["Der Kriegsfall Boccioni" is not included in the English edition. —Trans.]

4.   See more in Guido M. Gatti, "In memoria di Ferruccio Busoni," *Revista Musicale Italiana* (1924): 565–80.

5.   Hans Pfitzner, *Futuristengefahr* (1917); *Die neue Ästhetik der musikalischen Impotenz* (1919). Both pamphlets were later reprinted in a collection of the author's works. Hans Pfitzner, *Gesammelte Schriften* (Augsburg: Filser-Verlag, 1926). Pfitzner's esthetic views were quickly picked up by the Nazis, who purged all musical institutions of Busoni's students and followers shortly after coming to power. They lauded Pfitzner for being the "spiritual forerunner of National-Socialist ideas" who fought against "infection" in music long before the founding of Hitler's party. *Die Musik* (December 1933). [It must be stated in Pfitzner's defense that, although at first very popular with the powers that be within the Third Reich, he soon fell out of favor, mostly for the offense of his musical association with the Jewish Bruno Walter, as well as stating publicly that the equally Jewish Mendelssohn was a greater composer than he could be himself. —Trans.]

6.   E. Refardt, ed., *Briefe Busonis an Hans Huber* (Zurich: Verlag Hug, 1939), 44.

7.   Busoni, *Von der Einheit der Musik*, 242–43.

8.   See Richard Aldington's novel *Vse liudi—Vragi* (Moscow: Goslitizdat, 1959). [Richard Aldington, *All Men Are Enemies* (London: Chatto & Windus, 1933). Aldington is that strange example of a writer who is better known in translation than in his homeland. After the scandal caused by his *Lawrence of Arabia*, he became quite unpopular in Britain

and could not find a publisher. However, several of his works were translated into Russian and, to his surprise, Aldington became all the rage in the Soviet Union, and was invited to visit there in 1962. —Trans.]

9. Noisily, with spirit, with bravura, fiery; measured, lightly, with freshness.

10. Paul Bekker, *Klang und Eros* (Berlin: Deutsche Verlags-Anstalt, 1922); *Die Musik* XVI; *Musikblätter des Anbruch* (October 1924).

11. Streaming, whispering, shimmery, sparkling, whispering, gliding, grainy, pearly.

12. "Constant defiance, desire for the resolution of dissonance, and running his head against a wall," Busoni notes.

13. F. Busoni, "Wie gab uns Beethoven," in *Von der Einheit der Musik*, 291–95. [Busoni, "What Did Beethoven Give Us?" in *The Essence of Music*, 130–32. —Trans.]

14. F. Busoni, "Mozart: Aphorismen," in *Von der Einheit der Musik*, 80. [Busoni, "Mozart: Aphorisms," in *The Essence of Music*, 105. —Trans.]

15. Refardt, *Briefe Busonis an Hans Huber*, 41–42.

16. [It is important to remember that Beethoven was V. I. Lenin's favorite composer; therefore, any criticism of the "human" Ludwig would be seen as heresy by the censor. —Trans.]

17. *Die Musik* XVI/12.

18. Preface to Volume II of the *Well-Tempered Clavier.*

19. [Of course!—Trans.]

20. Which was not appreciated by the composer.

21. Comparing his impression of the "matinee" in question with the usual boredom reigning at traditional academic concerts: "In any case, different from that of a sonata recital given by two court professors." (Meaning professors of any Royal German Conservatory.) F. Busoni, "Schönberg: Matinée," in *Von der Einheit der Musik*, 171. [Busoni, "Schönberg Matinée," in *The Essence of Music*, 177. —Trans.]

22. F. Busoni, "Die neue Harmonik," in *Von der Einheit der Musik*, 160. [Busoni, "The New Harmony," in *The Essence of Music*, 24. —Trans.]

23. F. Busoni, "Offener Musikbrief," in *Von der Einheit der Musik*, 345–47. [Busoni, "The New Harmony," in *The Essence of Music*, 26–27. —Trans.]

24. "Why," Busoni asked jokingly, "do the Dadaists double (in the name of their group) only the first syllable of the Italian musical term *da capo?*" (in the collection *Die Schlapperklange*). [Actually, the origin and the meaning of the term Dadaism are unclear. Opinions vary: some believe the word is nonsensical, or that it is derived from the Slavic word *da* (for yes, something like *yeah, yeah*), or the French word for "hobby." None, besides Kogan (and Busoni), seem to think that *da capo* has anything to do with it. See more in Marc Dachy, "Dada & les dadaïsmes," in *Folio Essais* (Paris: Gallimard, 1994), and Aurélie Verdier, *L'ABCdaire de Dada* (Paris: Flammarion, 2005). —Trans.]

25. F. Busoni, "Junge Klassizität," in *Von der Einheit der Musik*, 277–78. [Busoni, "Young Classicism," in *The Essence of Music*, 172–73. —Trans.]

26. F. Busoni, "Aufzeichnungen," in *Von der Einheit der Musik*, 277–78. [In the English edition, this essay appears in a very abbreviated form as "Simplicity of Music in the Future."—Trans.]

27. F. Busoni, "Von den Proportionen," in *Von der Einheit der Musik*, 357. [Busoni, "Proportion," in *The Essence of Music*, 34. —Trans.]

28. Book 2 of the *Indian Diaries.*

29. "Entwurf eines Vorwortes zur Partitur des 'Doktor Faust,' enthaltend einige Betrachtungen über die Möglichkeiten der Oper," in *Von der Einheit der Musik*, 314–15. [Busoni, "The Oneness of Music and the Possibilities of the Opera," in *The Essence of Music*, 5. —Trans.]

30.   "Von der Zukunst der Oper," 190. ["The Future of Opera," 39–40. —Trans.] It is easy to notice that the views expressed here are very close to the principles of the famous Vakhtangov Theater production of *Princess Turandot*. It is curious also that, to put his ideas into practice, Busoni selected, as we shall see, the same subject matter. [This is Yevgeny Vakhtangov's most distinctive production, in 1922, the year of his death, of Carlo Gozzi's *Turandot*, with its abstract costumes, avant-garde sets, masks, music, and dance. It must have been especially pleasant for Kogan to be able to mention and admire Vakhtangov openly, after all the years his name would have been taboo. —Trans.]

31.   F. Busoni, *Entwurf eitner neuen Ästhetik der Tonkunst*, 16–17. [Busoni, *Sketch*, 14. —Trans.]

32.   December 1914.

33.   Gisella Selden-Goth, *Ferruccio Busoni*, 114.

34.   See more about these comedies in the collection *Legenda o doktore Fauste* [The Legend of Doctor Faust], ed. V. M. Zhirmunskii (Moscow-Leningrad: AN SSSR, 1958), 167–259, 452–92, 537–53.

35.   See more about him in the following chapter. [A more complete version was created in the 1980s by Anthony Beaumont, who was able to have access to previously unknown material. —Trans.]

36.   [Boris Vladimirovich Asafiev (1884–1949), prolific composer, musicologist, laureate of important Soviet prizes and titles, and functionary, is thought to be the father of Soviet music theory and one the of most important Soviet musicians of the first half of the twentieth century. —Trans.]

37.   [Fantasie für eine Orgelwalze, K. 608. —Trans.]

38.   *[Duettino Concertante*, arrangement for two pianos of Mozart's Piano Concerto, no. 19, K. 459. —Trans.]

Chapter 18

1.   [Paul Bekker and Rudolf Kastner were the most important and influential German music critics of the time. —Trans.]

2.   [Franz Schreker (1878–1934) attained his greatest fame as a composer during the Weimar Republic as the most popular living opera composer after Richard Strauss. As the political situation changed, the Jewish Schreker could no longer get his operas performed, and was removed from his position as director of the Hochschule in 1932. —Trans.]

3.   [Leo Kestenberg was a revolutionary in the field of music education in the Weimar Republic. His appointments were a testament to his far-reaching vision and open mind— among the musicians he supported were Arnold Schoenberg, Paul Hindemith, and Artur Schnabel. A dedicated socialist, he was forced out of office by the Third Reich. —Trans.]

4.   Two of these concerts had Busoni conducting his orchestral works, and the third consisted of his performing of his compositions for piano and orchestra: The Concertino, the *Indian Fantasy*, and the Concerto.

5.   This program included the Bach Chorale improvisation, the above-mentioned transcriptions of Mozart's works, and the *Fantasia contrappuntistica*.

6.   Gisella Selden-Goth, *Ferruccio Busoni* (Leipzig: E. P. Tal, 1922). This is the second book about Busoni; the first, Hugo Leichtentritt, *Ferruccio Busoni* (Leipzig: Breitkopf und Härtel, 1916), came out earlier during the war years was dedicated to Busoni's fiftieth birthday.

7.   Ferruccio Busoni, *Von der Einheit der Musik*.

8.   Selden-Goth, *Ferruccio Busoni*, 50.

9.   I. Philipp, "Quelques considérations sur l'art du piano," *Le Courrier musical et théatral,* November 15, 1927.

10.   Busoni, *Von der Einheit der Musik*, 247, 275, 279, 293; first Appendix to Book I of the *Well-Tempered Clavier.* [Busoni, "Open Letter to Hans Pritzner," and "Young Classicism," 17–20. —Trans.]

11.   Adolf Weissmann, *Der Virtuose*, 136.

12.   Militza V. Witt, "Aus Briefen Busonis," *Deutsche Allgemeine Zeitung*, May 8, 1931.

13.   Stefan Zweig, *Begegnungen mit Menschen, Büchern, Städten* (Berlin: S. Fischer, 1956), 111–12.

14.   Adolf Weissmann, in *Die Musik* 12 (XVI).

15.   Among the most outstanding concerts of those years is a Berlin cycle of three evenings of nine Mozart concertos with Busoni's own cadenzas.

16.   [One cannot help but wonder what must have gone through Kogan's mind as he wrote this. It is quite true that the "aims of gain" played a very small part in the consciousness of a normal Soviet citizen at the time—mainly because most legal and honorable avenues of employment offered none! There is a Russian saying, already venerable during my own childhood, that explains: "The government pretends that it pays us, and we pretend that we work." The inimitable Isaiah Berlin puts it best: ". . . most of the standard vices so monotonously attributed by Marxists to capitalism are to be found in their purest form only in the Soviet Union itself. We are familiar with such stock Marxist categories as capitalist exploitation, the iron law of wages, etc. . . . Party officials act far more like the capitalists of Marxist mythology than any living capitalists in the West today. The Soviet rulers really do see to it that the workers are supplied with that precise minimum of food, shelter, clothing, entertainment, education and so forth that they are thought to require in order to produce the maximum quantity of the goods and services at which the State planners are aiming." Isaiah Berlin and Henry Hardy, *The Soviet Mind: Russian Culture Under Communism* (Washington, D.C.: Brookings Institution Press, 2004), 150–51. At this book's writing, in 1964, Khrushchev's efforts to raise the production of food and consumer goods in the Soviet Union and thus to raise the standard of living had failed signally. "Gain," or at least "toil" rewarded by material comfort, were available only to the Party nomenklatura and their chosen favorites. —Trans.]

17.   F. Busoni, *Briefe an seine Frau*, 359–60; Militza V. Witt, *Aus Briefen Busonis.*

18.   F. Busoni, *Über die Möglichkeiten der Oper und über die Partitur des Doktor Faust* (Leipzig: Breitkopf und Härtel, 1926). The earlier version of this essay, under the title "Entwurf eines Vorwortes zur Partitur des Doktor Faust, enthaltend einige Betrachtungeg über die Möglichkeiten der Oper" was included in the first edition of *Von der Einheit der Musik.* [In the English edition, the earlier essay is divided into two parts: "The Oneness of Music and the Possibilities of the Opera," and "The Score of *Doktor Faust*."—Trans.]

19.   Jarnach, who studied with Busoni back in Zurich, of course, was the same student who finished *Doctor Faust* after Busoni's death. Later, Jarnach became a professor of the Cologne, and, eventually, the director of the Hamburg Hochschule für Musik.

20.   Emil Debusmann, *Ferruccio Busoni* (Wiesbaden: Brucknerverlag, 1949), 34.

21.   *Melos* 1 (IV); reprinted in Ferruccio Busoni, *Wesen und Einheit der Musik. Newausgabe der Schriften und Aufzeichnungen Busonis revidiert und ergänzt von Joachim Herrmann* (Berlin: Max Hesses Verlag, 1956).

22.   [George Bernard Shaw (1856–1950) hardly needs an introduction as a playwright and critic. Throughout his life he was a devoted Socialist and member of the Fabian Society (which supports promoting Socialism by peaceful means). Like many European Socialist

intellectuals, he became enamored with Stalin, whom he met during his visits to the USSR in the 1930s. Peaceful means or not, Shaw became an ardent supporter of the Stalinist USSR and an apologist for Stalin. He went so far as to attempt to justify the pogroms and the purges in the preface to his play *On the Rocks* (1933). Worse yet, he refused to acknowledge reports about the Ukraine famine (which took millions of lives)—Shaw called them slanderous falsehoods in an open letter to the *Manchester Guardian*. See more in "Letter to the Editor: Social Conditions in Russia by George Bernard Shaw," *Manchester Guardian*, March 2, 1933. But then Shaw could not bring himself to believe in the German death camps either; he could not accept the fact that the Nazis killed almost all the Jews in occupied Europe. Emrys Hughes, *Bernard Shaw* (Moscow, 1966), 272. On a less serious note, Shaw, who also wrote that smallpox inoculations are a crime against humanity, defended Stalin's espousal of Lysenko (who rejected Mendelian genetics in favor of his theory of heritability of acquired characteristics, and held back Soviet science for generations). G. B. Shaw, "The Lysenko Muddle," *Labour Monthly* (January 1949). —Trans.]

Conclusion

1.   I will not bother with the more laughable attempts to explain Busoni's duality by the struggle between "spirit" and "body," his "creative will" and "material essence." See, for example, Busoni's obituaries in *Die Musik* 12 (XVI) and *Musikblätter der Anbruch* (October 1924).

2.   R. Farber, *Zhizn´ iskusstva* 33, no. 1007 (1924).

3.   See, for instance, the discussion between Herbert Gerigk and the Master's son Benvenuto Busoni in *Die Musik* 11 (XXVI) and 3 and Karl Holl's article in *Frankfurter Zeitung*, September 9, 1934. [Herbert Gerigk (1905–96), was the "Leader of the Music Branch by order of the Führer for the Supervision of the Entire Intellectual and Ideological Enlightenment of the Nazi Party" and the author of one of the most notorious books in Nazi musicology, the *Lexicon der Juden in der Music* [The Lexicon of Jews in Music]. Karl Holl (1892–1972) was the influential music critic of the *Frankfurter Zeitung*. —Trans.]

4.   Paul Bekker, *Klang und Eros*. Adolf Weissmann, "Ferruccio Busoni," *Die Musik* 12 (XVI).

5.   Guido M. Gatti, "In memoria di Ferruccio Busoni," *Revista Musicale Italiana* (1924), 565–80; Edward J. Dent, "Ferruccio Busoni 'Italiano,'" *La Rassegna Musicale* 3 (January 1930): 44–53.

6.   K. Marx and F. Engels, *Works*, 2d ed., vol. 27 (Moscow: Gospolitizdat, 1962), 412.

7.   See more in Chapter 10.

8.   N. Chushkin, "Gamlet—Kachalov" [Hamlet—Kachalov], *Teatral´nyi almanakh*, vol. 2 (Moscow: VTO: 1947), 244.

9.   F. Busoni, "Wie lange soll das gehen?" in *Von der Einheit der Musik*, 158. [Busoni, "How Long Will It Go On?" in *The Essence of Music*, 184. —Trans.]

Annotated Discography

1.   Busoni's acoustic recordings and piano rolls are described in Larry Sitsky, *Busoni and the Piano* (Westport, CT: Greenwood Press, 1986), 326–33.

2.   The translator expresses profound gratitude to George Livadas for his help in compiling this discography.

Bibliography

Allgemeine Musikzeitung 1, 44 (1910); 44 (1911).

Aisberg, E. "Iz oblasti soveremennovo pianisma" [About Contemporary Pianism]. *Muzyka* 157 (1913).

Bach, Johann Sebastian. *Two and Three-Part Inventions*. Rev. and ed. Ferruccio Busoni. New York: Breitkopf und Härtel, 1892; repr., New York: Carl Fischer, n.d.

———. *Well-Tempered Clavier*. Revised, annotated, and provided with parallel examples and suggestions for the study of modern pianoforte technique by Ferruccio Busoni. New York: Schirmer, 1894.

Bardas, V. *Psikhologiia fortepiannoi tekhniki* [The Psychology of Piano Technique]. Moscow: Muzsektor Gosizdata, 1928.

Barenboim, L. *Anton Grigor´evich Rubinshtein* [Anton Grigorevich Rubinstein]. Leningrad: Muzgiz, 1962.

Barinova, M. N. *Vospominaniia o Gofmane i Buzoni* [Reminiscences about Hofmann and Busoni]. Moscow: Muzyka, 1964.

Bekker, Paul. "Busoni." *25 Jahre neue Musik*. Jahrbuch 1926 der Universal-Edition.

———. "Busoni." In *Klang und Eros*. Berlin: Deutsche Verlags-Anstalt, 1922.

———. "Busoni." *Musikblätter des Anbruch* 6 (October 1924).

———. "Busoni." In *Neue Musik*. Berlin: Erich Reiss, 1920.

———. "Busonis Bach-Ausgabe." In *Klang und Eros*. Berlin: Deutsche [Verlags-Anstalt], 1922.

———. "Futuristengefahr." *Kritische Zeitbilder*. Berlin: Schuster und Loeffler, 1921.

———. "Impotenz oder Potenz? Eine Antwort an Herr Professor Dr. Hans Pfitzner." *Frankfurt Zeitung*, January 15 and 16, 1920. Also in *Kritische Zeitbilder*. Berlin: Schuster und Loeffler, 1921.

———. In *Klang und Eros*. Berlin: Deutsche [Verlags-Anstalt], 1922.

———. "Nachruf für Busoni." *Musikblätter des Anbruch* (October 1924).

———. "Neue Musik." *Tribüne der Kunst und Zeit*. Berlin: n.p., 1919.

———. "Über Busoni." In *Klang und Eros*. Berlin: Deutsche [Verlags-Anstalt], 1922.

Berg, Alban. "Die Musikalische Impotenz der 'neuen Ästhetick' Hans Pfitzners." *Musikblätter des Anbruch* (June 1920).

Boissier, Auguste. *Liszt-pédagogue*. Paris: Honoré Champion, 1927.

Brée, Malwine. *Die Grundlage der Methode Leschetizky*. Mainz: B. Schott's Söhne, 1903.

Breithaupt, R. M. *Die natürliche Klaviertechnik*. Leipzig: C. F. Kahnt, 1927.

Busoni, Benvenuto. "Um Das Erbe Busonis." *Die Musik* 27 (1935): 187.

Busoni, Ferruccio. *Briefe an seine Frau*. Zurich: Rotapfel, 1935.

———. *Entwurf einer neuen Ästhetik der Tonkunst*. Trieste: Carl Schmidl, 1907; repr., Leipzig: Insel, 1916; repr., Wiesbanden: Insel-Bücherei, 1954.

———. *Klavierübung*. N.p.: Breitkopf und Härtel, n.d.

———. "Letter to the Editor." *Signale für die musikalische Welt* 4 (January 1909): 125.

———. *Versuch einer organischen Klavier-Noten-Schrift.* Leipzig: Breitkopf und Härtel, 1910.

———. *Von der Einheit der Musik, von Dritteltönen und junger Klassizität, von Bühnen, und Bauten, und anschliessended Bezirken.* Berlin: Max Hesses, 1922.

———. "Zwei autobiographische Fragmente. Mitgeteilt von Friedrich Schnapp." *Die Musik* 21 (1929): 1.

Busoni, Gerda. *Erinnerungen an Ferruccio Busoni.* Berlin: AFAS Musik, 1958.

———. "Il mio incontro con Ferruccio Busoni." Trans. M. Lollini. *Musica Oggi* 3 (January 1960): 8–20.

Capellan, Georg. "Ferruccio Busoni: Versuch einer organischen Klaviernotenschrift." *Die Musik* 10 (1910/1911): 41.

Caporali, Rudolfo. "Le Trascrizioni pianistiche delle opera di Bach." *La Rassegna Musicale* 20 (1950): 241–42.

Casella, Alfredo. "Busoni Pianista." *Il Pianoforte,* June 5, 1921.

———. *Il Pianoforte.* Milan: Ricordi, 1937.

Chaikovskii, Petr I. [Tchaikovsky, Peter I]. *Muzykal'no-kriticheskie stat'i* [Musical-Critical Essays]. Moscow: Muzgiz, 1953.

Chantavoine, Jean. "Busoni." *Musical Quarterly* 7 (1921): 331–43.

———. "Ferruccio Busoni." *Revue Hebdomadaire,* April 17, 1920.

———. "Ferruccio Busoni." *Il Pianoforte* (June 1920).

———. "Ferruccio Busoni." *Musikblätter des Anbruch* 3 (January 1921).

———. "Ferruccio Busoni." *La Revue musicale* 11 (October 1924): 235–43.

Chesterman, D. "Boult Remembers Busoni." *Music and Musicians* 14 (April 1966): 25.

Cortot, Alfred. *Cours d'interprétation.* Paris: Legouix, 1934.

———. *Éditions de travail.* Paris: Maurice Senart, various dates.

Dalhaus, Carl. "Von der Einheit der Musik. Bemerkungen zur Ästhetik Ferruccio Busoni." *Deutsche Universitatszeitung* 10 (1956): 19.

Dandelot, A. *Francis Planté.* Paris: Dupont, 1920.

Debusmann, Emil. *Ferruccio Busoni.* Wiesbaden: Brucknerverlag, 1949.

Dent, Edward J. "Busoni." *London Mercury* 11 (August 1920): 488–91.

———. "Busoni and the Pianoforte." *Atheneum,* October 24, 1919.

———. "Busoni: A Posthumous Paper." *Monthly Musical Record* 62 (June 1932): 99–100.

———. "Busoni on Musical Aesthetics." *Monthly Musical Record* 39 (September 1909): 197–98.

———. "Busoni's Pianoforte Music." *Listener,* November 25, 1936.

———. *Ferruccio Busoni: A Biography.* London: Oxford University Press, 1933.

———. "Ferruccio Busoni 'Italiano.'" *La Rassegna Musicale* 3 (January 1930): 44–53.

———. "Ferruccio Busoni." *Listener,* October 16, 1935.

———. "Ferruccio Busoni." *Music and Letters* 14 (1933): 186–87.

———. "The Italian Busoni." *Monthly Musical Record* 61 (September 1931): 57.

———. "Mozart and Busoni." *Truth* (February 22, 1921).

———. "On the Interpretation of Chopin." *Atheneum* (July 9, 1920).

Die Musik. 2 (1902); 4 (1904); 6 (1906); 9 (1909); 16 (1924); 19 (1927).

Diesterweg, A. "Futuristen-Dämmerung. Ein offener Brief und sein Widerhall." *Allgemeine Musikzeitung* 49 (December 1922): 375.

Ertei, Paul. "Ferruccio Busoni." *Neue Musikzeitung* 11 (March 1908): 19.

Fischer, Edwin. *Von den Aufgaben des Musikers.* Wiesbaden: Insel, 1960.

Flesch, Carl. *The Memoirs of Carl Flesch.* Trans. Hans Keller. London: Rockliff, 1957; repr., New York: Macmillan, 1958.

Friedheim, Arthur. "Busoni und Liszt–Interpretation." *Signale für die musikalische Welt* 5 (February 10, 1909): 202–3.

Fryer, H. "Celebrated Pianists I Have Known." *Music Teacher* 33 (June 1954): 285–86.

Gerigk-Danzig, Herbert. "Bemerkungen über Busoni." *Die Musik* 26 (1934): 807.

Godowsky, Leopold. *Studien über die Etuden von Chopin.* Berlin: Schlesinger, 1914.

Goebbels, Franzpeter. *Der Neue Busoni: Übungen und Studien für Klavier, zusammengestellt und eingeleitet von Franzpeter Goebbels.* Wiesbaden: Breitkopf und Härtel, 1968.

Goldenweiser, Alexander. *Voprosy muzykal'nogo iskusstva* [Questions of Musical Art]. Moscow: Muzgiz, 1958.

Gray, Cecil. *A Survey of Contemporary Music.* London: Oxford University Press, 1924.

Gutmann, Albert. "Eingesandt 'Wie lange soll das gehen.'" *Signale für die musikalische Welt* 9 (March 1, 1911): 88–89.

Halm, August. "Busonis Bachausgabe." *Melos* 2 (1921): 207, 239.

Hanslick, Eduard. *Am Ende des Jahrhunderts.* Berlin: n.p., 1899.

———. *Konzerte, Komponisten und Virtuosen der letzen fünfzehn Jahre* (1870–85). Berlin: N.p., 1996.

———."Kritik über zehnjärigen Busoni." *Neue Freie Press,* February 13, 1887.

Henderson, A. M. "Busoni as Artist and Teacher." *Music Teacher* 35 (November 1956): 515.

Heuss, Alfred. "Nachruf auf Busoni." *Zeitschrift für Musik* 91 (August 1924): 435.

Hofmann, Josef. *Fortepiannaia igra* [*otvety na voprosy o fortepiannoi igre*] [Piano Playing: Answers to Questions About Piano Playing]. Moscow: Muzgiz, 1961.

Jarnach, Philipp. "Ferruccio Busoni." *Zeitschrift für Musik* 12 (December 1932): 1050.

Kammerer, R. "Philipp Compares Pianists Past and Present." *Musical America* 75 (December 1955): 16.

Kempff, Wilhelm. "Busoni." *Wilhelm Kempff, Unter dem Zimbelstern.* Stuttgart: n.p., 1951.

———. *Cette note grave . . .* Paris: Plon, 1955.

———. "Vstrechi s E. D'Alberom i F. Busoni" [Encounters with E. d'Albert and F. Busoni]. *Sovetskaia muzyka* 31, no. 1 (1967): 60.

Kerr, R. "Arrau as Beethoven Cyclist." *Music Magazine* 164 (September 1962): 13.

Kindermann, Jürgen. *Thematisch-chronologisches Verzeichnis der musikalischen Werke von Ferruccio Busoni.* Regensburg: Gustav Bosse, 1980.

Klemperer, Otto. *Erinnerungen an Gustav Mahler und andere autobiographische Skizzen.* Zurich: Atlantis, 1960.

Knorozovksy, [Isai Moiseevich]. "Muzykal'nye zametki" [Musical Notes]. *Teatr i iskusstvo* 47 (1912): 915–16.

Kogan, Grigorii [Grigory]. "d'Albert, Busoni i sovremennost´" [d'Albert, Busoni, and Modernity]. *Sovetskaia muzyka* 31 (January 1967): 58–60.

———. *Izbrannye stat´i* [Selected Essays]. Moscow: Sovetskii kompozitor, 1972.

———. "Pianisticheskii put´ Lista" [Liszt's Pianistic Path]. *Sovetskaia muzyka* 9 (1956).

―――. *Rabota pianista* [The Pianist's Work]. Moscow: Muzgiz, 1963.

―――. "Vidennoe i slyshannoe" [Seen and Heard]. With a Foreword by Dmitry Bashkirov. *Sovetskaia muzyka* 8 (1980): 95.

Kosnick, H. "Busoni. Ein bahnbrechender Meister in der Geschichte des Klavierspiels." *Allgemeine Musikzeitung* 30/31 (June 1934): 429.

―――. *Busoni Gestaltung durch Gestalt.* Regensburg: Gustav Bosse, 1971.

Krellmann, Hanspeter. *Studien zu den Bearbeitungen Ferruccio Busonis.* Regensburg: Gustav Bosse, 1966.

Leichtentritt, Hugo. "Busoni und Bach." *Musikblätter des Anbruch* 1–2/3 (January 1–15, 1921): 1216.

―――. *Ferruccio Busoni.* Leipzig: Breitkopf und Härtel, 1916.

―――. "Ferruccio Busoni." *Music Review* 6 (1945): 206.

Leitzmann, Albert. "Ferruccio Busoni: Sonatina." *Die Musik* 10 (1910/1911): 296.

Lessmann, Otto. "Aus dem Konzertsaal (Kritiken über Busoni)." *Allgemeine Musikzeitung* 12 (1885): 152, and 21 (1894): 606.

―――. "Gibt es noch eine weitere Entwickelung des Klavierspiels? Betrachtungen nach dem jüngsten Busoni Klavierabend." *Allgemeine Musikzeitung* 1 (January 1910): 6.

―――. Concert Review. *Allgemeine Musikzeitung* 45 (November 1911): 1154.

―――. Concert Review. *Allgemeine Musikzeitung* 51/52 (December 1911): 1325.

Malnev, S. "O sovremennoi virtuoznosti. K smerti Ferruchcho Buzoni" [About Contemporary Virtuosity. On the Death of Ferruccio Busoni]. *Muzykal'naia kul'tura* 2 (1924).

Marcus, M. "Busoni Revisited." *Music and Musicians* 10 (July 1962): 42.

Martienssen, C[arl] A[dolf]. *Die individuelle Klaviertechnik auf der Grundlage des schöperferischen Klang-willens.* Leipzig: Breitkopf und Härtel, 1930.

Mersmann, Hans. "Entwurf einer neuen ästhetik der Tonkunst." *Allgemeine Musikzeitung* 44 (October 1917): 79–95.

―――. "Pfitzner und Busoni." *Neue Musikzeitung* 38 (July 1917): 447.

Meyer, Heinz. *Die Klaviermusik Ferruccio Busonis.* Wolfenbüttel: Möseler, 1969.

[Meyer-Greffe, Julius. *The Impressionists.* Moscow: (N.p)., 1913), 136–37.]

[Moos, Paul. *Die Philosophie der Musik von Kant bis Eduard von Hartmann; ein Jahrhundert deutscher Geistesarbeit.* Stuttgart: Deutsche Verlags-Anstalt, 1922.]

Nadel, Arno. "Arnold Schönberg." *Die Musik* 11 (1912): 356–57.

―――. *Ferruccio Busoni.* Leipzig: Breitkopf und Härtel, 1931.

―――. "Neue Notensysteme." *Signale für die musikalische Welt* 47 (November 23, 1910): 1771–72.

Nestyev, Israel. *Sergei Prokofiev: His Musical Life.* Trans. Rose Prokofieva. New York: Knopf, 1946.

Niemann, Walter. *Meister des Klaviers.* Berlin: Schuster und Loeffler, 1919.

[Nikolaev, A. *Mastera sovetskoi pianisticheskoi shkoly* [Masters of the Soviet Pianistic School]. Moscow: Muzgiz, 1954.]

Pannain, Guido. "Ferruccio Busoni." *La Rassegna Musicale* 1, no. 6 (June 1928): 352–64.

Perrachio, Luigi. "Bach-Busoni." *La Rassegna Musicale* 1 (1928): 415–18.

Petri, Egon. "Principles of Piano Practice." *Proceedings of the MTNA,* Thirty-Fourth Series, December 27–30, 1939. N.p., 1939, 275–83.

Pfitzner, Hans. "Die neue Ästhetick der musikalichen Impotenz. Ein Verwesungssymptom?" *Gesammelte Schriften.* Augsburg: Filser [Verlag], 1926.

———. "Futuristengefahr. Bei Gelegenheit von Busonis Ästhetick." In *Gesammelte Schriften.* Augsburg: Filser [Verlag], 1926.

Philomele (pseudonym) "Muzyka za granitsei" [Music Abroad]. *Russkaia muzykal'naia gazeta* 4 (1904): 1061.

Piano Quarterly 108 (Winter 1979–1980). Busoni issue (articles by Franco Agostini, Larry Sitsky, Peter Armstrong, Anthony Beaumont, Daniel Raessler, Gunnar Johansen, Dolores Hsu, F. E. Kirby, and Guido Agosti).

Ponnelle, Lazare. *At Munich: Gustave Mahler, Richard Strauss, Ferruccio Busoni.* Paris: Librairie Fischbacher, 1913.

Prechtl, Robert. "Zweig auf Busonis Grab." *Melos* 4, no. 2 (September 1, 1924).

Prelinger, Melanie Mayer. "Erinnerungen und Briefe aus Ferruccio Busonis Jugendzeit." *Neue Muzikzeitung* 48 (October 1927): 6–10; 48 (November 1927): 37–40; 57–61.

Prokofiev, Grigorii. *Igra na fortep'iano* [Playing the Piano]. Moscow: Muzsector Gosizdata, 1928.

———. "Kontserti v Moskve" [Concerts in Moscow]. *Russkaia muzykal'naia gazeta* 48 (1912): 1046–48.

———. "Kontserti v Moskve" [Concerts in Moscow]. *Russkaia muzykal'naia gazeta* 50 (1913): 1166–69.

[Refardt, E., ed. *Briefe Busonis an Hans Huber.* Zurich: Verlag Hug, 1939.]

Rothe, Friede F. "How Ferruccio Busoni Taught: An Interview with the Distinguished Dutch Pianist, Egon Petri." *Etude* 58 (October 1940): 657.

Rules of the International Competition for the Musical Prizes of Anton Rubinstein. Comp. N. M. Lisovski. St. Petersburg: M. Bernard, 1889.

Santelli, Alfonso. *Busoni.* Rome: Carlo Colombo, 1938.

Schnabel, Artur. *My Life and Music.* London: Longmans, 1961.

Schnapp, Friedrich. "Anekdoten um Busoni." *Zeitschrift für Musik* 12 (December 1932): 1094.

———. "Busonis musikalisches Schaffen." *Zeitschrift für Musik* 12 (December 1932): 1045.

———. "Busonis persönaliche Beziehungen [zu] Anton Rusinstein." *Zeitschrift für Musik* 12 (December 1932): 1053.

———. "Ferruccio Busoni e Antonio Rubinstein." *La Rassegna Musicale* 13, no. 1 (June 1940.)

Schonberg, Harold C. *The Great Pianists.* New York: Simon and Schuster, 1963.

———. "Recalling Busoni: Mitropoulos Remembers Teacher with Affection." *New York Times,* October 7, 1951, sec. 2.

Schünemann, Georg. "Aus den Berliner Konzertzälen." *Allgemeine Musikzeitung* 6 (February 1909): 119.

———. Concert Review. *Allgemeine Musikzeitung* 48 (December 1911): 1238.

Schweitzer, Albert. *J. S. Bach.* Moscow: Muzgiz, 1934.

Schwers, Paul. "Aus den Berliner Konzertzälen." *Allgemeine Musikzeitung* 3 (January 1909): 53.

Selden-Goth, Gisella. "Das Goethesche in Busoni." *Musikblätter des Anbruch* 3, nos. 1–2 (January 1–15, 1921): 37.

————. *Ferruccio Busoni: Der Versuch eines Porträts*. Leipzig: E. P. Tal, 1922.

————. "Ferruccio Busoni: Un Profilo." *Historiae Musicae Cultores*. Ed. Leo S. Olschki, no. 20. Florence: N.p., 1964.

Seletskii, P. D. *Zapiski* [Notes]. Kiev: N.p., 1884.

Signale für die musikalische Welt 45 (November 1911). S.v. "Busoni's liszt-Feier," 1566–67.

Signale für die musikalische Welt 2, 6 (1909); 44 (1910); 45, 51 (1911); 21 (1913).

Sorabji, K. S. *Around Music*. London: Unicorn Press, 1932.

Spanuth, August. "Der verdächtigte Busoni." *Signale für die musikalische Welt* 9 (November 1, 1911): 327–28.

————. Review of January 6, 1909, concert. *Signale für die musikalische Welt* 2 (January 1909): 51–52.

Stuckenschmidt, H. H. "Busoni." In *Schopfer der Neuen Musik*. Munich: Suhrkamp, 1962.

————. *Ferruccio Busoni: Chronicle of a European*. Zurich: Atlantis, 1967. Trans. Sandra Morris. London: Calder & Boyars, 1970; repr., New York: St. Martin's Press, 1970.

Szigeti, Joseph. "Busoni." *With Strings Attached*. London: Cassel, 1949.

Tagliapietra, Gino. "Ferruccio Busoni Trascrittore e revisore." *La Rassegna Musicale* 13, no. 1 (June 1940).

Thiessen, Karl. "Busoni als Erfinder einer neuen Notenschrift." *Signale für die musikalische Welt* 45 (November 9, 1910): 1685–88.

Weissmann, Adolf. *Berlin als Musikstadt*. Berlin: Schuster und Loeffler, 1911.

————. "Busoni." In *Der Virtuose*. Berlin: Paul Cassirer, 1918.

————. "Die Musik der Weltstadt." *Die Musik* 11 (1911): 1–76.

————. "Ferruccio Busoni." *Die Musik* 16 (1924): 887.

Wetzel, Hermann. "Kritik-Konzert." *Die Musik* 8 (1908/1909): 188.

[Witt, Militza V. "Aus Briefen Busonis." *Deutsche Allgemeine Zeitung,* May 8, 1931.]

Yavorsky, B. "Posle moskovskikh kontsertov Ferruchcho Buzoni" [After the Moscow Concerts of Ferruccio Busoni]. *Muzyka* 104, 105 (October–November 1912).

Ziloti, Alexander. *Moi vospominaniia o F. Liste* [My Memories of Liszt]. St. Petersburg: N.p., 1911.

Zweig, Stefan. *Begegnungen mit Menschen, Büchern, Städten*. Berlin: S. Fischer, 1956.

Translator's Bibliography

Annenkov, Yuri. *Dnevnik moikh vstrech. Tsikl tragedii* [Diary of My Encounters. The Cycle of Tragedy]. New York: Mezhdunarodnoe literaturnoe sodruzhestvo, 1966.

Artizov, Andrei, and Oleg Naumov, comp. *Vlast´ i khudozhestvennaia intelligentsia. Dokumenty TsK RKP(b), VChK-OGPU-NKVD o kul´turnoi politike. 1917–1953 gg.* [Government and the Artistic Intelligentsia. The Documents of the TsK RKP(b), VChK-OGPU-NKVD Regarding Cultural Politics. 1917 to 1953]. Moscow: Mezhdunarodnyi fond "Demokratiia," 2002. English translation under Clark, Katerina et al.

Bach, C. P. E. *Essay on the True Art of Playing Keyboard Instruments.* Trans. and ed. William J. Mitchell. New York: Norton, 1949.

Bashkirov, Dmitry. Preface to "Vidennoe i slyshannoe" [Seen and Heard], by Grigory Kogan. *Sovetskaia muzyka* 8 (1980): 95–6.

Beaumont, Antony. *Busoni the Composer.* Bloomington: Indiana University Press, 1985.

Bennet, Will. *Telegraph,* June 18, 2003, Arts section.

Berlin, Isaiah, and Henry Hardy. *The Soviet Mind: Russian Culture Under Communism.* Washington, DC: Brookings Institution Press, 2004.

Busoni, Ferruccio. *The Essence of Music and Other Papers.* Trans. Rosamond Ley. London: Rockliff, 1957; repr., Mineola, NY: Dover, 1965.

———. *Letters to His Wife.* Trans. Rosamond Ley. London: Edward Arnold, 1938; repr., New York: Da Capo Press, 1975.

———. *Sketch of a New Esthetic of Music.* Trans. T. Baker. New York: Schirmer, 1911.

———. *Put´ k fortepiannomu masterstvu* [Klavierübung]. With a Foreword by Busoni. Ed. Y. Milstein. Moscow: Muzyka, 1968 and 1973.

Chukovskaya, Lydia. *The Akhmatova Journals,* trans. Milena Michalski, Peter Norman, and Sylva Rubashova. Evanston, IL: Northwestern University Press, 2002.

Chukovsky, Kornei. *Diary, 1901–1969.* New Haven: Yale University Press, 2005.

Clark, Katerina; E. A. Dobrenko; Andrei Artizov; and Oleg V. Naumov. *Soviet Culture and Power: A History in Documents, 1917–1953. Annals of Communism.* New Haven: Yale University Press, 2007.

Dachy, Marc. "Dada & les dadaïsmes." In *Folio Essais.* Paris: Gallimard, 1994.

Donnington, Robert. *The Interpretation of Early Music.* New York: Norton, 1992.

Edmunds, Neil, ed. *Soviet Music and Society Under Lenin and Stalin: The Baton and Sickle.* BASEES/RoutledgeCurzon series on Russian and East European studies, 9. New York: RoutledgeCurzon, 2004.

Feuchtwanger, Lion, and Irene Josephy. *Moscow, 1937: My Visit Described for My Friends.* New York: Viking Press, 1937.

Fleishman, Lazar. *Boris Pasternak v tridtsatye gody* [Pasternak in the Thirties]. Jerusalem: Magnes Press, Hebrew University, 1984.

Frankland, Mark. *Khrushchev.* Introd., Harry Schwartz. New York: Stein and Day, 1967.

Fytika, Athina. "A Historical Overview of the Philosophy Behind Keyboard Fingering Instruction from the Sixteenth Century to the Present." Electronic treatise, Florida State University School of Music, 2004.

Gay, Peter. *Modernism: The Lure of Heresy.* New York: Norton, 2008.

Goethe's Faust. Trans. Walter Kaufmann. Garden City, NY: Doubleday, 1961.

Gould, Glenn. *The Glenn Gould Reader.* Ed. and with a Foreword by Tim Page. New York: Knopf, 1984.

Hughes, Emrys. *Bernard Shou* [Bernard Shaw]. Moscow: Molodaia gvardiia, 1966.

Iakimenko, Iu. N. "Iz istorii 'chistok apparata': Akademiia khudozhestvennykh nauk v 1929–1932." *Novyi istoricheskii vestnik,* no. 1/12 (2005), www.nivestnik.ru/2005_1/11.shtml.

Iankovskii, Mark, ed. *Rimskii-Korsakov: issledovaniia, materialy, pis'ma* [Rimsky-Korsakov: Research, Materials, Letters]. Moscow: AN SSSR, 1954.

Ivinskaia, Ol'ga Vsevolodovna. *V plenu vremeni: gody s Borisom Pasternakom* [A Captive of Time: My Years with Pasternak]. Paris: Fayard, 1978.

Ivinskaya, Olga, and Max Hayward. *A Captive of Time: My Years with Pasternak.* London: Collins and Harvill Press, 1978.

Koestler, Arthur, and R. H. S. Crossman. *The God That Failed.* New York: Harper, 1949.

Lemke, M.K. *Nikolaevskie zhandarmy i literatura 1826–1855 gg.: po podlinnym delam Tretiago otdeleniia SEIV Kantseliarii* [Nicholas's Gendarmes and Literature 1826–1855: Authentic documents of the Third Division of His Imperial Majesty's Own Chancellory]. St. Petersburg: Izdatel'stvo S. V. Bunina, 1908.

Levitz, Tamara. *Teaching New Classicality: Busoni's Master Class in Composition, 1921–1924.* Frankfurt am Main: Lang, 1996.

Literaturnaya gazeta, March 10, 1936.

Mandelshtam, Nadezhda. *Hope against Hope: A Memoir.* New York: Atheneum, 1970.

Matthews, Joseph. "Busoni's Contribution to Piano Pedagogy." DM diss., Indiana University, 1977.

Mayakovsky, Vladimir, and V. V. Vinogradov. *Novoe o Maiakovskom. Literaturnoe nasledstvo,* t. 65 [New about Mayakovsky. Literary Legacy, vol. 65]. Moscow: Izdatel'stvo Akademii nauk SSSR, 1988.

Medvedev, Roy. *Let History Judge: The Origins and Consequences of Stalinism.* New York: Columbia University Press, 1989.

Nestyev, Israel. *Sergei Prokofiev: His Musical Life,* trans. Rose Prokofieva. New York: Knopf, 1946.

Neuhaus, Heinrich. Foreword to *U vrat masterstva* [At the Gates of Mastery] by Grigory Kogan. Moscow: Muzgiz, 1958.

Novy mir 1 (1966), 233–35.

Ord-Hume, Arthur. *Player Piano.* New York: A. S. Barnes, 1970.

Pechat' i revolutsiia 1 (1930): 85–86.

Petrak, Albert. "Busoni: His Life and Times." *Mechanical Music Digest* (March 7, 2004), www.rprf.org/PDF/Busoni_Bio.pdf.

Pravda, March 3, 1936; October 26, 1958.

Rappaport, Helen. *Joseph Stalin: A Biographical Companion.* Santa Barbara, CA: ABC-CLIO, 1999.

Régnier, Herni de. *Le Divertissement Provincial.* Paris: Paul Dupont, 1925.

Roberge, Marc-André. *Ferruccio Busoni: A Bio-Bibliography.* Westport, CT: Greenwood Press, 1991.

Roehl, Harvey. *Player Piano Treasury.* New York: Vestal Press, 1973.

Rosen, Charles. *The Romantic Generation.* Cambridge, MA: Harvard University Press, 1995.

Sayers, Michael, and Albert Eugene Kahn. *The Great Conspiracy against Russia.* New York: Boni & Gaer, 1946.

Schmitt, Kurt. "Busoni als Pädagoge und Interpretdargestellt an seiner Bearbeitung der Klavierwerke J. S. Bach." Diss., Saarbrüchen, 1965.

Schwarz, Boris. *Music and Musical Life in Soviet Russia, 1917–1981.* Bloomington: Indiana University Press, 1983.

Schuman, Frederick Lewis. *Soviet Politics at Home and Abroad.* New York: Knopf, 1946.

Schweitzer, Albert. *J. S. Bach.* Moscow: Muzgiz, 1934.

Shaw, George Bernard. "Letter to the Editor: Social Conditions in Russia." *Manchester Guardian,* March 2, 1933.

———. "The Lysenko Muddle." *Labour Monthly* (January 1949).

Sitsky, Larry. "Busoni." *Dictionary of Contemporary Music.* New York: Dutton, 1974.

———. "Busoni and the New Music." *Quadrant* 33 (January–February 1965).

———. *Busoni and the Piano.* Westport, CT: Greenwood Press, 1986.

———. "Transcriptions and the Eunuch." *Quadrant* 43 (September–October 1966).

Sovetskaia muzyka 1 (1948), 117; 2 (1948) 35, 45.

Taruskin, Richard. *The Oxford History of Western Music,* vol. 4. Oxford: Oxford University Press, 2005.

———. *Text and Act.* New York: Oxford University Press, 1995.

TSK KPSS. *O partiinoi i sovetskoi pechati. Sbornik dokumentov* [On Matters of the Party and the Soviet Press. Collected Documents]. Moscow: Pravda, 1954.

Tsukkerman, Viktor Abramovich. Preface to *Izbrannye stat'i* [Selected Essays], by Grigory Kogan. Moscow: Sovetskii Kompozitor, 1985.

Vechernyaya Moskva, August 1, 1930.

Verdier, Aurélie. *L'ABCdaire de Dada.* Paris: Flammarion, 2005.

Volkov, Solomon, and Antonina W. Bouis. *Shostakovich and Stalin: The Extraordinary Relationship between the Great Composer and the Brutal Dictator.* New York: Knopf, 2004.

Volkov, Solomon, and Vladimir Spivakov. *Shostakovich i Stalin: khudozhnik i tsar'* [Shoshtakovich and Stalin: Artist and Tsar]. Moscow: EKSMO, 2006.

Walton, J. M. *Craig on Theatre.* London: Methuen,1983.

Williams, Peter. "Keyboards." In *Performance Practice: Music After 1600,* ed. Howard Mayer Brown and Stanley Sadie. New York: Norton, 1990.

Wimbush, R. "Busoni." *Gramophone* 43 (April 1966): 486.

Zamiatin, Evgenii [Zamyatin, Evgeny]. *Sochineniia* [Works]. Moscow, 1988.

Index

Ferruccio Busoni is most widely known today as the composer of such works as the Second Violin Sonata, the incidental music for Gozzi's Turandot, and the most monumental piano concerto in the repertory (some 80 minutes long, with male chorus in the finale). But Busoni was also renowned in his day as an author and pedagogue and, most especially, as a pianist. Busoni's recordings of pieces by Chopin and Liszt—and of his own arrangements of keyboard works by Bach and Beethoven—are much prized and studied today by connoisseurs of piano playing. Yet even his most important biographers have cast only a cursory glance at the pianistic aspect of Busoni's fascinating career.

Grigory Kogan's book *Busoni as Pianist* (published in Russian in 1964, and here translated for the first time) was and remains the first and only study to concentrate exclusively on Busoni's contributions to the world of the piano. *Busoni as Pianist* summarizes reviews of Busoni's playing and Busoni's own writings on the subject. It also closely analyzes the surviving piano rolls and recordings, and examines Busoni's editions, arrangements, and pedagogical output. As such, it will be of interest to pianists, teachers and students of the piano, historians, and all who love piano music and the art of piano playing.

Grigory Kogan (1901–79) was a leading Soviet pianist and music critic. A conservatory professor at the age of twenty-one, Kogan created the first-ever course in Russia dealing with the history and theory of pianism. Through his brilliant lectures, his concert performances, and his many books, articles, and reviews, Kogan influenced an entire generation of Soviet pianists.

Svetlana Belsky is a teacher and performer, and is coordinator of Piano Studies at the University of Chicago.

"Busoni's immense significance in the history of pianism, and the perceptive, illuminating observations of the late Grigory Kogan, make this volume a major addition to the existing literature on this fascinating, enigmatic musical personality. Svetlana Belsky's annotated translation is admirable."

—Donald Manildi, curator,
International Piano Archives,
University of Maryland

"Illuminating, and brilliantly translated. Kogan's book sheds invaluable light on the life and career of a unique creative genius. Busoni's awe-inspiring artistry and personality are here described in riveting analytical detail. We are indebted to Svetlana Belsky for making this important work available in English, to the lasting benefit of students, scholars, and performers."

—Ann Schein, noted concert pianist and educator